LEGENDARY LOCALS

OF

ASBURY PARK

NEW JERSEY

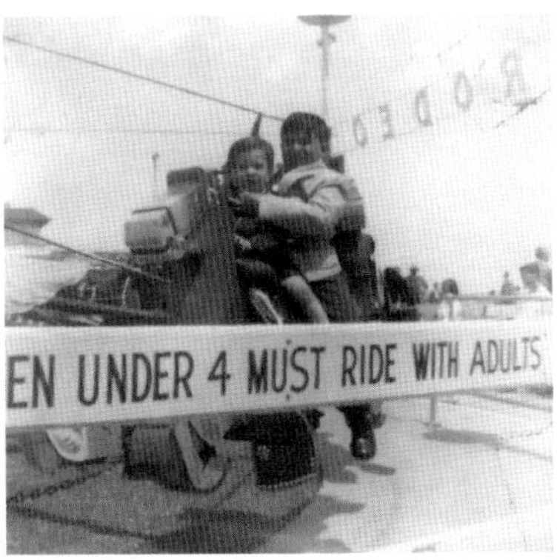

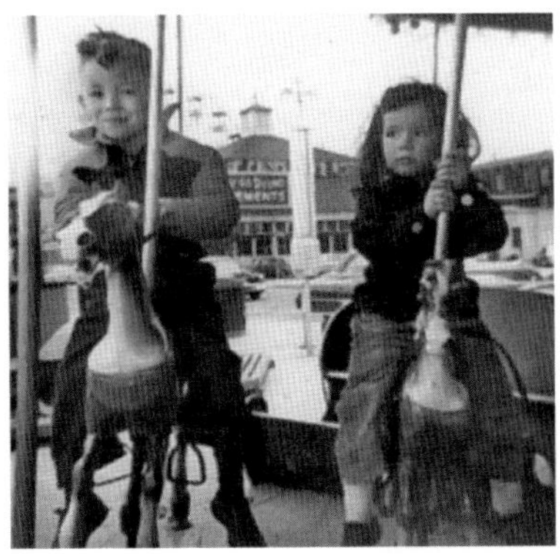

I0805770

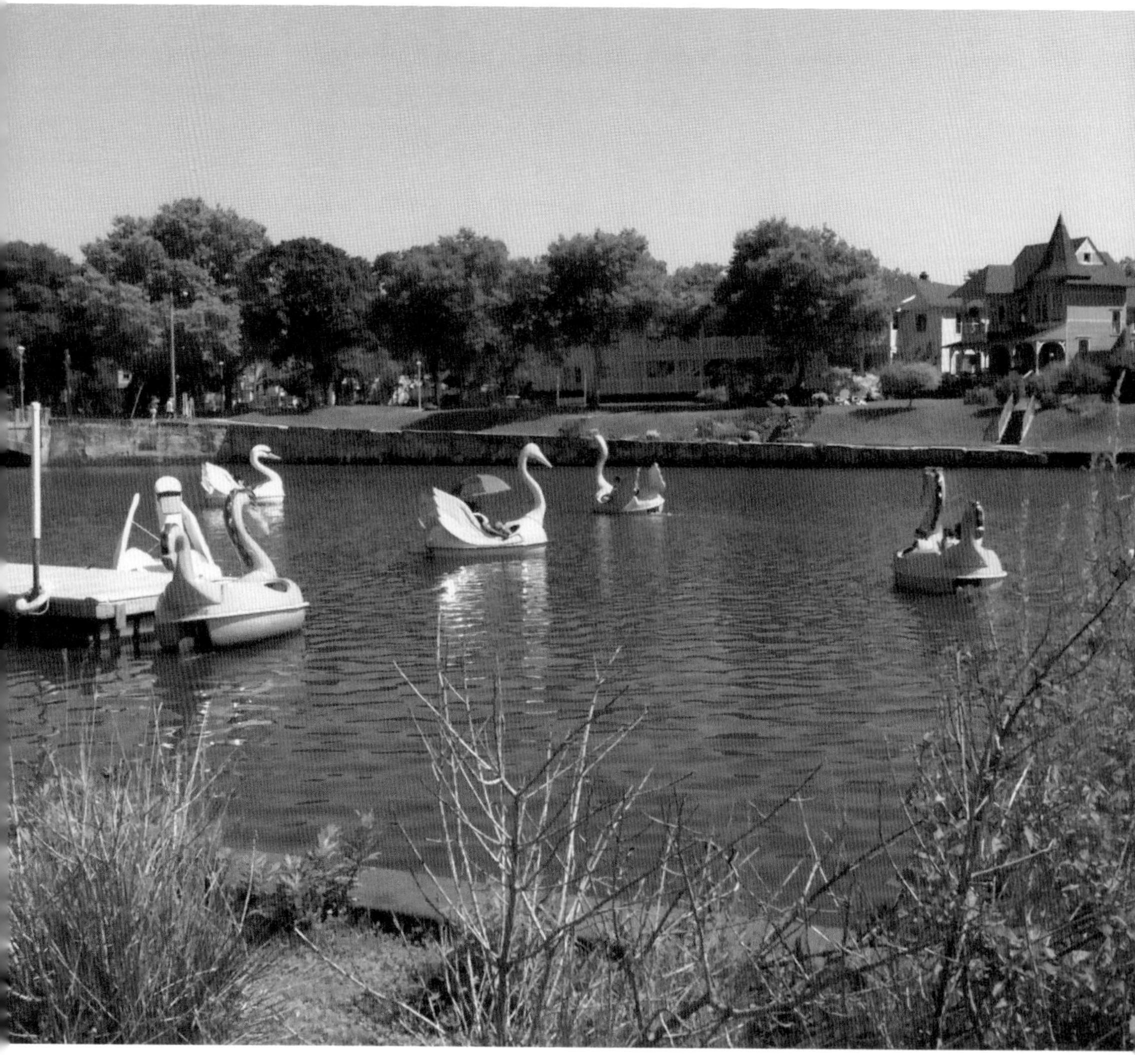

Swan Lake

The swans returned to Wesley Lake (with the blue herons, pink flamingos, and green dragons), when Linda Occhipinti opened her Asbury Park Pedal Boats attraction in spring 2011. (Photograph by the author.)

Page 1: Growin' Up

Young Danny DeVito (left image, behind cousin Peter) and five-year old Bruce Springsteen (right image, with sister Virginia) enjoy the rides at the Asbury Park boardwalk in the early 1950s. (Courtesy of Peter Lucia, Billy Smith Collection.)

LEGENDARY LOCALS

OF

ASBURY PARK

NEW JERSEY

TOM CHESEK

LEGENDARY LOCALS

ISBN 978-1-4671-0194-3

Legendary Locals is an imprint of Arcadia Publishing
Charleston, South Carolina

Printed in the United States of America

Library of Congress Control Number: 2014947947

For all general information, please contact Arcadia Publishing:
Telephone 843-853-2070
Fax 843-853-0044
E-mail sales@arcadiapublishing.com
For customer service and orders:
Toll-Free 1-888-313-2665

Visit us on the Internet at www.arcadiapublishing.com

Dedication
To Mister D

On the Front Cover: Clockwise from top left:
Bruce Springsteen at Convention Hall, 2006 (Courtesy of the *Coaster*; see page 73), the Bouncing Souls outside their studio (Courtesy of Kate Hiltz; see page 117), Village Person Felipe Rose in Paradise (Courtesy of the *Coaster*; see page 115), off-season Doggie Yappy Hour at the Wonder Bar (Courtesy of the *Coaster*; see page 105), local children get a special guest reader in their classroom (Courtesy of the *Coaster*; see page 123), sand sculptor Lorenzo Harris (Courtesy of Kay Harris; see page 36), Danny DeVito hosts a homecoming movie premiere (Courtesy of Peter Lucia; see page 92), the inimitable "Mr. Fashions" (Courtesy of the *Coaster*; see page 70), teenaged Stephen Crane (Courtesy of University of Virginia; see page 22).

On the Back Cover: From left to right:
Pop artist "Porkchop" stands before his oft-photographed mural inside the shell of the boardwalk casino (Courtesy of Mike Lavallee), one of the original "Tillie" faces from the old Palace Amusements is removed from the landmark building's facade prior to its 2004 demolition and relocated to a storage berth at the city sewage treatment plant (Courtesy of Michael Booth and the *Coaster*).

CONTENTS

ACKNOWLEDGMENTS

There have been numerous books written about Asbury Park—certainly far more than one might expect from a town of its small size—but two in particular proved genuinely inspirational for the development of this project. Helen-Chantal Pike's *Asbury Park's Glory Days* is a richly detailed tour through the places, people, and public institutions of this complex community—one that draws from a variety of voices and witnesses—while Daniel Wolff's *4th of July, Asbury Park* is a devastating view from the underside of the boardwalk; an examination of the harsh dichotomies and self deceptions that form the rotted pilings of an American city's promised land. Both are absolutely essential reading for all those looking to further their study of the place Where the City Meets the Sea.

The author is additionally indebted to the good work and input of historians, archivists, and Asbury aficionados that include John Cavanaugh, Eileen Chapman, Bob Crane, Frank D'Alessandro, Milton Edelman, Kay Harris, Pam and Charlie Horner, Madonna Carter Jackson, Peter Lucia, Kate Mellina, Dan Moore, Tony Pallagrosi, Mike Richison, Billy Smith, Bob Stewart, Don Stine, Carol Torre, Donna Troppoli, Henry Vaccaro, Gary Wien, Harry Ziegler and Joe Bilby, as well as the late Fritz Cleary.

While every photograph and illustration credit in this book represents a debt of gratitude, special kudos must go to Michael J. Booth, publisher of Asbury Park's weekly *Coaster* newspaper, for contributions above and beyond the call of duty. The awesomely talented artists Susan Culbert, Kathy Polenberg, and Jason Robinson graced (and in several cases saved) this project with their amazing portrait work. A tip of the vintage straw boater as well to the unfortunately un-credited (but supremely skilled) artist who rendered the images drawn from the pre-1910 antique portfolio *Just for Fun: Caricatures of Jersey Shore Pioneers*.

Special thanks to Erin Vosgien, Lily Watkins, and the staff at Arcadia Publishing for the opportunity to compose this labor-intensive love letter to the author's adopted city. A shout-out to the Asbury Park Historical Society and love to Stuffy, for being so supportive and understanding during a frantically busy "Lost Summer" of nonstop work.

—Tom Chesek
The Stephen Crane House
Asbury Park, NJ
Follow Legendary Locals of Asbury Park on Facebook

INTRODUCTION

Let me take you to a place where the sun warms your face,
And the sound of the waves takes you away
The ghosts on the boardwalk will keep you company
Where the city meets the sea, where the city meets the sea

—"Ghosts on the Boardwalk,"
by the Bouncing Souls

Take a trip to the Asbury Park Boardwalk and download the operating app for Augmented Asbury Park, the virtual tour project created by a team from Monmouth and Kean Universities. Fire up some Bouncing Souls (or the boardwalk-tested troubadour of your choice) and marvel as the panorama of present-day town and surf is overlaid with spectral images of the Casino complex in its full glory, the iconic Palace Amusements, the sprawling Monterey Hotel, carousels and rides in motion, and the charred corpse of the SS *Morro Castle* in its place of rest. Then, track the passing people and the seabirds oblivious to the ghosts that loom just out of sight.

Asbury Park, New Jersey, is a place that is experienced in layers; a place where every street corner, storefront, or sandy stretch comes weighted with the sorrowful echoes of cherished but vanished monuments or comes alive with vision, potential, and the promise of new and exciting things around the corner. It is not a very big town, nor has it really been around for all that long, but such is its hold that even those who have never lived a day of their lives here can feel a bit proprietary about Asbury Park. From the lifelong resident whose family connection goes back generations, to the day-tripper who's "seeing how it has come back" for the first time in years, to the relative newbie who just arrived in town with an idea, everyone believes they own a piece of the place.

At the same time, Asbury Park—divided in half by design, demographically diverse and ever-morphing—remains delightfully, even devastatingly confounding to all who dare to rope it, brand it, put it on a leash. Even founder James Bradley's planned paradise crumbled before market and social forces that he could not control. Mayor Clarence Hetrick, as textbook a boss as any little city has ever seen, faded from this world without so much as a park bench plated in his honor. Movie-house mogul Walter Reade, a purveyor of dreams and would-be shaper of public opinion, seemed no more substantial than a dusty projected image when the final credits rolled. And too many generations of ambitious developers, deal-making public servants, and self-appointed leaders have learned what happens when the grandest sandcastle plans wash up against changing times and economic tides.

That said, it is the fingerprints of those who dared to shape the town to their ends—or who simply sought, often against all odds, to make a year-round life in this city of summers—that define Asbury Park every bit as much as the footprints of landmark buildings. This book, *Legendary Locals of Asbury Park*, is a whirlwind tour through the history of what just might be the most famous, yet most misunderstood, 1.5 square miles on the map. It is a story told through the visionaries and the vagabonds, the shopkeepers and the show people, the pillars of the community and the passers-through who could not wait to get out while they can, the activists and advocates on the front lines of social change, and the stalwart stewards of the status quo. The witnesses who chronicled and commented on the passing parade through words and images and art and music.

While it is impossible to tell the full story of Asbury Park without factoring in a few rogues, con artists, and corrupt politicos, or ignoring ongoing fiscal struggles, school issues, redevelopment controversies, and crime headlines, an attempt has been made here to skew things toward the positive. Particularly as regards the true believers who stood by and stayed in the city during those years when it seemed almost to have been wrenched from the mainstream of life. Then there are the 21st-century legendaries, each of whom is endeavoring in their own way to move things forward, bring it all together, and make it work somehow for the greater good. Because just as a shot fired from somewhere in the city can seem to come from all directions at once, a burst of positive energy can ripple through a community in the most intriguing ways.

If this author's own experience as a relatively recent arrival carries with it more of an outsider's perspective than that of someone who grew up, graduated, and grew old here, it has also served to find us instantly among friends. There is the sense that Asbury is ready to reinvent itself once more, and the belief that this current cast of characters is among the finest, most truly transformative ever assembled within city limits.

There are many more Asbury Park stories to be told of course, and hopefully, other opportunities to tell them. For now, there are some memorable personalities to meet, neighbors to greet, good times to be had, and friends to be made.

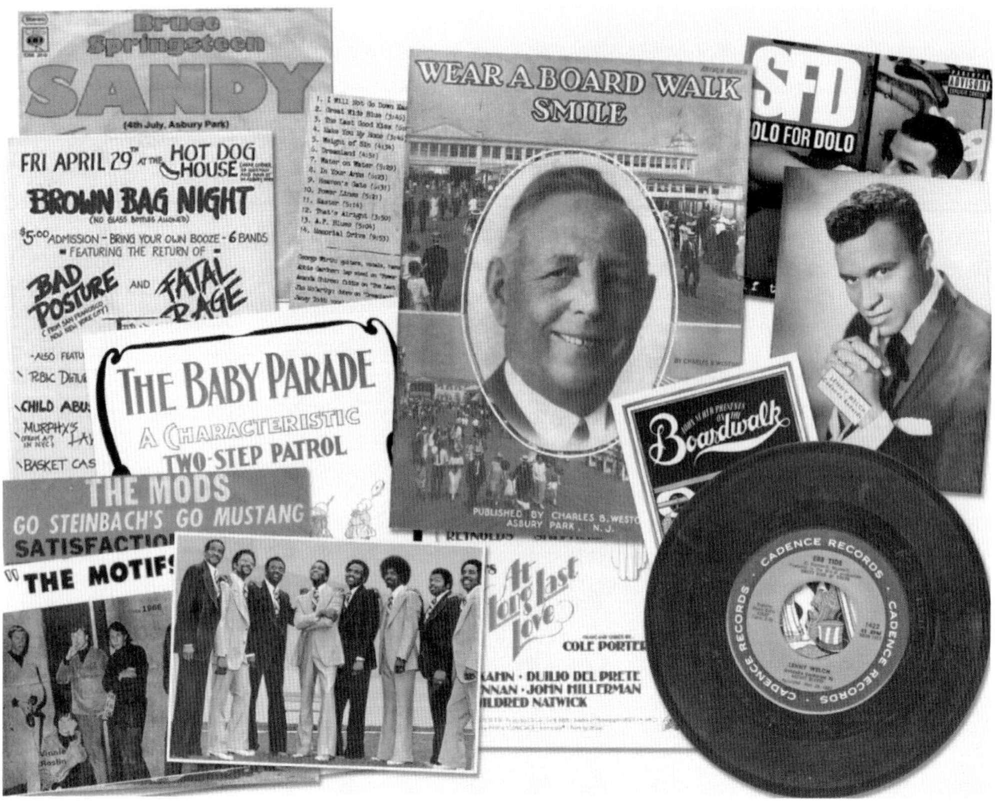

Soundtown

Whether sparked by God or the devil, rising up from the neighborhoods or rolling through on a never-ending tour, music has long been the lifeblood of this seldom-quiet city, and the saga of the place "Where Music Lives" demands an eclectic soundtrack. The chapters in this book are keynoted with a period-perfect piece of musical history—a song that serves to illuminate a corner of the Asbury Park story and that makes a glorious noise even as words and images on the page. Step right up, and listen in. (Author's collection.)

CHAPTER ONE

The Baby Parade

1870–1903

The Baby Parade started in July 1890, nearly 20 years to the day that a brush manufacturer named James A. Bradley gazed upon an untamed patch of sand, scrub, and surf near the camp meeting grounds of Ocean Grove and conjured a pious paradise that the passionate Methodist named for pioneer "Bishop on Horseback" Francis Asbury.

A generation had come of age since the wealthy war profiteer bought up those wild acres, cut down the tangled growth, paced off the "Bradley lots" and boulevards, and planned a city of lakeside parks and wide, shaded streets open to the sea and connected (with difficulty at first) to the region's crowded cities.

The Baby Parade started at Wesley Lake, the narrow body of water that separates Asbury Park from Ocean Grove, and promenaded north on the boardwalk; an army of some 200 mothers, nurses, toddlers, and carriage-bound infants. The *New York Times* estimated that 15,000 onlookers lined the route that afternoon, while "the band from the steamship *Trenton* led the procession." Founder Bradley himself graced the proceedings.

The Baby Parade also started something bigger even than the man who owned the boards. Within a few seasons, the event would reportedly attract crowds of more than 100,000 to view a procession of ever more elaborately decorated go-carts and floats, "lifelike dolls," and tots attired as historical figures or period celebs. There were best-of-show prizes, a court of honor presided over by Titania, Queen of the Fairies, a "carpeted roadway," and faux-Corinthian columns. Photographer William Stauffer captured the action, and by 1904 the pageant would be preserved via motion pictures.

Additionally, the music came to be furnished by one of the most popular bands in the land, that of Asbury's own Arthur Pryor. The trombonist, conductor, and composer of "On Jersey Shore" and "Down at Asbury Park" used the occasion to introduce originals like "Queen Titania" and of course "The Baby Parade," a "two-step patrol" that he would wax for the Victor label in 1906.

It was a spotlight moment for a town that had only just taken its first tentative baby steps and had keyed into a middle-class wave of increasingly mobile urban customers for its hotels, beaches, and amusements. Soon, Asbury would boast a permanent boardwalk, a busy rail station, and more guest accommodations than Atlantic City, still years away from its first Miss America pageant.

For the founder of this feast, things were parading off in a direction that he had not foreseen. Asbury Park was a place on the threshold of what looked to be a real golden age—a place of prim pleasures and forbidden thrills alike; one that would soon enough welcome everyone from presidents to pugilists, day laborers to distinguished lecturers. It was also becoming a year-round town, albeit one with conflicts that seemed built into its DNA. All that Bradley could ultimately do was view the inexorable march into the 20th century and watch as his baby continued to grow at an alarming rate.

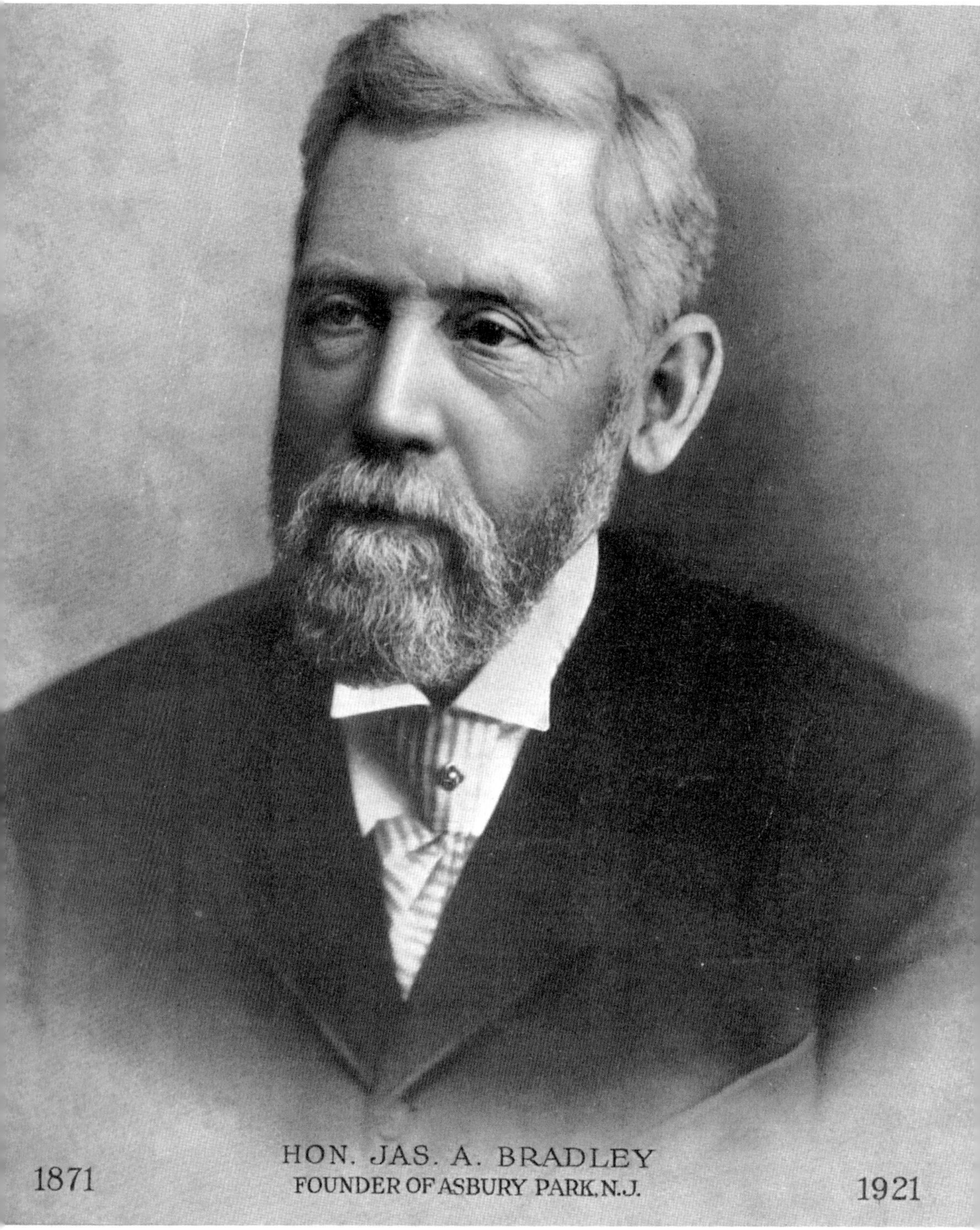
1871
HON. JAS. A. BRADLEY
FOUNDER OF ASBURY PARK, N.J.
1921

Daddy Warbrush (OPPOSITE PAGE)

The Springfield of television's *The Simpsons* has its Jedediah Springfield—and in life as in cartoons, the statue of the stone-faced "founder" has proven irresistible to parodists, protesters, and pigeons alike. But if there's one American city whose very existence is tied to the working hands, expansive imagination, and active checkbook of a single individual, it is Asbury Park and its Staten Island–born, Bowery-bred father, James A. Bradley.

Under Bradley's vision, Asbury Park was to be a middle-class resort community of model cleanliness, modest virtue, and moderately paced recreational pursuits. But, as the city's sole landowner began to sell off those lots and lease out those waterfront properties, something else would take shape behind the back of the man who frowned upon drink, gambling, racially integrated beaches, or ladies' bathing attire that was any more revealing than the heavy, woolen "Bradley Bag."

The self-appointed moral arbiter would personally patrol the lakesides and beaches, filling the sands with salvaged "curiosities" like old fire wagons, boats, and bird cages—and filling his *Asbury Park Journal* with racist editorials. His handwritten signs regarding proper public conduct would become subject to ridicule, with Stephen Crane writing, "His work has an air of philosophic thought about it . . . he is an artist."

The image of Bradley as aging eccentric was at odds with the fact that, as the town's majority landowner, newspaper publisher, and occasional mayor, he continued to exert enormous influence over municipal matters. He was even elected to the state senate in 1893, on a ticket that would successfully campaign to shut down the nearby Monmouth Park horse track. Still, increasing pressure from local merchants caused him to sell his beachfront interests by 1903.

Bradley would spend his last years regarding his town-building experiment as a failure, and his own name would come to grace nearby Bradley Beach, in which he was a significant early investor. Following his death in 1921, Asbury Park would dutifully erect a proper statue of the founder in an Ocean Avenue plaza designated as Bradley Park. It is there that he stands to this day, gazing toward a horizon obscured by Convention Hall. And just behind his back, a series of Skate and Surf Festivals, Pride Weekend celebrations, and Blues 'n Brews BBQs set the pace for an Asbury Park he never saw coming. (Courtesy of the Monmouth County Historical Association Library and Archive.)

The First Lady

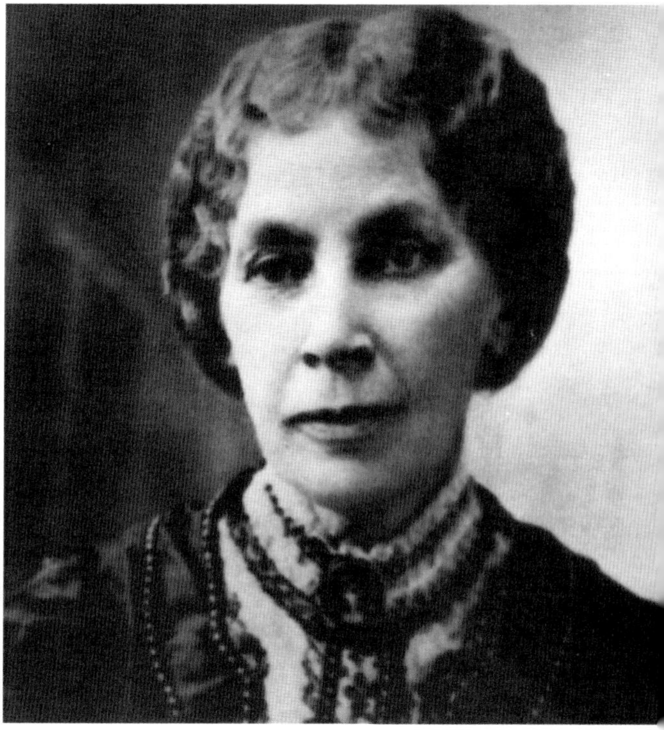

Upon Helen Packard Bradley's passing in 1915, the *Press* called her "The first lady of Asbury Park." Although flags would fly at half mast around town that February day, the Bradleys had largely returned to their life and business in New York City. Never a truly public figure, the Rutgers-educated Helen exerted a behind-the-scenes influence on the city's guiding vision. She is credited with converting her Irish Catholic husband to Methodism, and helping name Asbury streets after prominent Methodist clergy and laypersons. (Courtesy of the Asbury Park Public Library.)

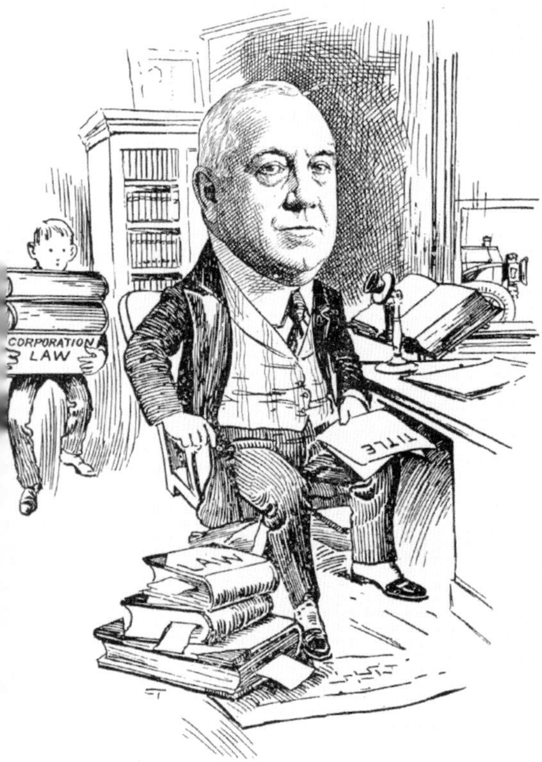

Kennedy Mystique

"The story of Isaac Kennedy is not that of the poor boy who makes good," wrote Fritz Cleary, but "the pampered rich boy who makes good on his own." The son of a Long Branch hotelier made a nationwide name for himself as a surveyor and city planner, laying out not only Asbury Park's wide and open-to-the-sea avenues, but also Ocean Grove's narrow pedestrian pathways. It was his innovative, modern design for the Bradley-owned municipal drainage system that got him, and Asbury, noticed in international circles—whereupon Kennedy switched careers, becoming Bradley's attorney of record. (Courtesy of the Asbury Park Public Library.)

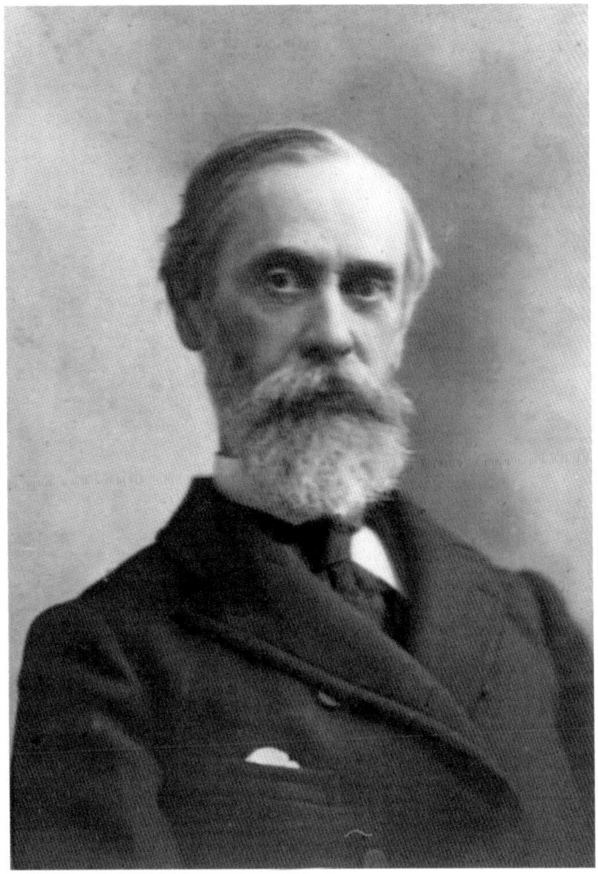

The Shadow City
As an upstanding citizen of Morristown, New Jersey, he bequeathed the community its beloved Burnham Park, and when he relocated to Canaan, New York, he founded the Burnham (later Berkshire) Industrial Farm for troubled city youth. One will not, however, find the name Frederick G. Burnham attached to anything in Asbury Park, where the wealthy attorney, philanthropist, and political player became the West Side's answer to Founder Bradley. Buying up 135 acres of farmland west of the tracks in 1882, and selling off small lots at a brisk clip, he created a shadow city to the micro-managed, painstakingly planned community to the east. With Springwood Avenue as its center, it was a place where working-class blacks, Jews, Italians, and Germans built homes and businesses of their own, despite not officially becoming part of Asbury Park until after Bradley's era. (Courtesy of Division of Rare and Manuscript Collections, Cornell University Library.)

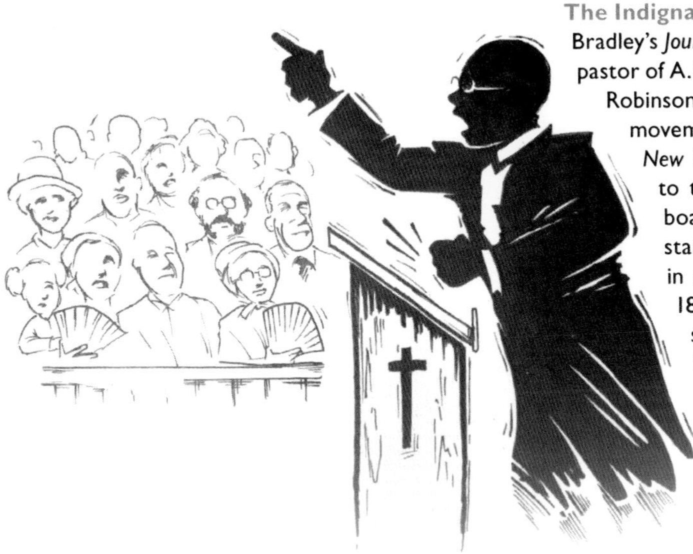

The Indignation Meeting
Bradley's *Journal* branded him an "agitator," but as pastor of A.M.E. Zion Church, Rev. James Francis Robinson found himself at the forefront of a movement and caught the attention of the *New York Times* when his bold opposition to the Founder's segregated beach and boardwalk policies found him taking a stand against "false religious sentiment" in the dry and pious resort. At a June 1887 "indignation meeting" (and a later sermon at NYC's St. Mark's Church), he declared, "We colored people fought for our liberty . . . we will not be dictated to in this manner by Mr. Bradley." (Illustration by the author.)

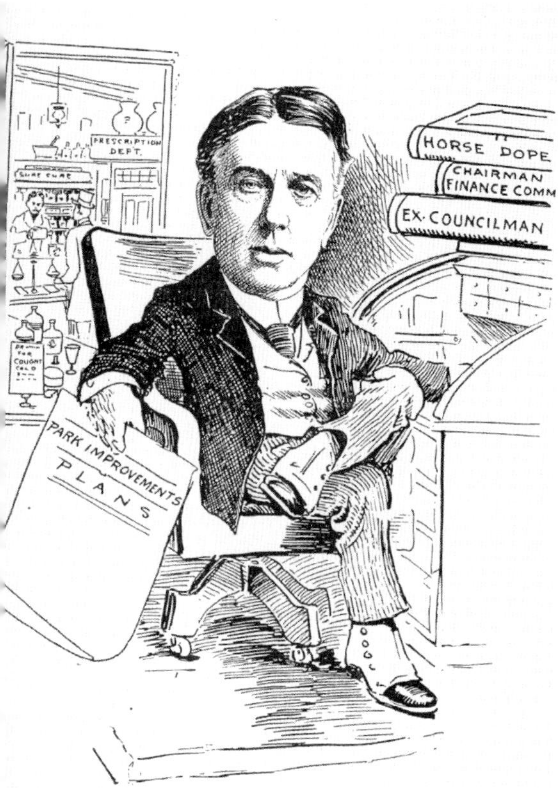

The Practitioner

He was a wounded veteran of the Civil War, or "The War of Rebellion," as Asbury Park's memorial states, but Dr. Hugh S. Kinmonth's greatest victories, setbacks, and scars were scored on the battlefields of Monmouth County politics and business. The former country doctor relocated to the new resort in 1872, becoming one of the town's first physicians and an early city council member. Kinmonth's professional and political callings kept him in contact with all walks of local life, and his legacy lives on in his cofounding of what became the *Asbury Park Press* and the still-standing Kinmonth Building on Mattison Avenue. Historian Fritz Cleary observed, "He played politics as he lived life, conducted his many business enterprises, and ran his medical practice and drug store—to get as much fun out of it as possible." (Courtesy of the Asbury Park Public Library.)

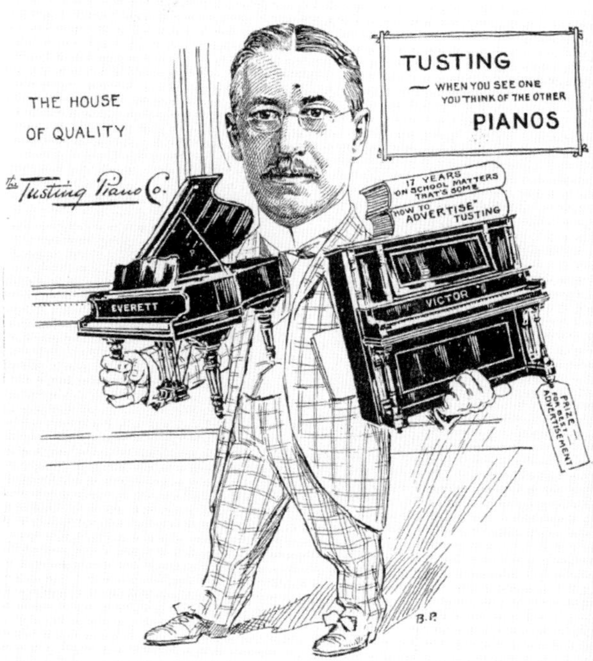

Ebony and Ivory

The *R* stood for Robert, but it could just as easily have stood for respectable, as R.A. Tusting was the very model of a late 19th century, small-town pillar-of-the-community type. Family man, schoolteacher, library trustee, board of education, Rotary Club, 32nd-degree Mason, and life member of the Asbury Lodge, he hit all the bases. But it is through his Tusting Piano Company that Robert achieved ubiquity in parlors throughout the area. The piano (and its insatiable appetite for sheet music) was an integral part of the middle-class American home in the days before phonographs and radio. (Courtesy of the Asbury Park Public Library.)

Go Steinbach's

It was a department store, back when that term conjured a sophisticated world beyond the cramped cubbies of the neighborhood shop. The evolution of a Long Branch–based dry goods business into what came to be known as Steinbach's Mammoth Department Store signaled the fact that Asbury Park was becoming a competitive commercial hub. Steinbach's, packed with the finest imported merchandise sprawling over a five-story Cookman Avenue building, would become the flagship of a regional chain.

The auto-centric age of highway shopping centers was not even on the horizon when brothers John (who operated a two-story emporium at the south end of town) and Henry (who opened the neighboring Ocean Palace) bet long on Asbury's viability as a year-round shopping destination. With the construction and expansion of their big store prior to the Great Depression, John and the next generation of Steinbachs (sons Arthur and Walter) also invested heavily in the notion that Asbury Park could sustain a one-stop center for upscale goods marketed to an affluent customer base. Meanwhile, an out-of-towner named Frank W. Woolworth would open his very first five and dime up Cookman Avenue—quickly joined by like-minded outlets of the McCrory, Newberry, and H.L. Green chains, with the new wave of down-market retail only serving to define the Steinbach philosophy in sharp relief.

Like its prehistoric namesake, Steinbach's downtown Mammoth would face extinction at the end of the 1970s, having phased out operations in favor of a location at the new Seaview Square Mall in Ocean Township. The Steinbach name soldiered on into the final years of the millennium under the ownership of a Midwest-based group. The Steinbach Building would live again, however, as the venerable flagship sailed into the new century as a luxury condo residence. Still, for many locals of a certain age, the notion of a trip to Steinbach's held a palpable appeal, best encapsulated by the 1960s band the Mods, whose pony-car worldview was captured in their original recording "Go Steinbach's Go Mustang." (Photograph by Milton Edelman, courtesy of Kay Harris.)

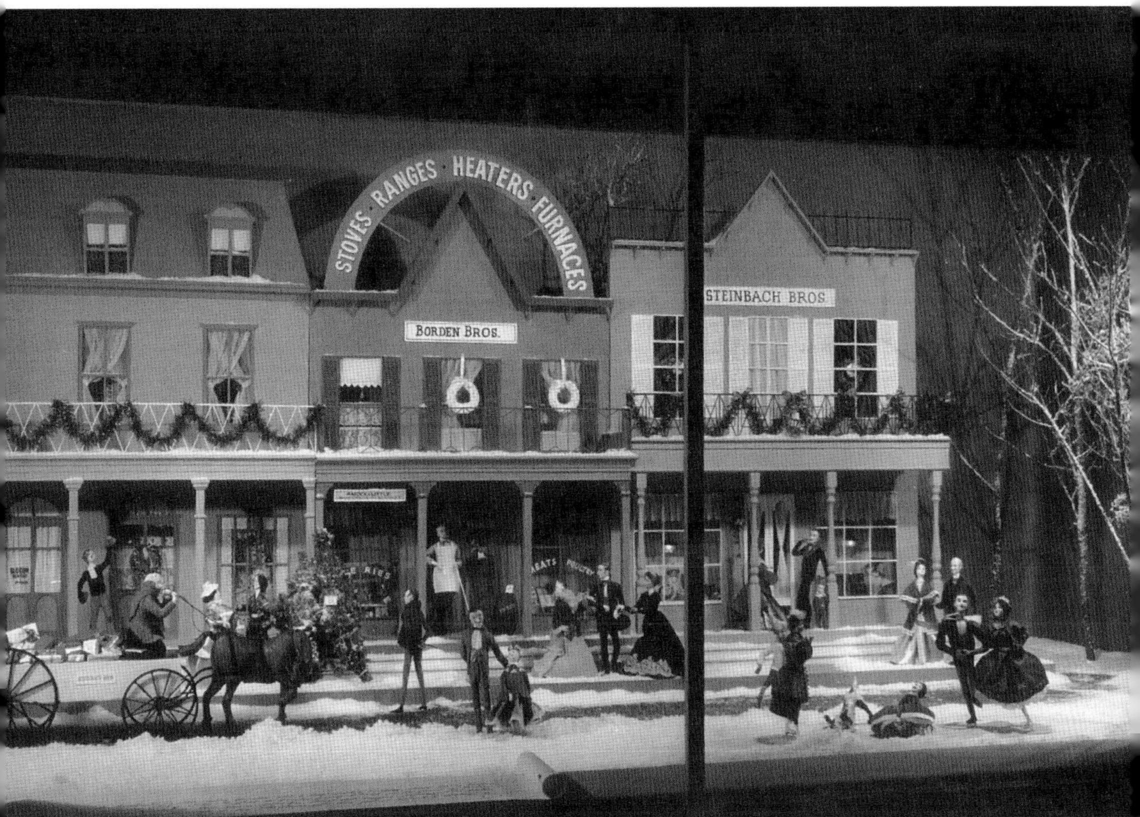

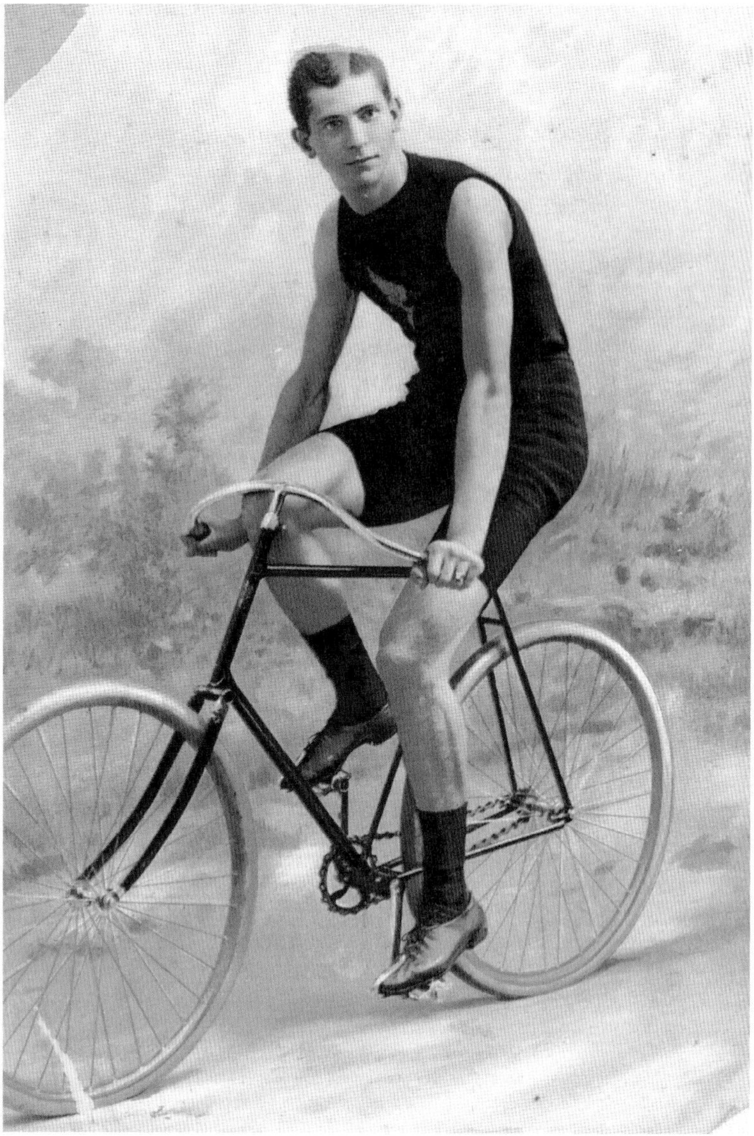

Call Him Zimmy

Europeans enthusiastically declared, "Not one single breath of suspicion has defiled the air as to the fairness of your riding, or the sportsmanship of your conduct." For Arthur Augustus Zimmerman, testimonials and audiences with royalty were secondary to the virtues of clean living, and in the 1890s, "Zimmy" came in second to no one. He held every bicycle-racing record (from the quarter mile to the 10 mile) in both the United States and Great Britain. The Camden native, who first caught the nation's attention at the 1893 Chicago World's Fair, moved to Asbury Park. It was there that he found community with his fellow members of the League of American Wheelmen, an organization whose 1894 national convention was hosted at a bike track and stadium built for the occasion near Deal Lake. Less fulfilling were his later business endeavors (including a locally manufactured bicycle known as the Zimmy), and by the time of his death in 1936, the one-time "World's Fastest Human" was reportedly working as a steward at the Belmar Moose Lodge. (Courtesy of the Monmouth County Historical Association Library and Archive.)

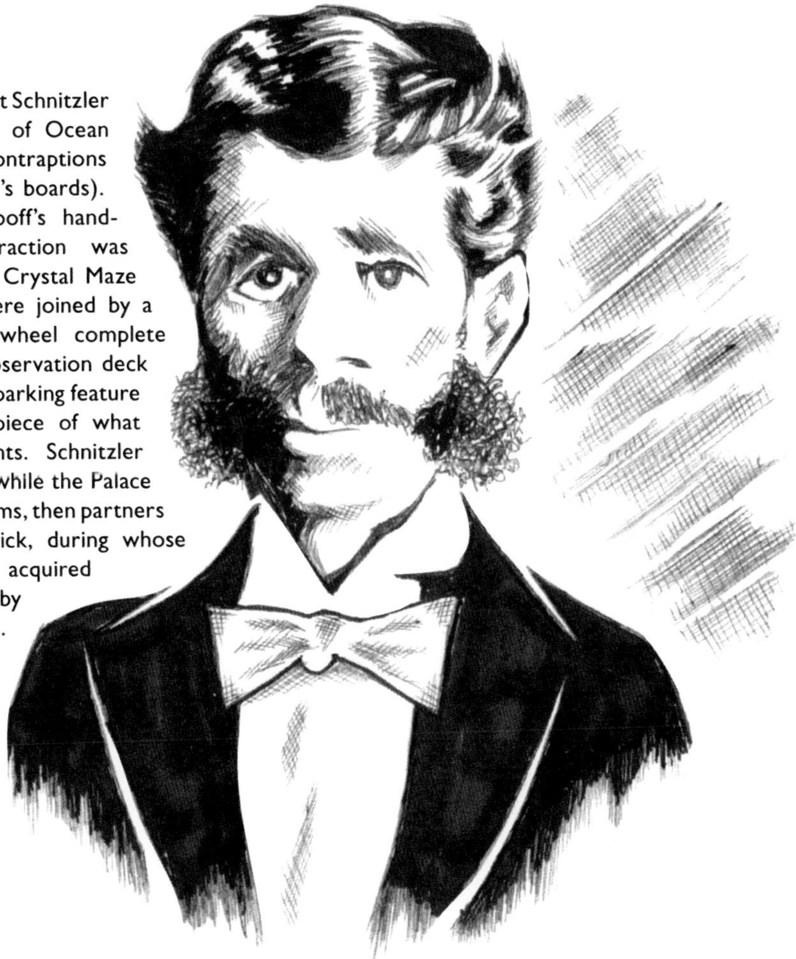

The Palace Guard

In 1888, German-born Ernest Schnitzler installed his carousel west of Ocean Avenue (such gaudy contraptions were prohibited on Bradley's boards). Equipped with Charles Looff's hand-carved animals, the attraction was augmented in 1890 by the Crystal Maze labyrinth. In 1895, they were joined by a 67-foot-tall, steam-driven wheel complete with Schnitzler-patented observation deck and electric lights; a noisy, sparking feature that remained the centerpiece of what became Palace Amusements. Schnitzler retired to Florida by 1920, while the Palace evolved under August Williams, then partners Ed Lange and Zimel Resnick, during whose tenure the indoor midway acquired the iconic "Tillie" faces by designer Worth Thomas. (Illustration by the author.)

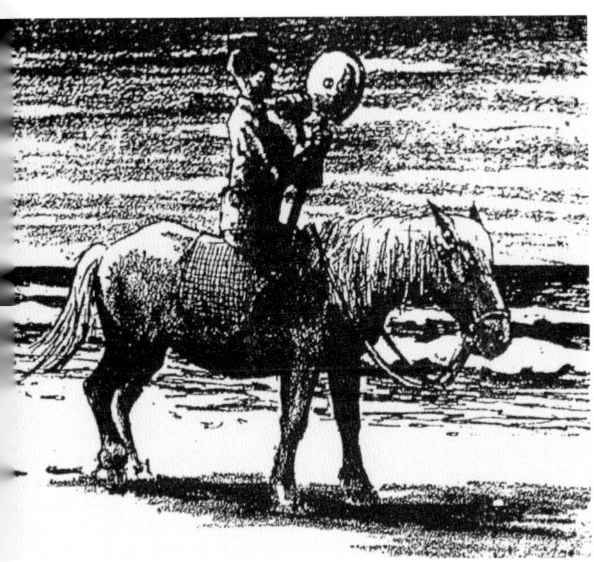

Bang a Gong

He was not exactly an officer of the law, more a night watchman or a town crier, but as per Founder Bradley, John Kittell was Asbury Park's first policeman. A Bradley employee rather than a public servant, Kittell patrolled the undeveloped beachfront on horseback, sounding the hour with a gong and mallet for the summer vacationers. In winter, he "kept an eye on the closed cottages and Mr. Bradley's tools." And, as keeper of the Fourth District station of the US Life-Saving Service, his quick response was credited with rescuing the crew of the schooner *Laura Bridgman* in June 1883. (Illustration by Bill King, courtesy of the Asbury Park Public Library.)

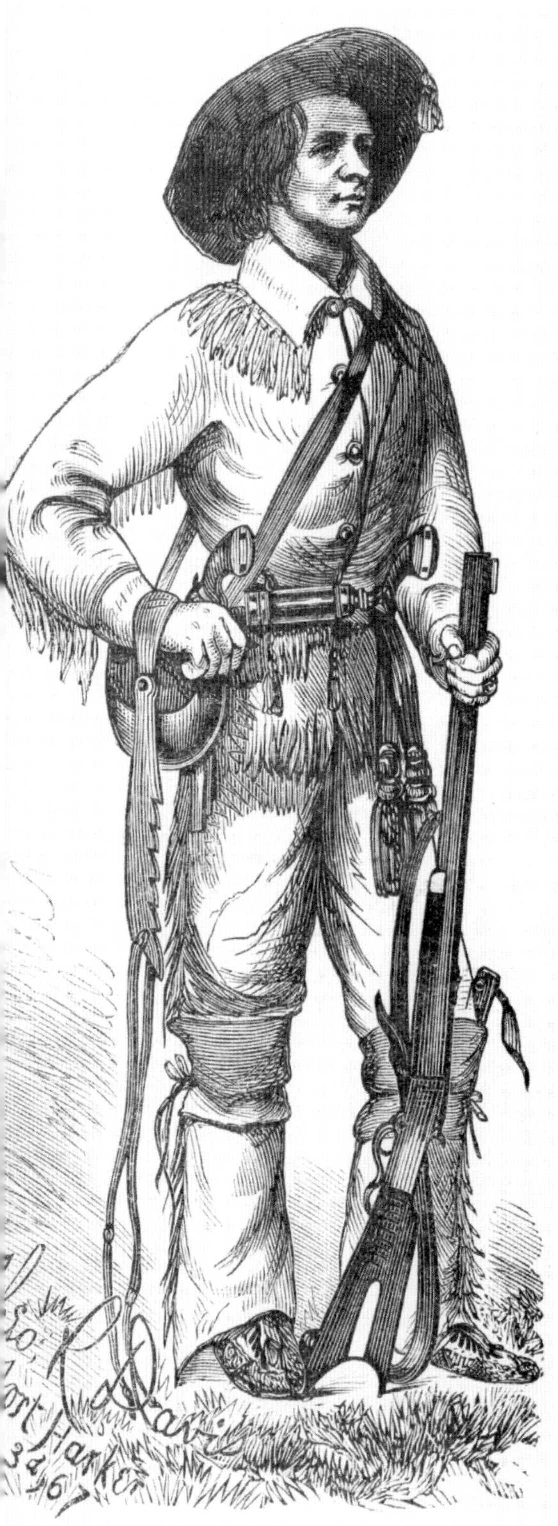

Man with a Pencil

"Theodore R. Davis, who died last week at his home in Asbury Park, N.J., was by no means the artist the obituarians of the daily press cracked him up to be," sniffed a November 1894 edition of the *Art Collector*. In actuality, Boston-born Davis was more than a fairly famous illustrator of his era, one whose skills were in demand from the White House to the "cyclorama" murals of the major expositions. He served as a sketching Civil War correspondent (for *Harper's* and others) during a time when news photography was in its impractical infancy, rode with Generals Sherman and McPherson, and was wounded on the field of battle. The young man who armed himself primarily with pencil and sketchbook was not the type to cover the conflict from the vantage of a big city office, believing that "to really see a battle . . . one must accept the most dangerous situations, for in most cases this can not possibly be avoided." And, when he retired to Asbury Park in 1879, his studio was not some cozy cottage on a shaded avenue but a beach hut so close to the surf that the breaking waves would often douse his fire as they crashed down the chimney.

Wiped out by a storm in 1888, the original Beach Studio (the place where the artist designed the new presidential china set ordered by First Lady Lucy Hayes) would be replaced by a repurposed bathhouse at Ocean and Sixth Avenues. An 1891 account in the *New York Times* describes the public curiosity attracted by the "dingy little brown-red building standing on piles on the beach outside the board walk." It is there that Davis would remain until his passing in 1894. A visit to present-day Asbury Park offers up a visible example of a design attributed to Davis: a large, Tiffany stained glass window on the west wall of the public library, inspired by the works of Henry Wadsworth Longfellow and dedicated to the memory of Dr. Henry Mitchell, the man who designed the city's sewer and sanitation system. (Courtesy of Prints & Photographs Division, Library of Congress.)

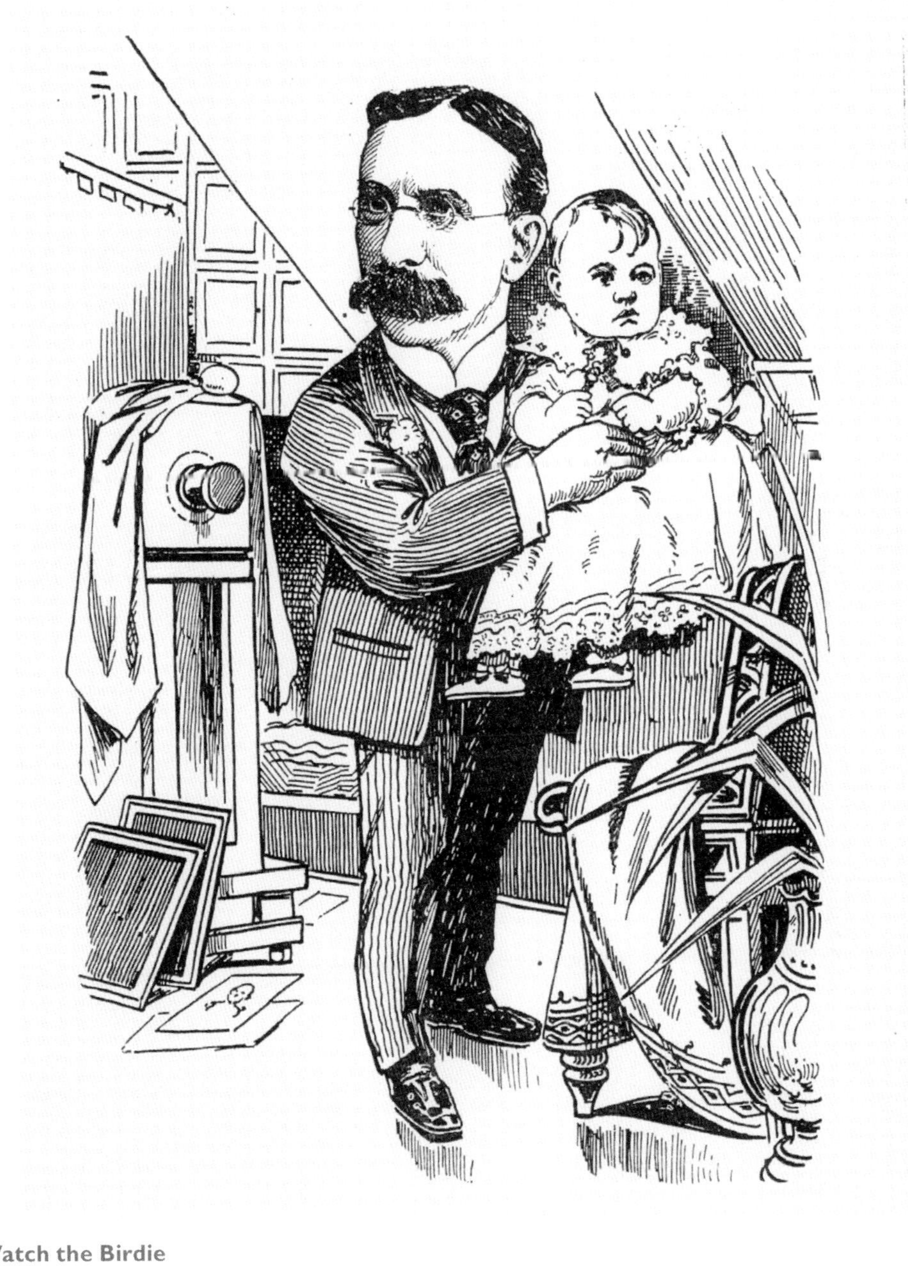

Watch the Birdie

William H. Stauffer had built a respectable career by the 1900s, establishing busy photography studios in Trenton and Asbury Park, patenting a new printing method, and taking portraits of everyone from janitors and waiters to famous athletes, entertainers, and writers (including a pre-fame Stephen Crane, see page 22). But it was in his capacity as "official Baby Parade photographer" that Stauffer would be best remembered; his images of the colorful annual event promoted the family-friendly virtues of the city's waterfront to the world beyond. His business would make him a local success story (he was reportedly one of the first people in town to own an automobile), but his late 1910s departure from Asbury Park was an abrupt and somewhat mysterious one, owing perhaps to "the intolerance against German descendants during World War I." (Courtesy of the Asbury Park Public Library.)

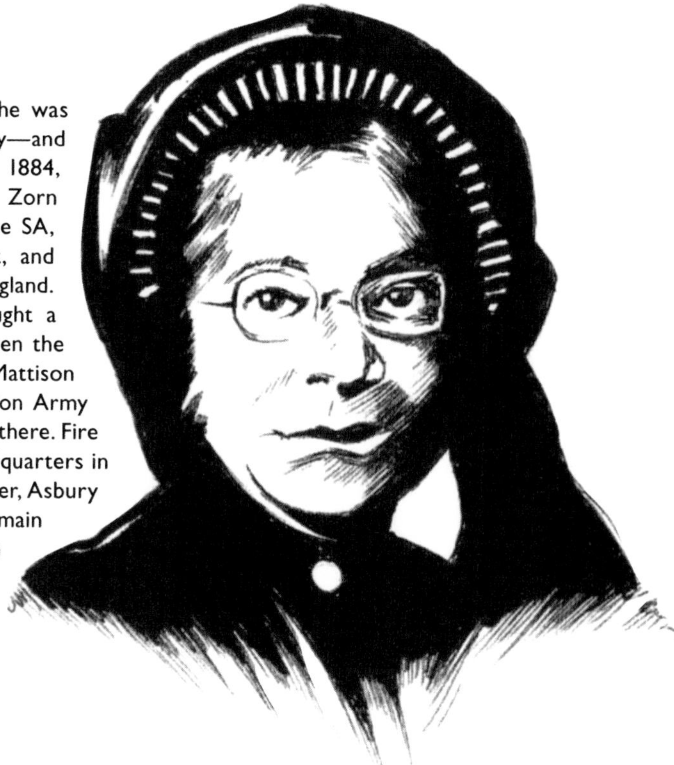

The Captain of His Heart

He was a local businessman; she was a captain in the Salvation Army—and when she came to town in 1884, bells rang. Before long, Jacob Zorn Stiles sold everything, joined the SA, married Capt. Elizabeth Pellatt, and honeymooned with her in England. Returning to Asbury, they sought a home for their mission, and when the organization dedicated its Mattison Avenue building in 1892, Salvation Army founder Gen. William Booth was there. Fire claimed that first of several headquarters in 1914, but more than 100 years later, Asbury Park and the Salvation Army remain a committed couple. (Illustration by the author.)

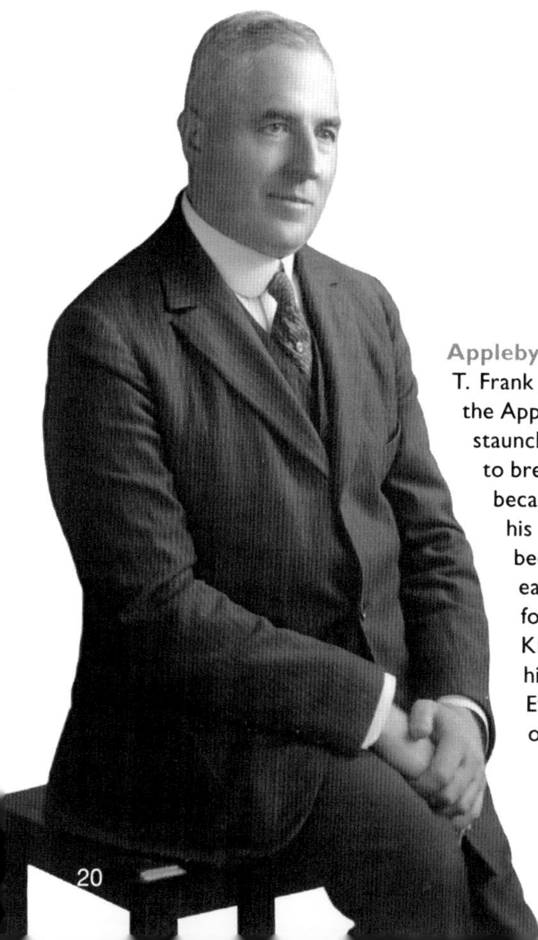

Appleby for Action

T. Frank Appleby was a 22-year-old councilman when he built the Appleby Building in 1886. As Bradley's realtor, he proved a staunch ally during the effort led by Councilman Bruce Keator to break the founder's grip on the waterfront. While Keator became mayor upon Bradley's resignation, Appleby had his turn by 1908. He was elected to Congress in 1920, becoming a vanguard supporter of some of the nation's earliest environmental legislation. Winning a 1924 bid for another term (during which he was endorsed by the KKK), he'd succumb to cancer before taking office, while his son would serve out his term. (Courtesy of Harris & Ewing Collection, Prints & Photographs Division, Library of Congress.)

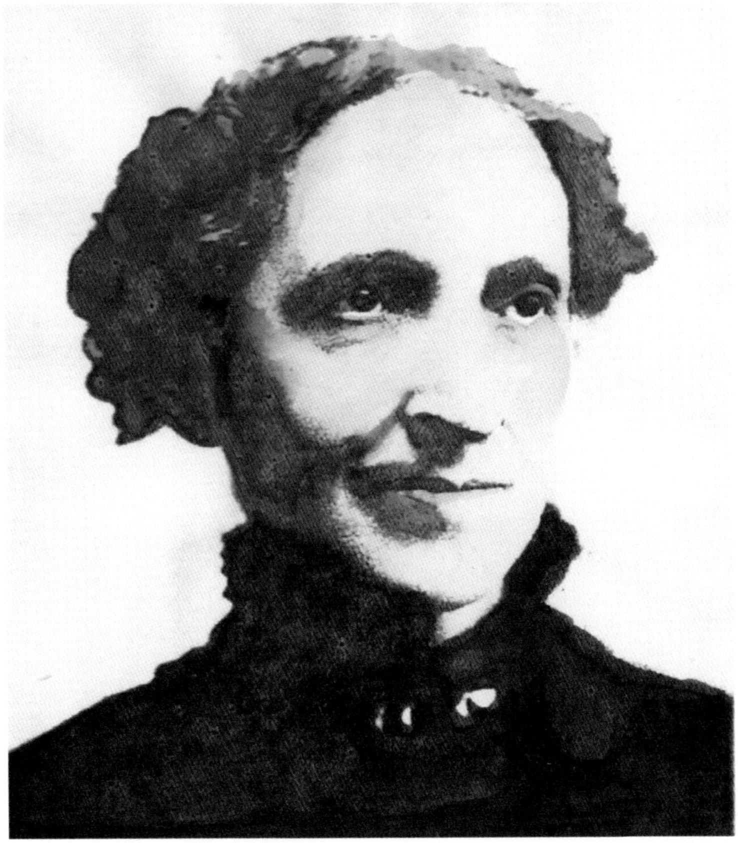

"More of a Christian than a Methodist"
A daughter of a "Methodist royalty" family and widow of a clergyman whose writings inveighed against the evils of slavery, intoxicating spirits, dancing, and chess, Mary Helen Peck Crane arrived in Methodist-friendly Asbury Park with her 27-year-old spinster daughter Agnes and 11-year-old son Stephen in the summer of 1883. They became the first year-round residents of Arbutus Cottage on Fourth Avenue, and she quickly assumed the presidency of the local Women's Christian Temperance Union chapter. A skilled communicator, both on the printed page and at the speaker's podium, "Helen" would augment her presentations on "The Effects of Alcohol on the Organs and Tissues of the Body" with creative touches, including dropping the white of an egg into a glass of liquor and explaining to her audience how the alcohol would harden the egg into a state that resembled "being cooked." She also advocated for women's rights, took in boarders (including an unwed mother-to-be), contributed dispatches to her son Townley Crane's locally based news service, and tried her hand at some comically folksy stories penned under the playful persona of "Jerusha Ann Stubbs, of the Skrub Oak Skule Deestrick."

Leaving the upbringing of her youngest child to Agnes, the first Crane to publish a work of fiction, Helen threw herself into her work with the WCTU, opening her home to its members (including cofounder Frances Willard, one of the most famous women of her day), delivering lectures, traveling to Union conventions in far-flung cities, and helping Crane daughter Nellie Van Nortwick set up what is thought to be the first art school in Asbury Park. In declining physical health and reportedly suffering from an "aberration of the mind," the Crane family matriarch passed away in December 1891. Stephen Crane would sell his share of the Asbury Park property to his older brother William in order to finance self-publication of his debut novel, *Maggie: A Girl of the Streets*. Arbutus Cottage, rechristened the Stephen Crane House in 1995, honors the legacy of Helen, Agnes, and the Crane clan. (Courtesy of the Stephen Crane House.)

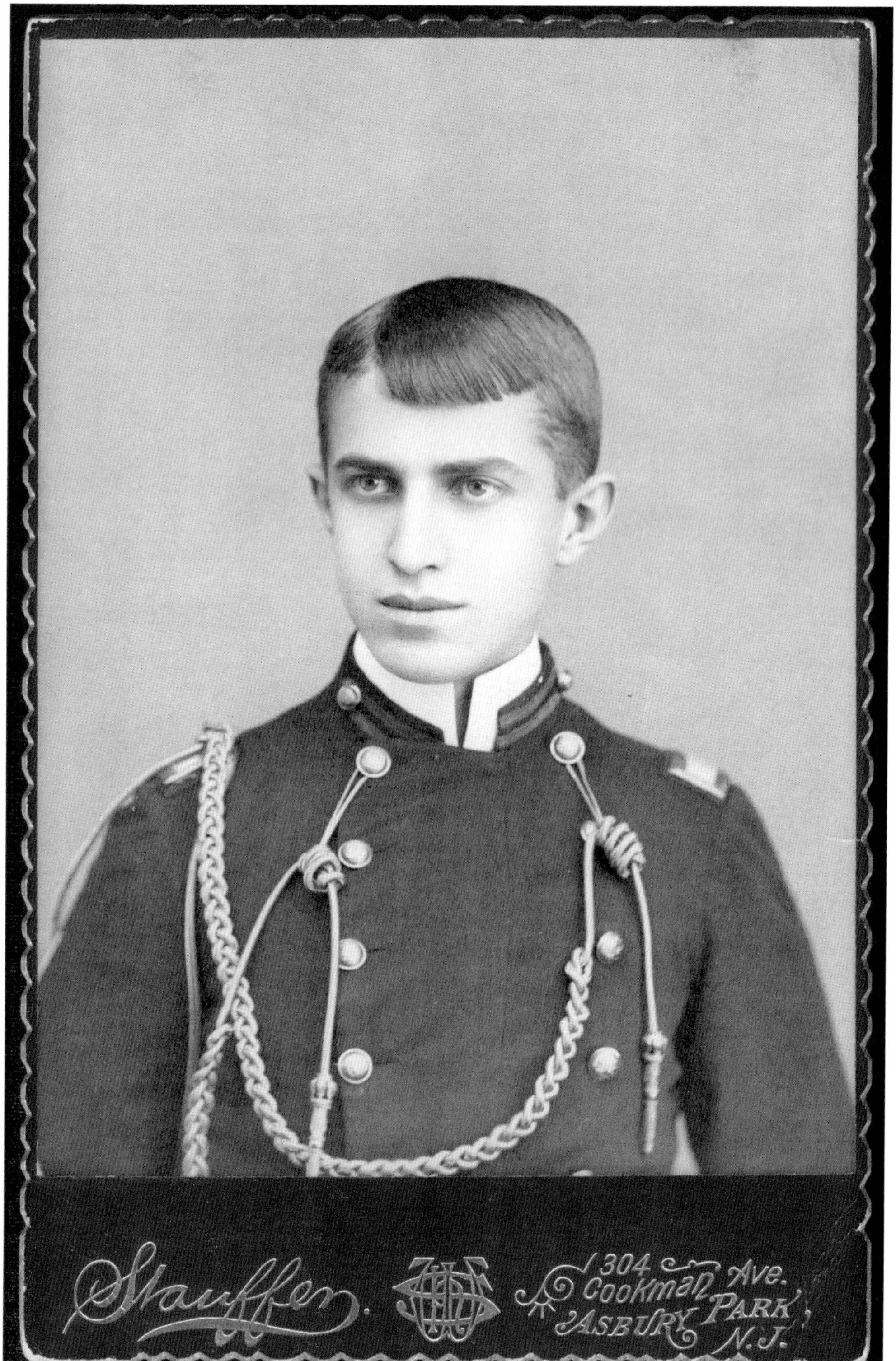
Stauffer.
304 Cookman Ave.
ASBURY PARK N.J.

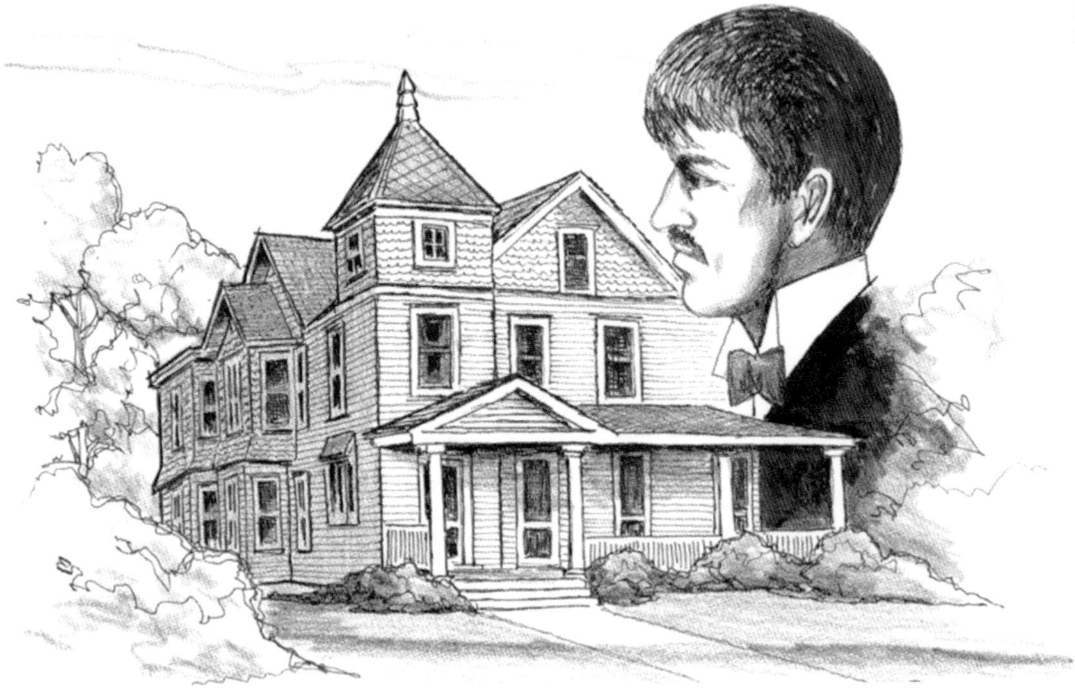

"A True Jerseyman" (OPPOSITE PAGE AND ABOVE)
In what is likely the only existing photograph taken of him in Asbury Park, a teenaged Stephen Crane is pictured (opposite page) as a lieutenant in the Hudson River Institute cadet corps. William Stauffer's portrait notwithstanding, "Stevie" never managed to graduate from military school, or from Syracuse University, the school that houses his archives. Crane preferred instead to receive his seminal education and find his calling on the summer-season boards and boulevards.

Born after the Civil War that he captured so vividly in his best-known novel, *The Red Badge of Courage*, and left to his own devices in a household headed by his activist mother, young Stevie acquired his first professional writing experience as an anonymous correspondent for his brother Townley's news service. He covered the comings and goings of the vacationing throngs and put his powers of observation to work in a series of sharply written dispatches. Local encounters with famous author-lecturers Jacob Riis and Hamlin Garland would catalyze his sense of social justice, and working drafts of his early books *Maggie* and *Sullivan County Sketches* would lead to his first fiction publications in major newspapers and magazines.

Stephen Crane and Asbury Park had evidently had enough of each other by summer of 1892, when his affair with a married woman came to light, and his controversial account of a civic parade by the Junior American Mechanics cost him his job (It was even said to have cost the Republicans the White House that year). Crane would return, famous if not exactly rich, to write one more provocative piece about the city he long claimed as his primary residence, and Asbury Park would continue to exert an influence on such later works as "The Pace of Youth." The rest of Crane's short life would see him traveling out West, covering foreign wars on two continents, being shipwrecked off the coast of Florida, and moving to Europe, where he hobnobbed with literary contemporaries Joseph Conrad, Henry James, and H.G. Wells. Crane died in 1900 at the age of 28, while the former Arbutus Cottage (the only standing residence in the United States associated with the man that Hemingway famously dubbed "one of the good writers") was rescued from demolition in the 1990s. The Stephen Crane House was named to the State Registry of Historic Places in 2014. (Photograph courtesy of Clifton Waller Barrett Library of American Literature, Albert and Shirley Small Special Collections Library, University of Virginia; illustration by Bill King, courtesy of the Stephen Crane House.)

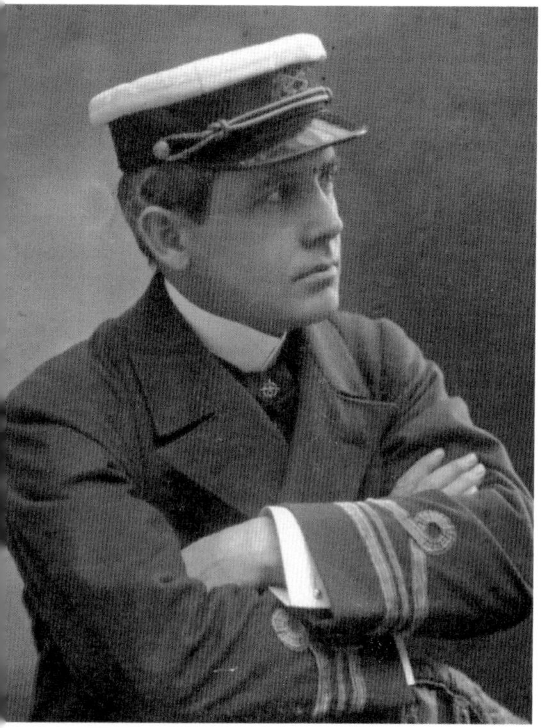

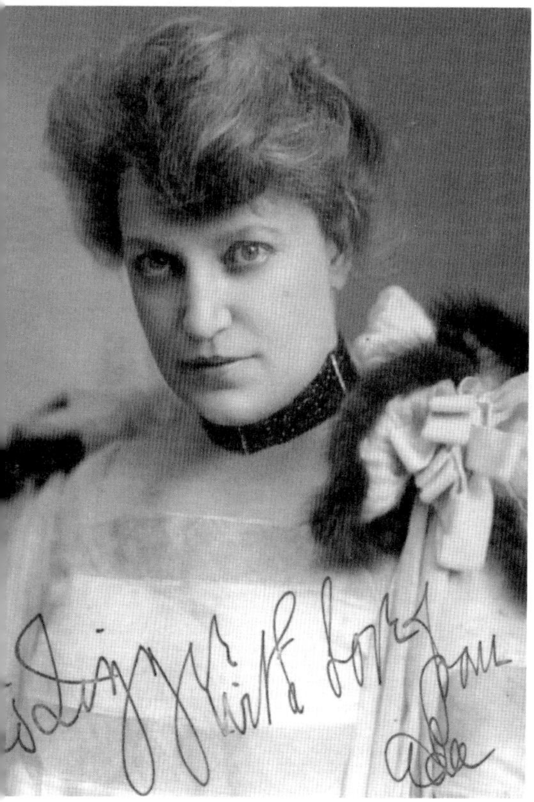

The Social Whirl

It is said that Charlie Ross, when asked if his mother was aware that he was an actor, responded, "Heavens, no! She'd be worried to death if she knew I was an actor; she thinks I'm a thief." Ross and his wife, Mabel Fenton, were hardly your average troupers, and their Asbury Park address was anything but a sedate cottage getaway. Blessed with leading-man looks and comedic gifts, Ross (born Charles J. Kelly) was an ex-jockey turned singing impressionist when he met and quickly married Fenton (née Ada May Towne) during a whistle-stop in Deadwood, South Dakota. It was not until the newlyweds teamed as Ross and Fenton that they ascended through the ranks of touring burlesque performers—their versatile skills serving them well in parody skits, silent shorts, and Broadway revues like *The Merry Widow Burlesque*, *The Social Whirl* and Flo Ziegfeld's inaugural *Follies*. When not on the road, the "congenial, delightful, well-matched comedy alliance" could be found holding court at Ross Fenton Farm, their home and hotel resort complex, which attracted a guest list of fellow entertainers and bohemians. It was there that Ross passed away in 1918 after a long illness, but Fenton continued to host the likes of Lillian Russell, Sophie Tucker, and John Philip Sousa. The farm resort would later come under the ownership of theater mogul Walter Reade, and Ross and Fenton would reteam one last time, when they were interred together in nearby West Long Branch, New Jersey. (Courtesy of Ocean Township Historical Society.)

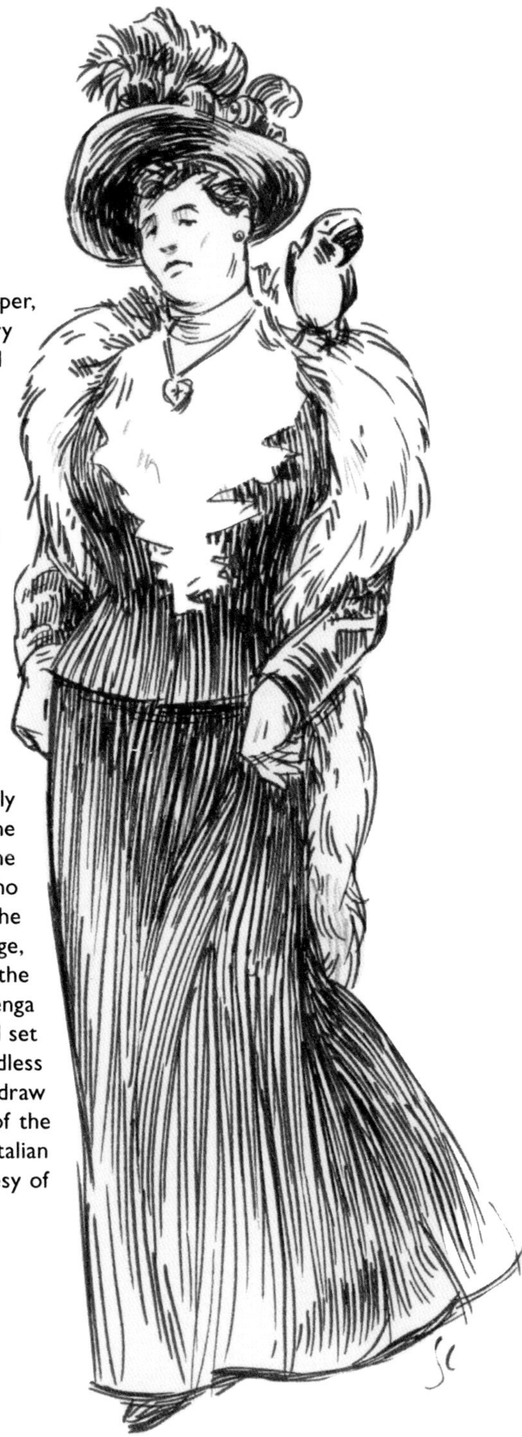

Call Her Padrone

The word *padrone* is defined variously as a boss, an innkeeper, a landlord, a protector, and, in many 19th-century immigrant communities, a trusted contact who served as anything from a banker to an employment agent for recent arrivals. The inference was that the padrone was a man, but in early Asbury Park's Italian neighborhood, the role of village padrone was fulfilled by Rosa Musto, reportedly the first Italian woman to settle on the young city's West Side. Following several of her male relatives who obtained jobs on the Shore railroad line, the baker's daughter quickly established a boardinghouse that may very well have been Monmouth County's first Italian eatery, a gathering place for fellow countrymen and a base from which Rosa would cement her standing as the undisputed Queen of Little Italy. Expanding into a grocery business, and investing in West Side real estate (in addition to handling the personal savings of her Little Italy charges), the "kind, loving, firm and fiercely pugnacious" Rosa Musto would reportedly become the wealthiest person in the Italian community by the time of her 1927 passing. She was a larger-than-life figure who "had a scar on her cheek and was always done up in the most elegant clothes and jewels . . . she had a carriage, a talking parrot, and would always be at the head of the church parade." In 1896, she became Rosa Musto Benvenga when she married a much younger man, and she helped set him up in the nightclub, hotel, and liquor business. Childless throughout her nearly 50-year reign, she would draw one of the largest funeral processions in the history of the city, reinforcing the fact that, in the end, "the entire Italian community here was her child." (Copyright and courtesy of Susan Culbert.)

Down at Asbury Park

He has been called "Asbury Park's first musical superstar," and even that does not come close to capturing the broad appeal and influence of Arthur Willard Pryor at the height of his fame. The Missouri-born trombonist, composer, and bandleader was second in popularity only to legendary "March King" John Philip Sousa at the dawn of the 20th century; in fact, Pryor had made his name as star soloist and assistant conductor for Sousa's organization before striking off on his own. Pryor's new band afforded him a chance to further showcase his innovative soloing technique as well as his then-radical affinity for the syncopations of the nascent ragtime styles. After several seasons of intensive coast-to-coast touring, he made the bold decision to base his activities permanently in Asbury Park, where he first put down roots in 1904.

Pryor had already been a frequent presence on the Asbury boardwalk, and the salt air would work its way into compositions such as "On Jersey Shore," "The Baby Parade," and "Down at Asbury Park." He became a long-running fixture in the summer of 1909. The notion of an entertainer as a destination attraction would presage latter-day Las Vegas, and it was during these years that Pryor would create his greatest hit, "The Whistler and His Dog," a jaunty march that New Yorkers of a certain advanced age will recall as the theme to the *Officer Joe Bolton* show.

Pryor retired to his Long Branch farm in 1933 and briefly served as a member of the Monmouth County Board of Chosen Freeholders. He passed the baton to protégée Frank Bryan, whose Asbury Park Municipal Band—a mix of high school students, local amateurs, and first-chair players from major symphony orchestras—would perform a full summer schedule at the 400-seat Arthur Pryor Band Shell on the boardwalk's north end. In 1961, a strikingly modern doo-wop pavilion at Fifth Avenue dedicated a new rooftop 1,400-seat band shell to Pryor. The venue is scheduled for renovation, after having fallen into neglect and decay. The old-timey sounds have continued into the 21st century, however, courtesy of John Luckenbill and the Asbury Park Concert Band. In 2012, Pryor was named as one of the first inductees to Asbury Angels and its musically minded memorial hall of fame. (Courtesy of the Asbury Park Historical Society.)

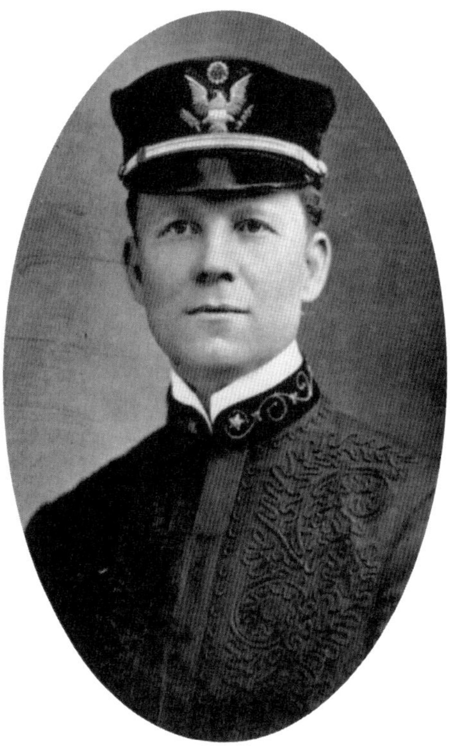

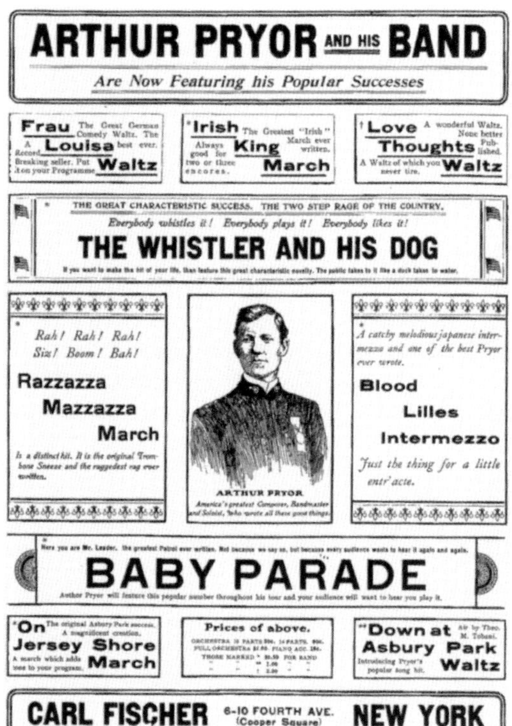

CHAPTER TWO

Wear a Boardwalk Smile

1904–1929

You'll meet Uncle Aunty too / There'll be Clara Rose and Sue / You'll meet Harry George and Jake / Then you stick right out your hand, make them feel so grand / With a warm hand shake / When the band begins to play / Every body seems so gay

—Charles B. Weston

Granted, this little-known ditty by forgotten songsmith Charles B. Weston failed to set the sheet music racks on fire when it appeared in 1926. But, with its postcard views of vintage boardwalk scenes on the cover, its jaunty implication that music was the essence of life in Asbury Park, and its possibly prescient nod to gay "Uncle Aunty," it is an anthem every bit as valid as Pryor's made-to-order marches.

The boardwalk itself was sporting a more polished smile in the early years of the new century, having cleaned up its act considerably in the wake of its divestiture by James Bradley. Bright lighting, dazzling amusements, new hotels, and grand pavilions would herald a post-Bradley age in the family-friendly summer resort, even as the nation moved toward a social model patched with the moralistic fiber of the founder.

The city's toothy public grin masked an Asbury Park that was hardly accommodating to certain diverse and growing segments of the populace. The institutionalized racism of the Bradley years—energized by a re-emergent Ku Klux Klan on the Jersey Shore—ensured that the beaches, bandstands, and other major amusements remained segregated and largely off limits to those who staffed its hotels, shops, and restaurants.

The irony was that the West Side was becoming a fast growing city-within-a-city with its own houses of worship and its own thriving center of commerce on Springwood Avenue, a mix of discount stores, neighborhood merchants, and entertainment establishments that ranged from upscale to down-market to downright illegal.

Inside the bars, billiard rooms and brothels, the land west of the tracks was also developing its own soundtrack—one that would get noticed by a couple of summering teens named Bill Basie and Edward Ellington (who would make friends here with the man who became his longtime drummer, Sonny Greer). The West Side was also noticed by an ambitious public servant named Clarence Hetrick, a man who would come to play that popular support like a grand movie-palace organ.

The smiles of campaigning politicians aside, there appeared to be real reasons for citizens of Asbury Park to take pride in their little town. It was becoming a place of breathtaking new buildings, first-class diversions, and thriving commercial enterprise—a place where the most famous people in America (Babe Ruth, Mary Pickford, and even the president) came to pay a visit, and where a new generation of year-round residents was going forth to make its mark in the world. Asbury Park wore a boardwalk smile and extended a hearty handshake, but in the background the skies grayed, the sea churned, and the storm clouds gathered in advance of some challenging seasons ahead.

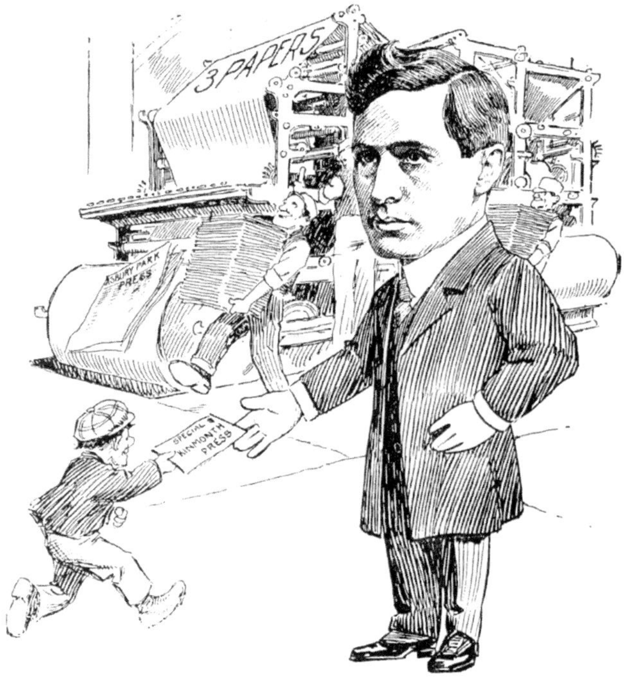

Power of the Press

Its masthead has changed several times over the years, and the current logo evokes an age of downloadable apps rather than the smell of hot type and the smear of ink on pulpy newsprint. But the *Asbury Park Press* traces a line to the 1879 founding of the summer weekly *Shore Press* by Dr. Hugh S. Kinmonth (see page 14). In 1895, the busy doctor sold the paper to his nephew Jesse Lyle Kinmonth, who shepherded the small-town intelligencer into year-round daily publication, surmounting challenges from rival publications owned by Bradley and movie-house mogul Walter Reade Sr. With printing and editorial operations consolidated within a formidable building straddling Mattison and Bangs Avenues, the *Press* became one of the city's major employers. J. Lyle Kinmonth was a pillar of the community, who headed the local Rotary Club, the Chamber of Commerce, and the New Jersey Press Association. While his one bid for a congressional seat was thwarted in 1925, "JLK" and his forum proved influential shapers of public opinion in the campaigns for public ownership of the beachfront, relaxation of anti-liquor statutes, and the easing of restrictions against Sunday train service to the Asbury station. Following Kinmonth's death in 1945, the company established a radio station with the call letters WJLK (a signature that the spun-off entity retains to this day).

The *Press* maintained a presence in downtown Asbury through the second half of the 20th century, lending its name to Press Plaza and kick-starting the careers of investigative journalist Fred Cook, Pulitzer-winning cartoonist Steve Breen, NPR's Eric Deggans, and the Grammy Museum's Robert Santelli. The publisher's chair transitioned to Wayne D. McMurry (1945), Ernest W. Lass (1955) and Jules L. Plangere Jr. (1977), and downtown operations were moved to a new building four miles west in Neptune. The nationwide media company Gannett purchased the *Press* and other properties in the late 1990s, and while the rapidly advancing digital age transformed the print product into a shade of its former self, it took Hurricane Sandy and the loss of power, phone, cable and Internet access to remind residents how the daily paper once kept the people of the Jersey Shore connected to and engaged with each other. (Courtesy of the Asbury Park Public Library.)

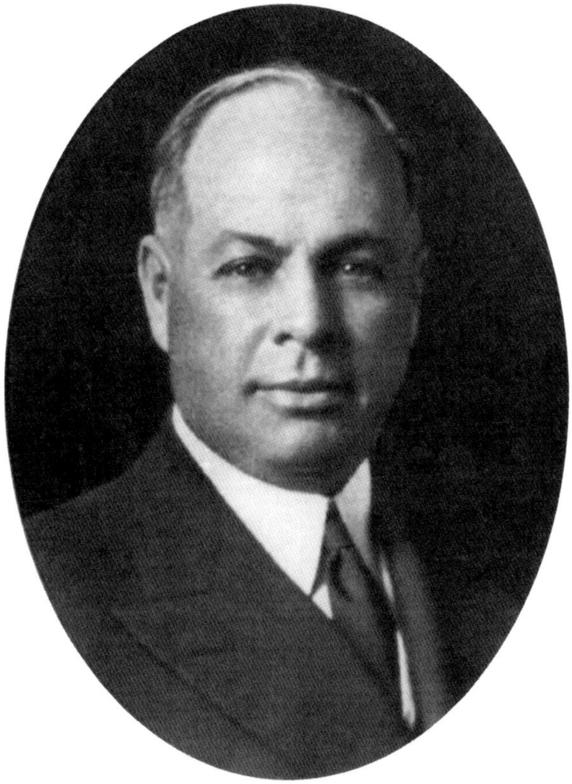

The Great Dictator

To the West Side Jews and African Americans who had only recently become full-fledged Asbury Parkers, Monmouth County sheriff Clarence E.F. Hetrick was "The Man Who Saved the City from the KKK." It was an accolade first earned when the investigation into the murder of 10-year-old Marie Smith cleared handyman "Black Diamond" Williams of the charge, and he spirited the accused man away from a lynch mob (A German-born florist named Frank Heidemann was eventually convicted of the crime).

It would be the West Side vote that put Clarence Hetrick over the top during the chaotic 1915 campaign for Asbury Park mayor, and the ethnic communities became his dependable power base. The fellow West Sider maintained a grip on the office that continued, off and on, for nearly 25 years. Hetrick would again run afoul of Klan-connected elements (and the Methodists, and the press, and the city's East Side) during a rollercoaster reign of nearly unchecked growth and consolidation of power. He earned the title of "dictator" for his expensive public construction projects, his efforts to put Asbury Park on an equal footing with Atlantic City and larger cities to the north, and his tendency to dig in against all opposition. The mayor also used his public pulpit to secure a position as a well-compensated lobbyist for a cabal of electrical utilities—a gig that would find Hetrick spending more time in Washington than at city hall while largely unaccountable backroom cronies in Depression-era Asbury would be issuing scrip to city employees by 1934.

A referendum that year created a new model of government, organized around nonpartisan council elections and a strong city manager position, which ousted Hetrick in favor of hotelier Sherman Dennis. The ex-mayor mounted a vigorous recall campaign—an effort that would be the impetus for Dennis's fatal heart attack and the return of Clarence Hetrick to office in 1935. It was an extended final act that saw the aging dictator fighting the state over its takeover of municipal finances, and he finally lost his seat when a reform slate won a council majority in 1941. The man who had ruled Asbury Park for a generation was now a mere councilman, and by October of that year, he was dead of diabetes-related complications at the age of 68. (Courtesy of the Asbury Park Historical Society.)

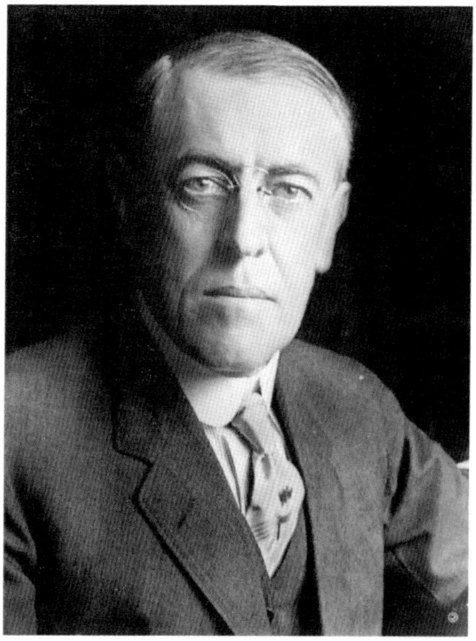

Summer of My President

He was not the first sitting president to visit Asbury Park—Taft reportedly enjoyed an operetta at the Savoy in 1911—and President Obama would declare the storm-battered boardwalk "open for business" in 2013. But, in the summer of 1916, Woodrow Wilson could be spotted at the downtown Byram building when not conducting business at the old Shadow Lawn estate in West Long Branch. While the former New Jersey governor's "White House Summer Executive Offices" in the onetime post office were more precisely a campaign headquarters, the rechristened Post Building now sports a plaque honoring that interlude when Asbury claimed Summer White House status. (Courtesy of Prints & Photographs Division, Library of Congress.)

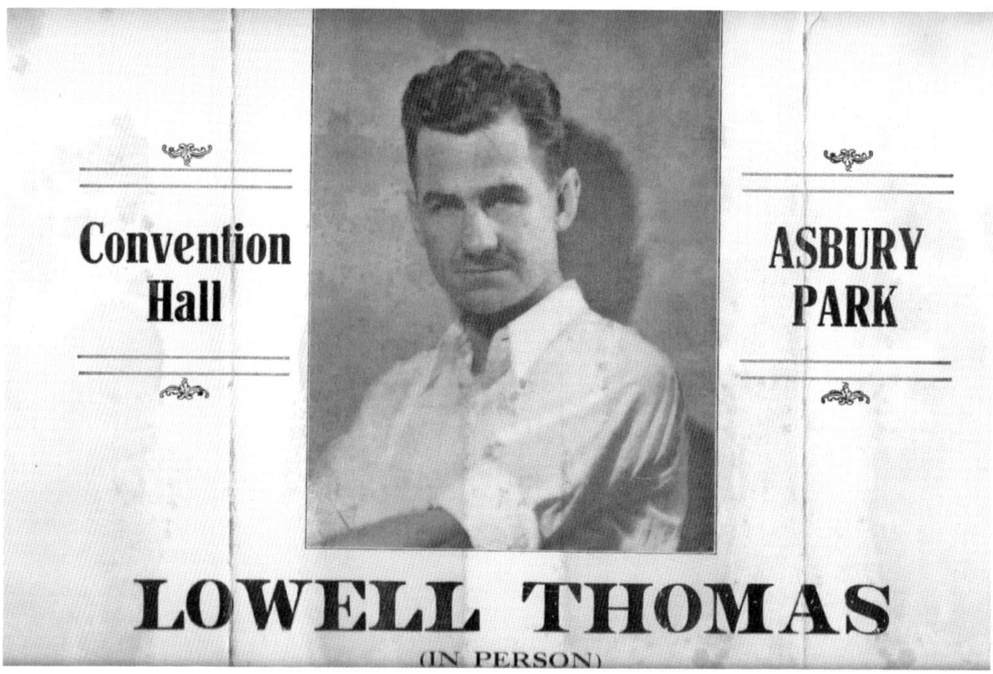

So Long, Until Tomorrow

He was "The World's Foremost Globetrotter," thanks to his travels with British soldier-adventurer T.E. Lawrence and the popular touring presentations drawn from his experience. Colorado-raised Lowell Thomas came east to attend Princeton and followed his parents, Dr. Harry and Harriet Thomas, when they became Asbury Park residents. It is while living with them between 1922 and 1923 that he penned his best-selling *With Lawrence in Arabia*. Even as Thomas found international renown as a broadcaster and newsreel narrator, he continued making return appearances in Asbury. The decades ahead saw Lowell dabble in television and author dozens of books, while his father made an unsuccessful bid for a city council seat in 1945. (Courtesy of Ocean Township Historical Society.)

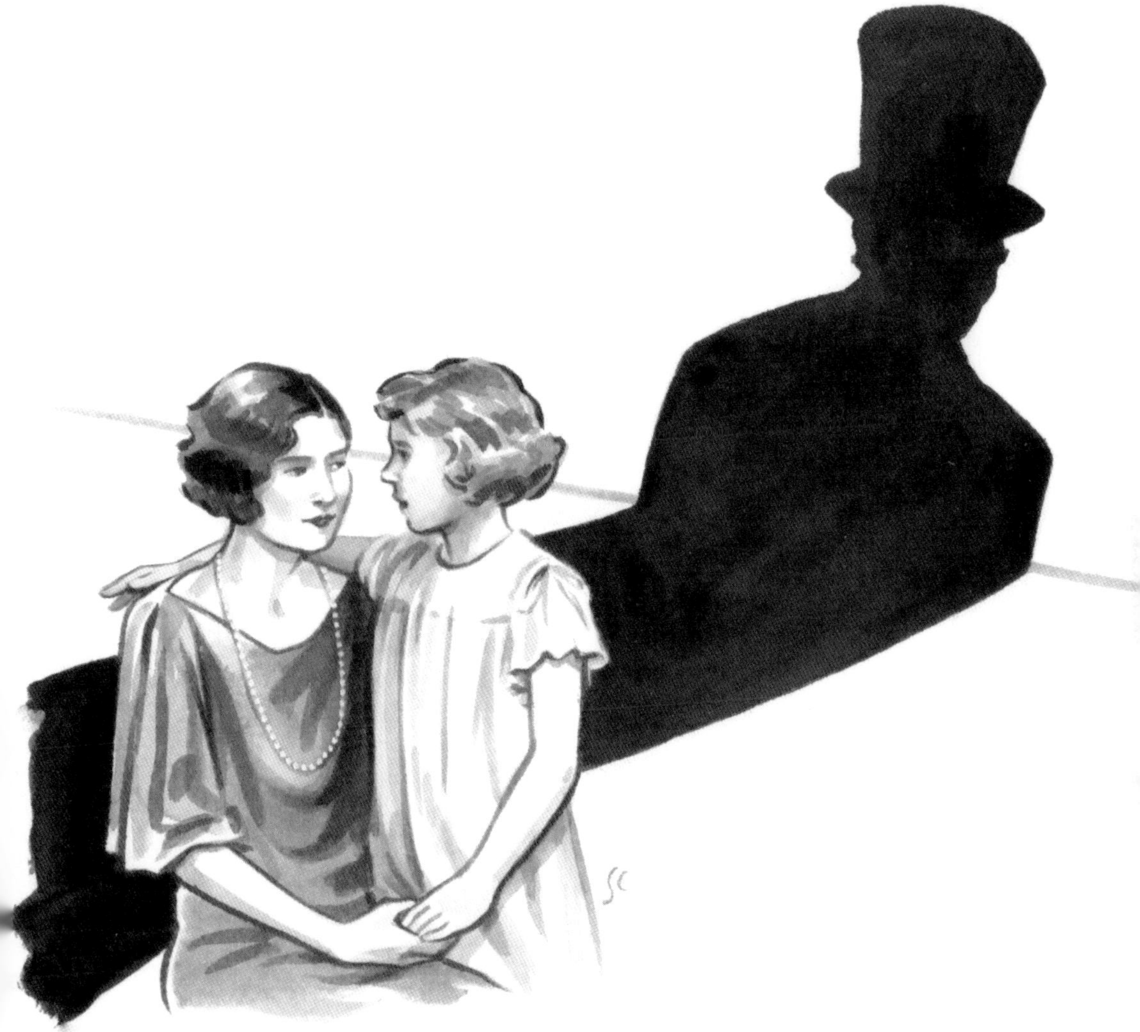

The President's Daughter

There is no record of what neighbors thought of the young, single lady who moved into the Bond Street cottage in the summer of 1919; no reports of her appearing in public; and no accounts of visitors prior to that October day when Dr. James Ackerman delivered a healthy baby girl. The mother was a former secretary named Nan Britton, and the child, according to "Nanny," was the illegitimate daughter of Warren G. Harding, then one year away from being elected president of the United States. Although she never proved that the senator from Ohio fathered the child who came to be known as Elizabeth Ann Britton Harding Blaesing, Nanny would insist until her passing in 1991 (beginning with her sensational memoir *The President's Daughter*, published five years after Harding's sudden death in 1923) that the baby was the product of an affair which continued well into the 29th president's time in office. Rebuffed in her attempts to collect support from Harding's estate, Nanny never said who installed her and a female chaperone on that quiet side street. Elizabeth, who died in 2005, never discussed the topic of her paternity in any public forum. (Copyright and courtesy of Susan Culbert.)

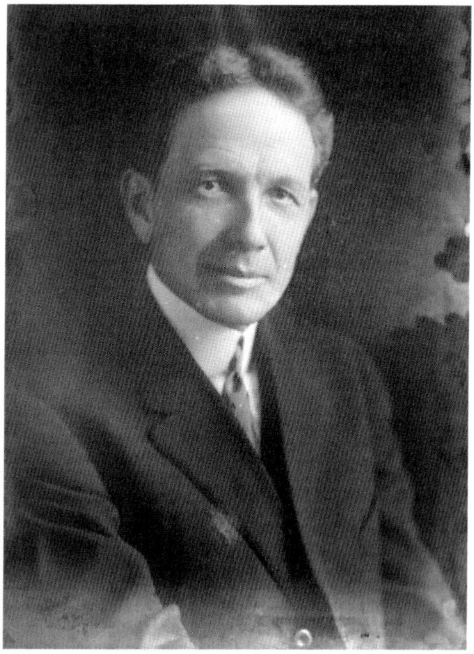

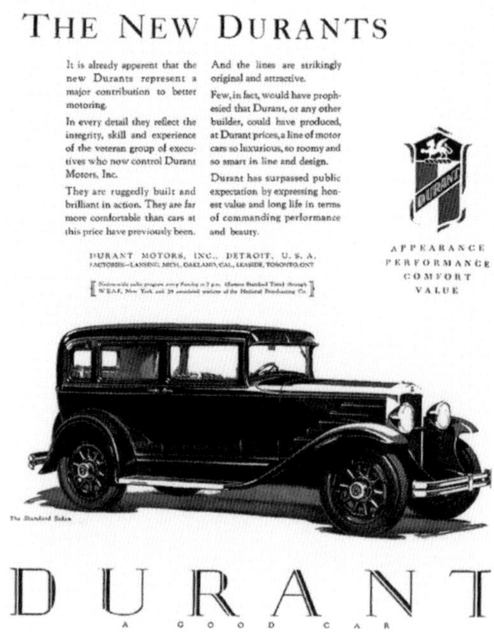

From Buicks to Burgers

Call him the John Z. DeLorean of his day; the former executive from General Motors whose attempts to launch an independent automotive line bearing his name would both forge his legacy and ruin him. His car was not built in Asbury Park; that honor would go exclusively to the Richelieu, only about 50 of which were made inside a Railroad Avenue garage between 1922 and 1923. But, for William C. Durant, Asbury was the logical location for the flagship dealership of his Durant Motor Car, a block-long showroom between Fifth and Sunset Avenues. Durant, who had assembled General Motors from Buick, Cadillac, Oldsmobile, and several other short-lived product lines, found himself ousted from the board in 1920. Just six months after incorporating his new company in 1921, the seasonal resident of nearby Deal was peddling his first Durant models at a brisk clip. He moved a respectable number of units in the early 1920s (in addition to Star cars, the Durant's four-cylinder, lower priced cousin), gaining him a spectacular mansion once owned by one of the Rothschilds. The 1929 stock market crash would sound the death knell for the Durant, however, and by the early 1940s a bankrupt Bill was reportedly running a bowling alley and burger stand in Flint, Michigan. (Courtesy of Bain Collection, Prints & Photographs Division, Library of Congress.)

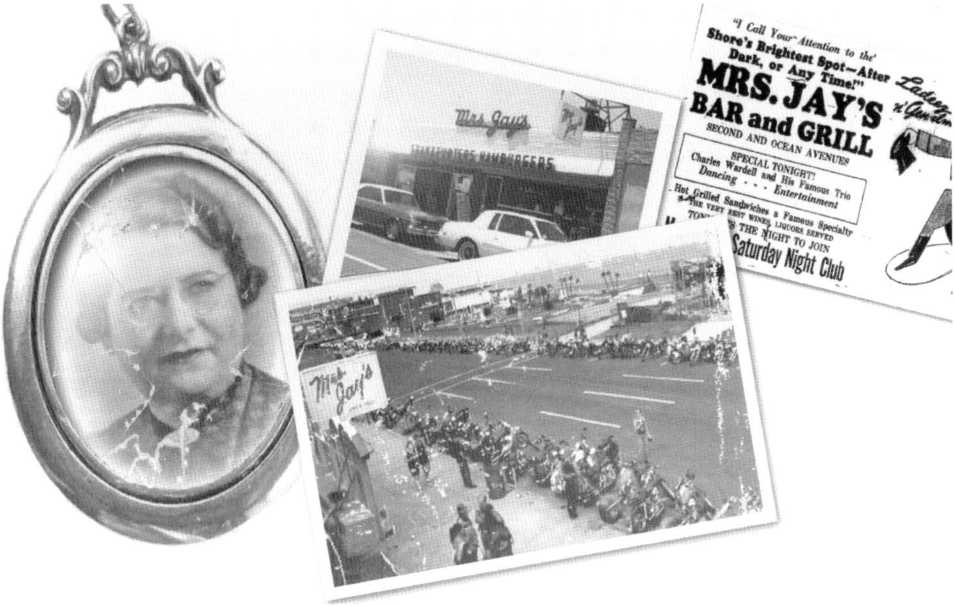

Ida's Garden

The lady whose name came to adorn the legendary biker bar Mrs. Jay's was not some swaggering frontier saloon-keep but a family restaurateur named Ida Jacobs. In the mid-1920s, Ida and her husband, John, transformed a hotdog stand at Ocean and Second Avenues into a full-service dining room, adding a "beer" garden, and, following Prohibition's repeal, an enclosed Circus Bar. Their daughter Jeanette Jacobs Weiner introduced the live entertainment, and Mrs. Jay's soldiered through the 1970s and 1980s as a place of seminal music and weird scenes, while today the beer garden footprint marks the site of the Stone Pony's Summer Stage enclosure. (Author's collection).

Coney Island Baby

Long before anyone endeavored to save Tillie, the iconic image and its quasi-official nickname were appropriated from a logo with deep roots in the amusements biz. With the leering caricature of Coney Island kingpin George Tilyou (or his brother Edward) as its mascot, Tilyou's Steeplechase empire stretched from Coney to Connecticut and Atlantic City to Asbury Park, where the veteran showman staked out a block of Ocean Avenue in 1915. Boasting a rollercoaster, underground ghost ride, and a walk-through "Insanitarium" (complete with notorious skirt-raising Blowhole Theater), the Steeplechase flared briefly but brightly, leaving Tillie's Cheshire grin behind. (Courtesy of the Asbury Park Public Library.)

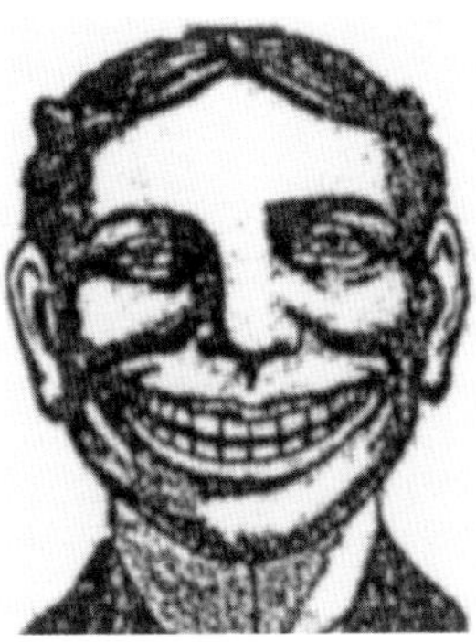

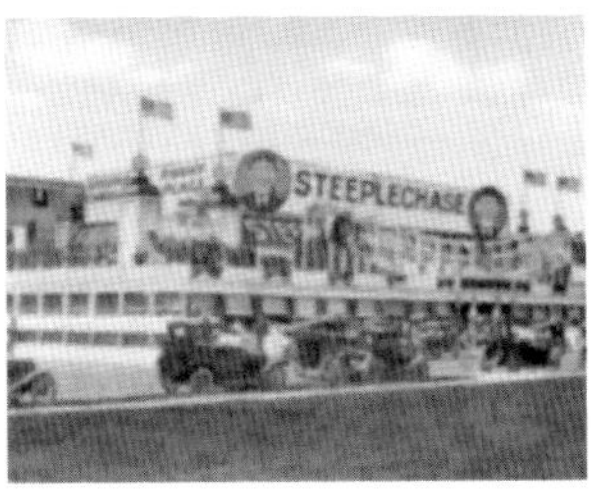

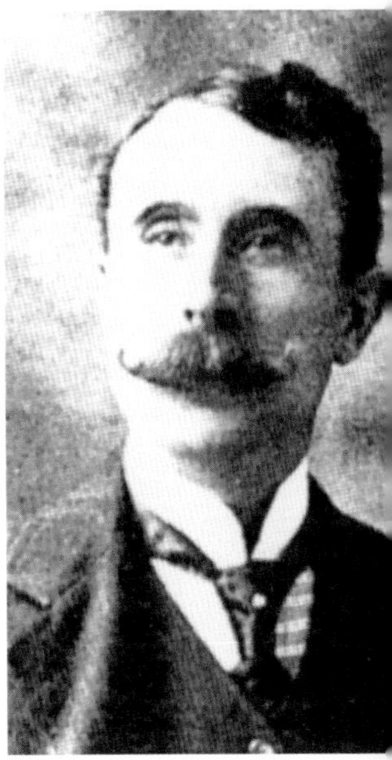

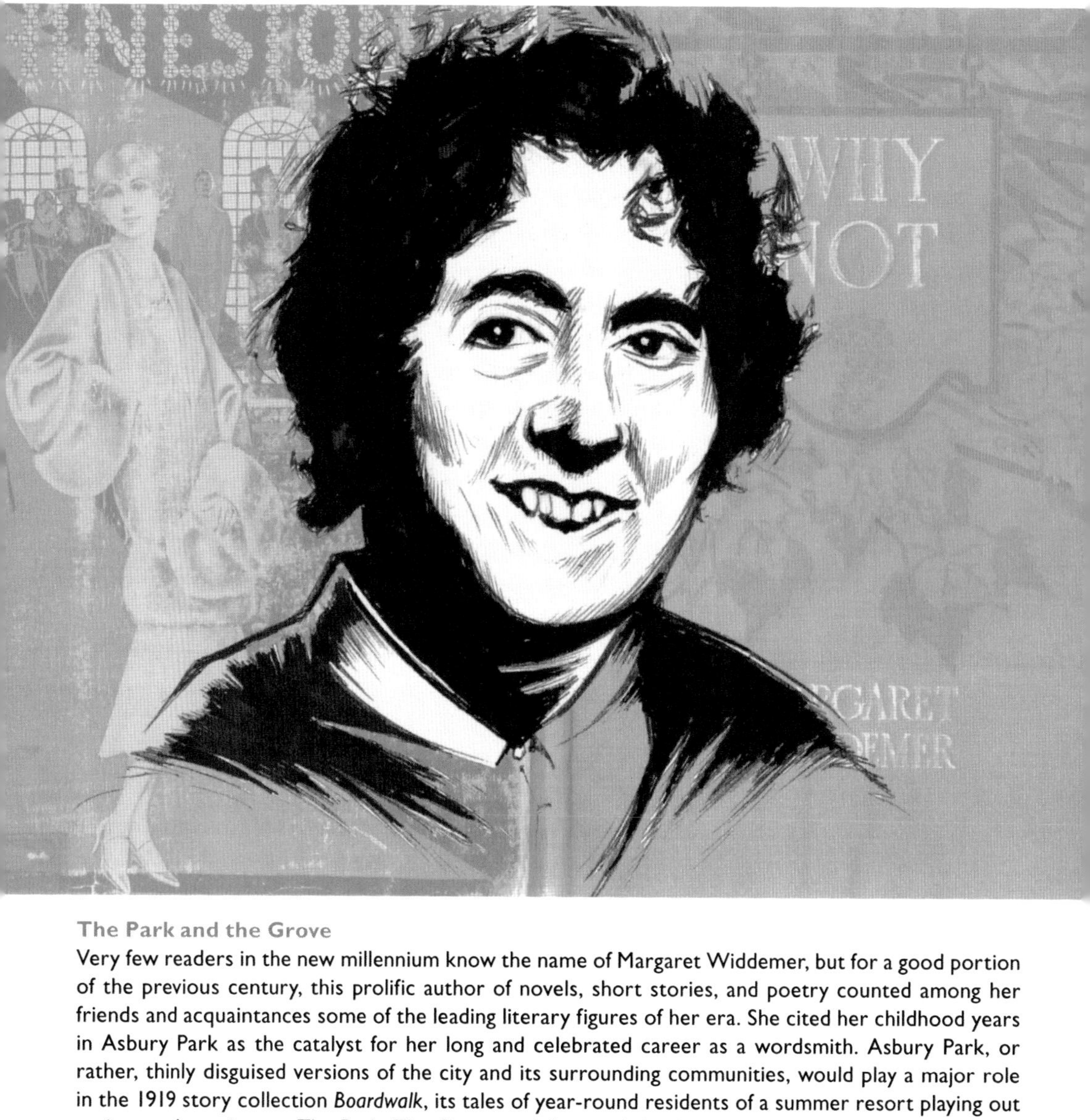

The Park and the Grove

Very few readers in the new millennium know the name of Margaret Widdemer, but for a good portion of the previous century, this prolific author of novels, short stories, and poetry counted among her friends and acquaintances some of the leading literary figures of her era. She cited her childhood years in Asbury Park as the catalyst for her long and celebrated career as a wordsmith. Asbury Park, or rather, thinly disguised versions of the city and its surrounding communities, would play a major role in the 1919 story collection *Boardwalk*, its tales of year-round residents of a summer resort playing out against such settings as The Park, The Grove, and Sunrise Lake. Her more than 30 novels include the 1915 romance *Why Not?*, which follows the adventures of a young woman in a lakefront community very much like Wanamassa. The daughter of Reverend E.P. Widdemer of Asbury's Congregational Church and a graduate of Asbury Park High School, Widdemer would win the Columbia University Prize for poetry (the Pulitzer Prize's predecessor), an honor she shared with fellow young poet Carl Sandburg. In 1964, her volume of memoir sketches *Golden Friends I Had* detailed her reminiscences of figures ranging from F. Scott Fitzgerald, T.S. Eliot, and Edna St. Vincent Millay to the notorious occultist Aleister Crowley. She was still active when she died at age 93 in 1978, leaving a novel called *A Rope to Hang My Love* unfinished at her home in upstate New York. (Illustration by the author.)

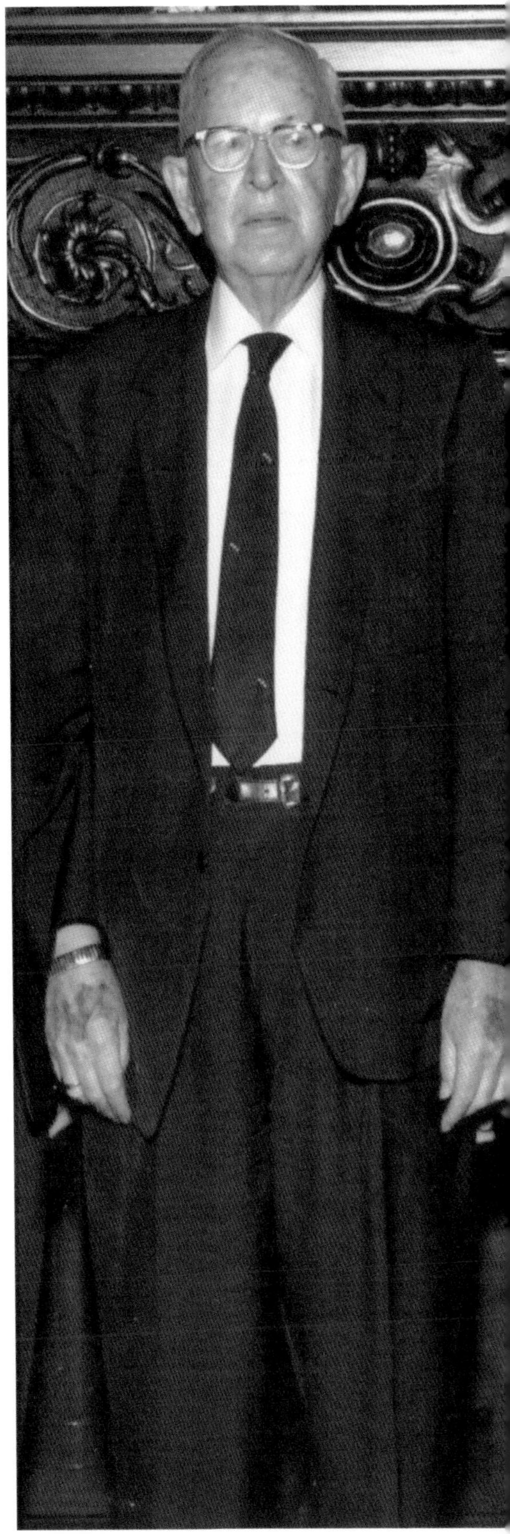

Blockbusters and Sequels
A larger-than-life figure even within the theater-building business, Walter Reade Sr. smelled opportunity in Asbury Park with the passing of the notoriously puritanical James Bradley, making Asbury the base of operations for his burgeoning regional theater empire. His acquisitions and constructions in the city range from the relatively modest Main Street and Lyric (later the pornography palace Park Cinema), to the St. James, the still-standing Savoy (a 1910s vaudeville house inside the Kinmonth Building) and, in 1927, the jewel in the crown known as the Mayfair: a massive 2,000-seat Lake Avenue movie temple that boasted Spanish-Moroccan décor, a $40,000 organ, a marble wishing well, and a ceiling projected with moving clouds and stars. The Paramount followed in 1930, a Deco-design partnership with the city that adjoined Convention Hall, and enjoyed personal appearances by the Marx Brothers, Ginger Rogers, Carole Lombard, and Fredric March.

Reade quickly came to operate some 40 sit-down and drive-in theaters across New Jersey, and in 1942 the ambitious entertainment mogul opened the spectacular Monte Carlo Pool off Ocean Avenue. The Jersey Shore's largest heated saltwater swimming hole boasted an attached stadium, a restaurant-lounge, and appearances by the likes of Buster Crabbe. Disgruntled by the administration of Mayor George Smock, Reade ran for city hall in 1945 on his own Citizens Victory League ticket, and, failing in his bid, he turned newspaper publisher for the brief but controversial 1946–1947 lifespan of fighting daily the *Asbury Park Sun.*

The senior Reade died in 1952, still branching out into new resort projects like the former Ross Fenton Farm (see page 22), even as Walter Reade Jr. was making his own mark. Junior acquired a sixth Asbury Park theater (the Ocean, later the Baronet), and went on a misadventure in hyper-local television with WRTV (Reade TV), Channel 58. In 1958, he erected a replica bridge across Cookman Avenue as a promotion for *The Bridge on the River Kwai.* Entering distribution in the 1950s, the Walter Reade Organization would expose audiences to fare that ranged from *Ulysses* and *Room at the Top* to *Ghidrah, the Three Headed Monster* and its greatest success, *Night of the Living Dead.* From a 1963 high of 89 theaters nationwide, 50 of them in New Jersey, the old Reade empire was showing signs of financial stress by the time of Reade Jr.'s 1973 death on the ski slopes of St. Moritz, Switzerland. (Courtesy of the Monmouth County Historical Association Library and Archive.)

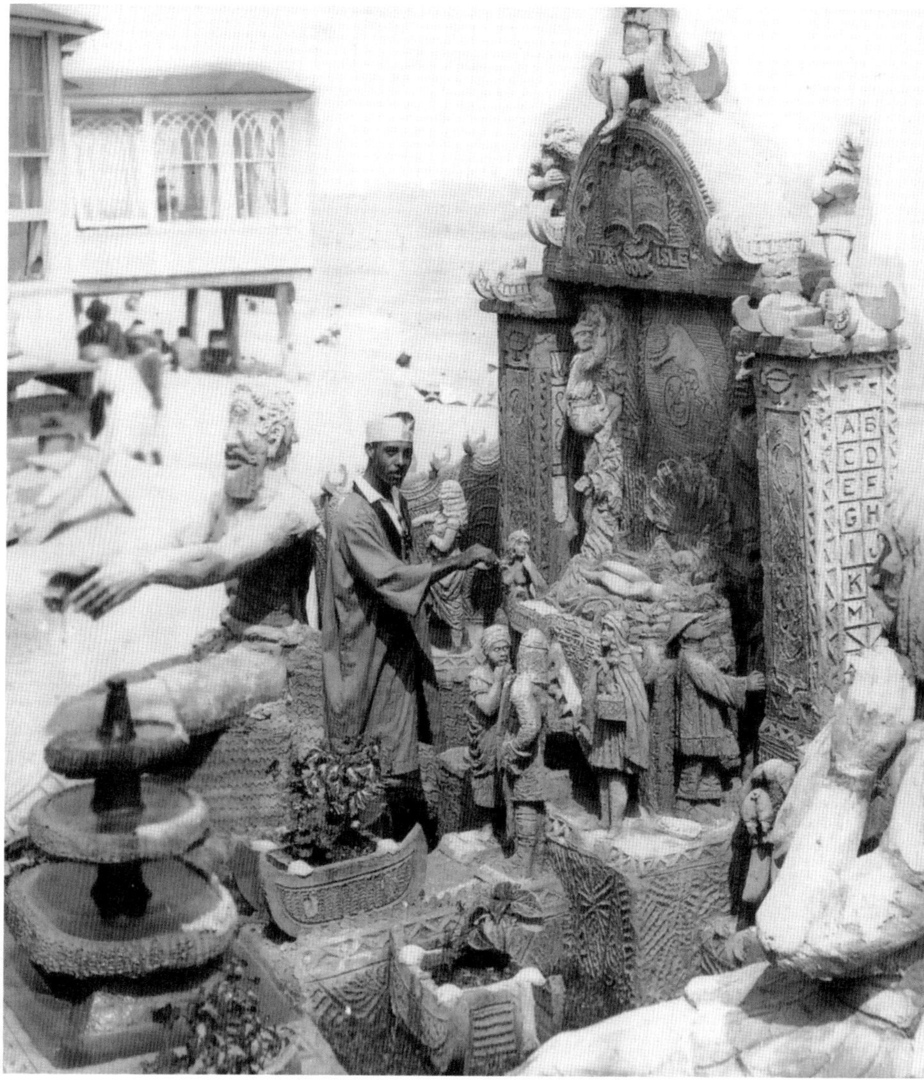

The One-Armed Arab

Visitors to the boards one July day in 1916 were astonished by an apparition: a giant pair of legs, modeled with great skill in wet sand, extending out from beneath the boardwalk as part of a huge figure. In the shadows labored an equally astonishing sight, "an Arab, dressed in fez and burnoose," the *Press* reported, answering queries in a tongue that was deemed to be Arabic. That this stranger had only his right arm with which to craft his intricate masterpieces was but one more mystifying element of what would become a fixture on the Asbury beach for the next 25 years. Those who took the Arab at face value missed out on the fact that Lorenzo Harris was a Virginia-born, college-educated African American gentleman who had lost his arm on a construction job and had never been anywhere near the Middle East. He originally plied his sand-sculpting trade in Atlantic City, where hostile crowds would repeatedly vandalize his work and drive him from the beach. Finding a far more welcoming canvas on the sands of Asbury, Harris would eventually put away the Arab trappings and become a prominent member of several regional African American civic organizations (and an unsuccessful candidate for the city council in 1945). His son Dr. Lorenzo Harris Jr. would become an internist and, in 1973, the city's first African American council member. (Courtesy of Kay Harris.)

CHAPTER THREE

At Long Last Love

1930–1949

Is it for all time, or simply a lark? / Is it Granada I see, or only Asbury Park?

—Cole Porter

The musical question posed by the great Cole Porter, with his usual topically witty wordplay, was more of a riddle—one with a punch line at the expense of Asbury Park.

If one had to endure a gentle drubbing, however, it paid to have it come at the hands of the very best, and Porter's breakout tune from the 1938 show *You Never Know* would float the name of Asbury Park through the decades. Memorable versions were recorded by Frank Sinatra, Ella Fitzgerald, Lena Horne, and Count Basie, who could very well have gotten a laugh out of the song's reference to the musical training ground of his pre-fame youth.

Asbury Park would continue to serve as a punch line over the years, on Jackie Gleason's *Honeymooners* and in Neil Simon's *The Odd Couple*, as well as a date-from-hell in the Doris Day-Cary Grant screwball *That Touch of Mink*. But, as the country struggled through the Great Depression and World War II, the Shore town that was aging and out of date in many ways, beaten down by decades of official corruption, and devastated by a massive 1944 hurricane would somehow manage to find a way. It could have sprung from an influx of military personnel and families during the thick of the war effort. It could have been the buzz generated by the spring-training stay of the 1943 New York Yankees. Or it could have been the tragic but fortuitous arrival of a major maritime disaster, right on the city's seaside doorstep.

Through it all, Asbury Park kept up appearances as a family-friendly destination and a functioning municipality as best it could. Actors, athletes, and entrepreneurs emerged from its neighborhoods to success in the big world beyond. Famous faces would pass through town on one night gigs, military assignments, and public relations tours. And a year-round base of working families, merchants, churchgoers, and students continued to perform the heroic task of forging a future from what must have seemed like a very uncertain here and now.

Was it, as Cole Porter's lyrics suggested, the real thing? Did a city constructed on fleeting amusement and devil-may-care diversion have any real place in an America that was rushing headlong into atom-age modernity? Or was it a baseless optimism, a funhouse distortion through a cocktail glass of nostalgia for a simpler time? For Asbury Park, such long-term thinking was a fancy not worth thinking of.

Writing decades later in the *Coaster* newspaper about the city's new wave of Latino-owned eateries, Frank D'Alessandro served it back to Cole Porter thusly:

"A juicy burrito, a flaming fajita, served by a beautiful sweet señorita, A Spanish paella, a plump empanada—Is this Asbury Park? Or only Granada?"

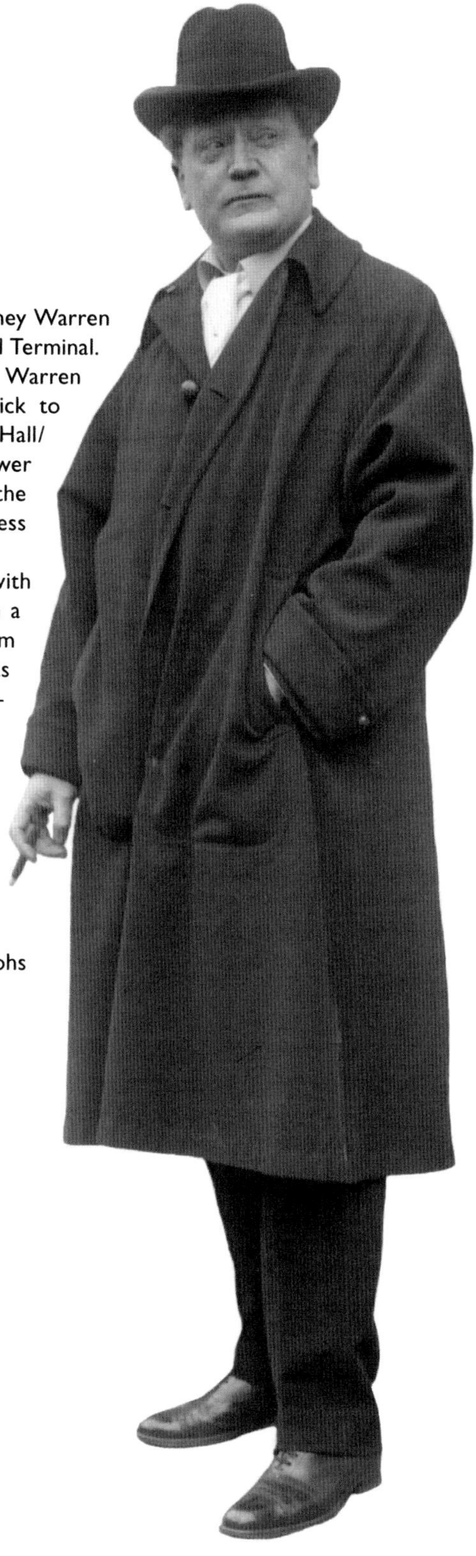

The Warren Commission

One of the most famous architects of his day, Whitney Warren is best remembered as the designer of Grand Central Terminal. In Asbury, the partner in the prestigious firm Warren and Wetmore was commissioned by Mayor Hetrick to blueprint several landmark buildings: the Convention Hall/ Paramount complex, the (second) Casino, the power plant, and the distinctive carousel roundhouse—the survivors of which have served as backdrop to countless wedding photographs and daytrip snapshots.

Prior to his waterfront projects, Warren worked with department store scion Arthur Steinbach to design a 420-room luxury hotel on Bradley's old auditorium block, and the Berkeley-Carteret Hotel opened its doors in 1925. Connected by walkway to a Warren-designed boardwalk pavilion that burned down in the early 1960s, the cross-shaped brick and steel Berkeley went on to host characters both upper-crust and underworld (Waxey Gordon, Sam Giancana), house British naval officers in wartime (including young Alec Guinness), and serve as setting for a *Shining*-themed Halloween party. It was owned by a myriad of people, from Johnny Cash to the Maharishi Mahesh Yogi. (Courtesy of Bain Collection, Prints & Photographs Division, Library of Congress.)

Tellin' Fortunes

Her 2008 passing was newsworthy enough to be noted by the Associated Press. That said, it seems as if the all-seeing, all-knowing, and ever so slightly mysterious Madam Marie is still with us, just as her presence in town predated by decades her famous cameo in Bruce Springsteen's "4th of July, Asbury Park (Sandy)," in which the cops "finally busted" her "for tellin' fortunes better than they do." The young Neptune City native Marie Castello (sometimes reported as Costello) had in fact arrived on the Asbury boards a full 40 years prior to Springsteen's song. From her tiny concrete-block Temple of Knowledge, the palmist would watch the boardwalk transition from a place of formally attired strollers to an increasingly down-market street parade. Her thousands of customers included not only Springsteen but Woody Allen, Ray Charles, Perry Como, Judy Garland, Elton John, and members of the Rolling Stones. Having outlasted nearly every other boardwalk merchant by the late 1990s, and with the passing of her husband of nearly 70 years, Marie would bid the boards a bittersweet goodbye in favor of a new location in nearby Ocean Township. The iconic temple would remain in the hands of her large family, however, and when the Asbury waterfront began showing signs of renewed life in 2004, Marie returned to join her granddaughter Sabrina at her familiar perch. Two generations of Castello descendants continue to operate the recently repainted landmark in addition to a downtown Madam Marie storefront in the heart of the Cookman corridor. The new stewards of the Asbury Park boardwalk flew the Asbury Park Convention Hall flag at half-mast following the news of Marie's crossing over to the other side, and Springsteen paid tribute to her in a website post that noted, "The world has lost enough mystery as it is—we need our fortunetellers." (Copyright and courtesy of Kathy Polenberg.)

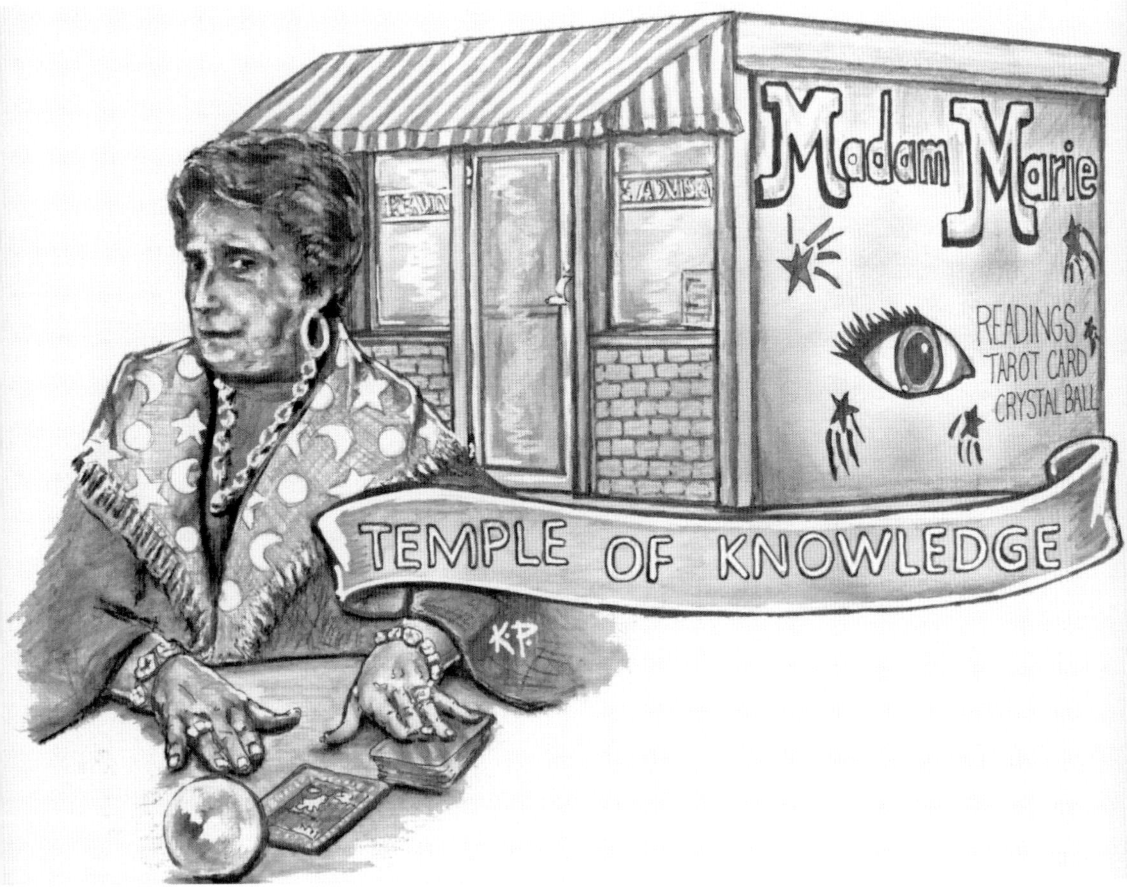

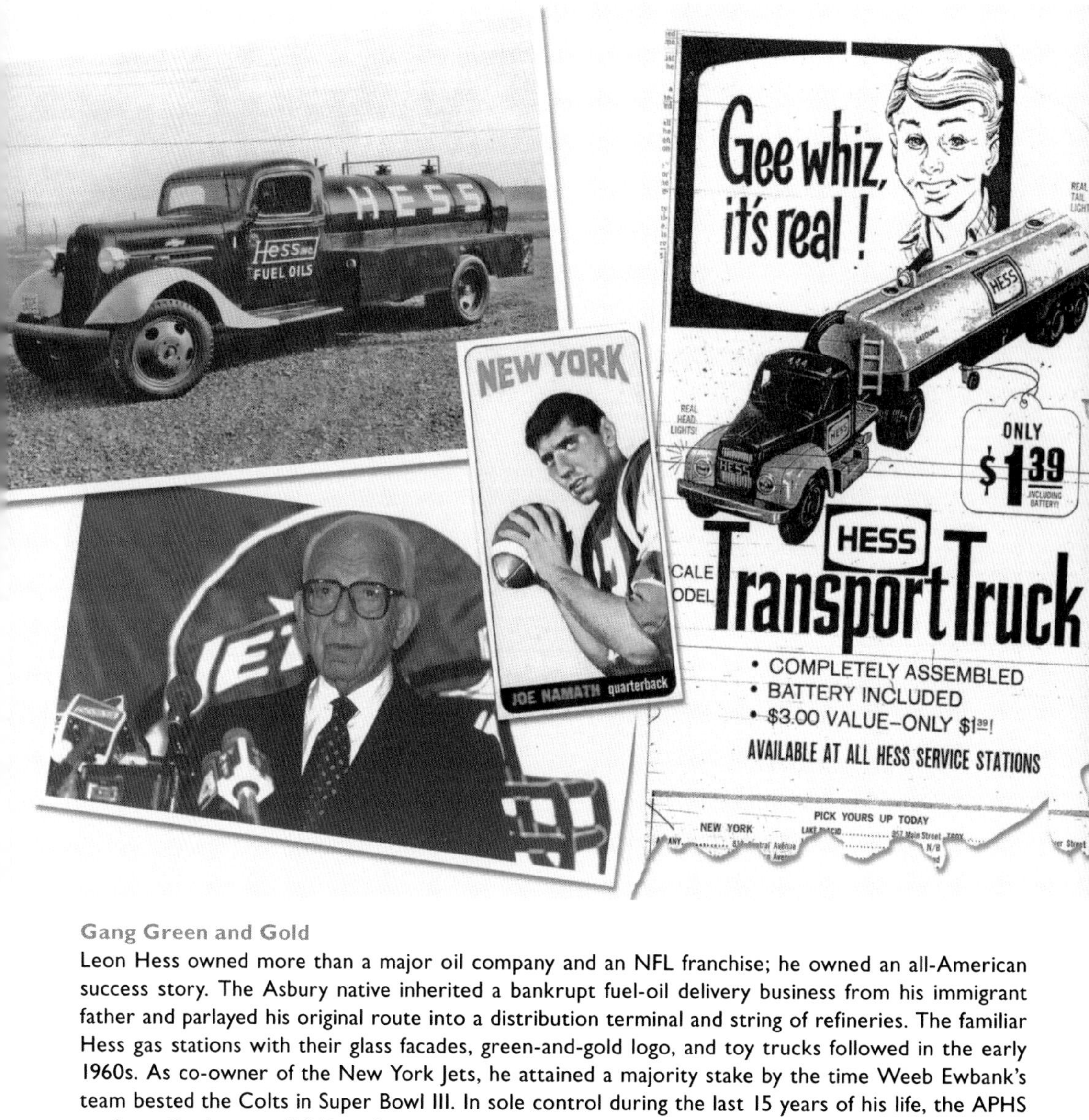

Gang Green and Gold

Leon Hess owned more than a major oil company and an NFL franchise; he owned an all-American success story. The Asbury native inherited a bankrupt fuel-oil delivery business from his immigrant father and parlayed his original route into a distribution terminal and string of refineries. The familiar Hess gas stations with their glass facades, green-and-gold logo, and toy trucks followed in the early 1960s. As co-owner of the New York Jets, he attained a majority stake by the time Weeb Ewbank's team bested the Colts in Super Bowl III. In sole control during the last 15 years of his life, the APHS graduate lived to see Bill Parcells return the Jets to the postseason in 1998. A regular presence on *Forbes*'s list of the richest Americans, his name adorns Monmouth University's Leon Hess Business School—while Asbury Park High School continued to graduate many future business leaders, including TV syndication kingpins Roger and Michael King; Baron Capital founder Ronald Baron, and medical professional/ investment innovator Dr. Henry Jarecki. (Author's collection.)

The Champ

Heavyweight Champion of the World for one day shy of one year in 1934–1935, Max Baer was a hard-hitting Hall of Famer who won high-profile bouts against Primo Carnera, Hitler-favorite Max Schmeling (a contest for which the half-Jewish fighter proudly entered the ring wearing the Star of David on his trunks), and Frankie Campbell, a young fighter whose subsequent death from brain injury saw a charge of manslaughter leveled against Baer. He also lost decisively to Joe Louis and surrendered his title to "Cinderella Man" long-shot Jim Braddock in a misplayed match that signaled a career decline. Nebraska-born and raised primarily in California, Baer was said to have briefly attended Asbury Park High School prior to beginning his professional boxing career in 1929, but it was his preference of Asbury Park as training camp site that put him in with the locally legendary. The camera-loving contender had already begun a side career as an actor; his many feature films include appearances alongside future Asbury resident Myrna Loy, city-born Bud Abbott (page 44), and Lou Costello. Newsreels caught him holding public-invited workouts at a temporary ring set up near the boardwalk and making publicity appearances with retired great Jack Dempsey. Going on to best Carnera in New York City, Baer would return to his Asbury camp several times afterward, continuing his film career and working as a radio announcer, referee, and wrestler following his retirement in 1941 (His brother, fellow boxer-actor Buddy Baer, would also appear with Abbott and Costello in *Jack and the Beanstalk*). Max died in 1959, never having seen his son Max Baer Jr. in the role of Jethro on the *Beverly Hillbillies*. (Courtesy of Bob Redfield.)

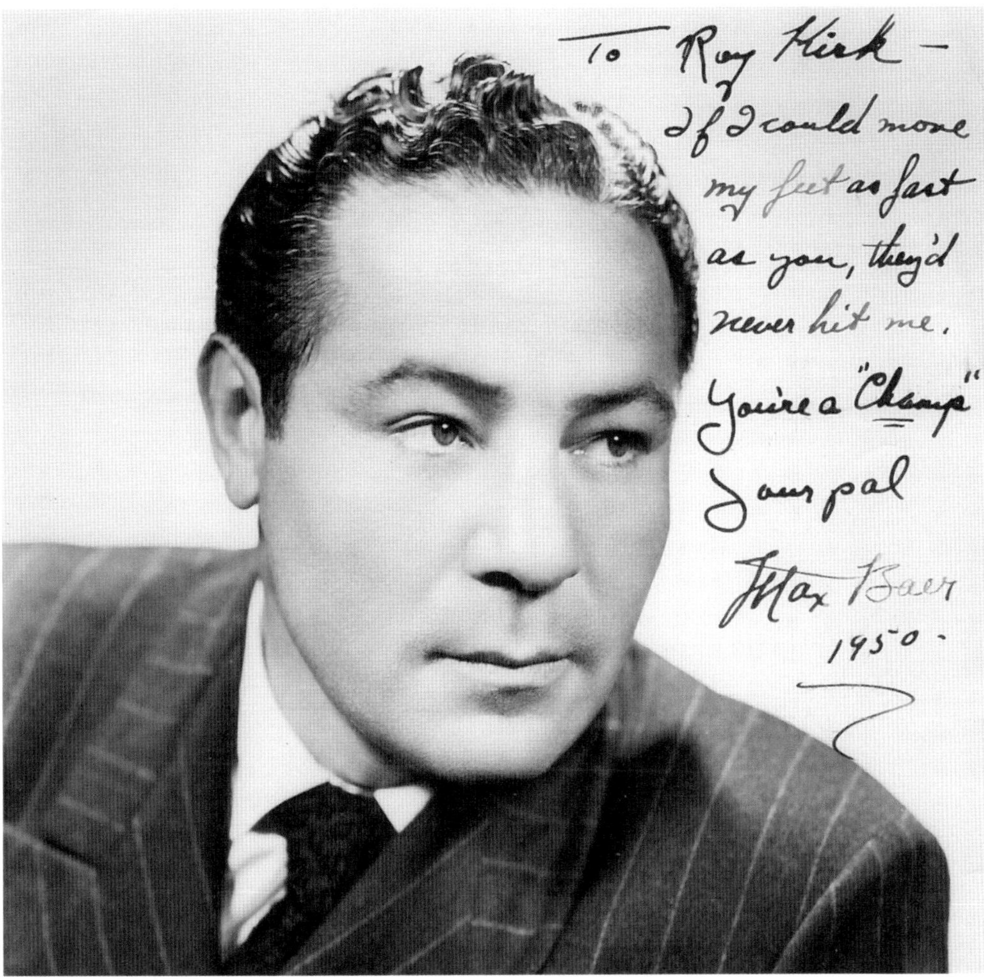

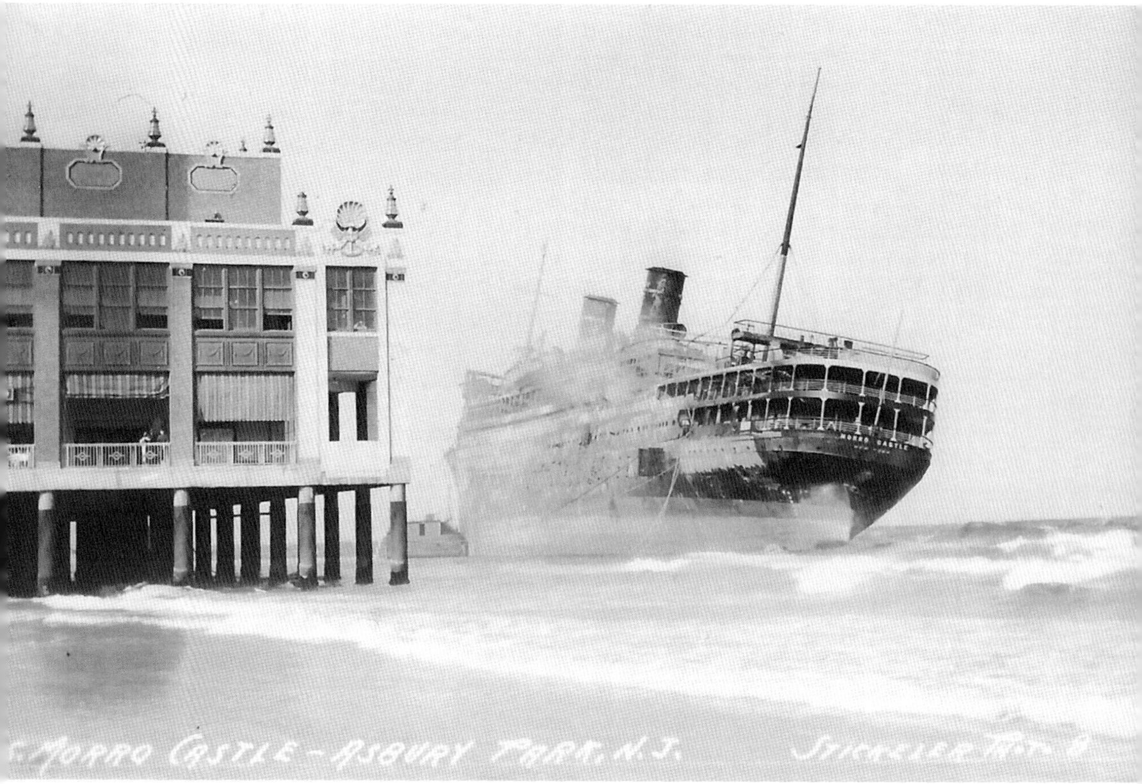

The Station Man

"My God! She's coming in right here!" yelled astonished radio announcer Thomas Burley on the stormy night of September 8, 1934, as he broadcast from the studios of WCAP inside Asbury Park's Convention Hall. "She" was the SS *Morro Castle*, a luxury liner that had burst into flames en route to New York from Havana, Cuba, and had drifted, off course and on fire (and with the loss of more than 130 passengers and crewmembers), only to beach itself not more than 100 yards from Burley's perch. While that momentous local broadcast failed to achieve the status of Herb Morrison's *Hindenburg* account, the unscheduled arrival of the *Castle* would prove to be something of a ghoulish godsend for the Depression-wracked economy of Asbury Park. The ship smoldered out of control in plain view of boardwalk hotels and restaurants, and for the next several months the blackened steel hulk would become a tourist attraction viewed by paying sightseers.

Occurring freakishly on the same spot as the *New Era* disaster of 1854, the shipwreck—involving the mysterious sudden death of the captain, and a murderous radio operator with a thing for incendiary devices—would furnish fuel for books and documentaries and catalyze the adoption of new guidelines and standards governing fire prevention and safety. Forgotten was the story of how Burley—a politically connected friend of Mayor Clarence Hetrick (see page 29)—had come to be owner, station manager, and on-air personality at WCAP, previously under the ownership of the city's (then-nonexistent) chamber of commerce. In the early 1930s, Burley enjoyed a paid position as secretary of the phantom chamber, while city hall paid the station tens of thousands of dollars to run sponsored programming, throwing in two prime Convention Hall storefronts with all rent and utilities at no charge. This, plus a salaried appointment as the city's beach director, would make Thomas F. Burley Jr. an especially well compensated crony. Following Hetrick's defeat by a reform ticket in the early 1940s, the man who would be credited as having originated the "sidewalk-interview type of broadcast" would sell out to a group headed by Walter Reid's Charms Candy Company. He died in 1944 at the age of 48. (Courtesy of Ocean Township Historical Society.)

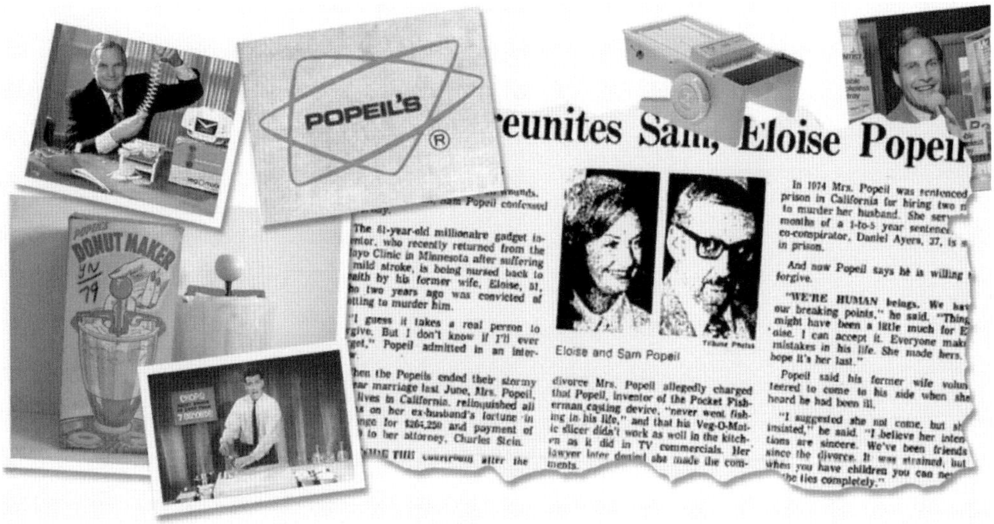

But That's Not All

His experience as an Asbury boardwalk pitchman (a gig he shared with young Ed McMahon) set the tone for Samuel J. Popeil's multimillion-dollar empire of ballyhoo, and his 1930s apprenticeship with Nathan Morris's local line of kitchen gadgets (including the "KwiKi-Pi") inspired him to found Chicago-based Popeil Brothers. The dynasty that famously introduced the Pocket Fisherman and Veg-O-Matic saw Sam's son Ron Popeil spin off into the competing Ronco (and rotisserie-fueled dominance in the age of infomercials). His daughter Lisa sang for Frank Zappa and others, and his ex-wife Eloise notoriously went to prison for ordering a hit on him. They remarried when she got out. When the elder Popeil died in 1984, the memorial service was held in Asbury Park, and the Prince of Pitchmen was interred in nearby Neptune. (Author's collection.)

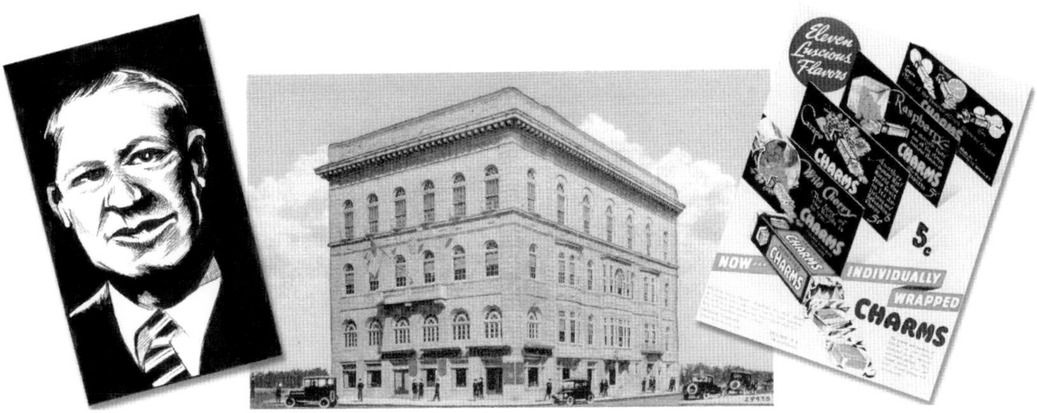

This Charming Man

As chairman of the Charms Candy Company, Walter W. Reid Jr. popularized the square, fruit-flavored hard candies that gave the business its name. Manufactured elsewhere in New Jersey, the candies were individually wrapped and packaged 10 to a roll in the former Elks Lodge on Heck Street, a four-story affair (later a popular gay disco) that would be known as the Charms Building. According to Helen Pike, Reid and his son Walter III also "had contracts to make medicines for such pharmaceutical companies as Playtex." The historic Charms Building would become the sweet stuff of nostalgia in 2009. (Courtesy of Asbury Park Historical Society and the author's collection.)

Bud's On Second

He was the son of circus folk and variously give his place of birth as Atlantic City, Coney Island, or Asbury Park. But it is Second Avenue in Asbury that claimed him as its own. William "Bud" Abbott became the city's first native-son screen star, an unlikely box-office champ, but a skilled dialogue comic whose partnership with Lou Costello hit the spot with 1940s movie and radio audiences. Abbott's career would not long outlast the breakup with Costello, and he passed away, plagued by poor health and money woes, in 1974. The city of Paterson, New Jersey, erected a statue in honor of hometown hero Costello, while in Asbury Park, a half-hearted "Bud Abbott Day" promotion was never attempted again (although the popular nightspot Porta would name its in-house dance club the Abbot Room). (Courtesy of the Asbury Park Historical Society.)

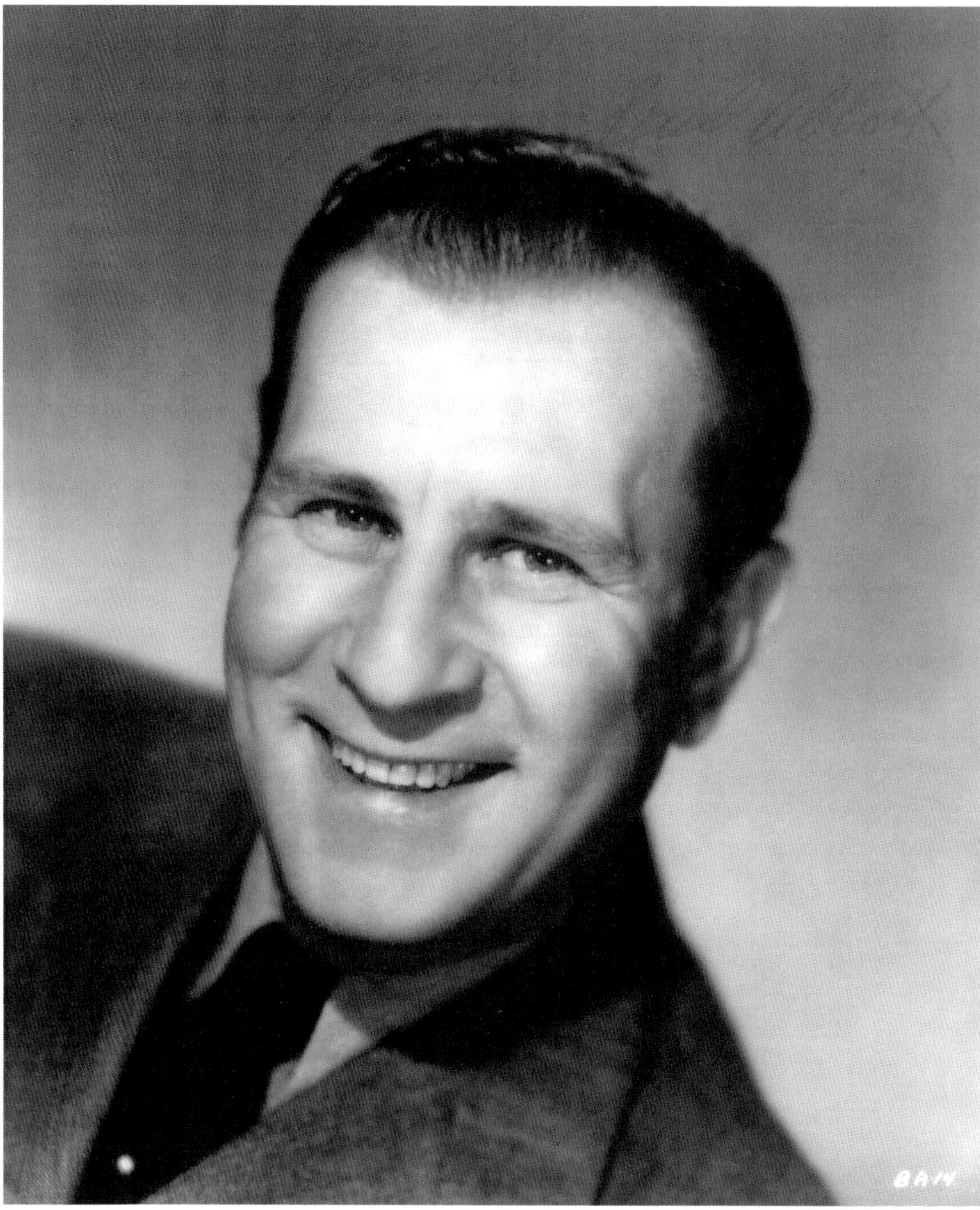

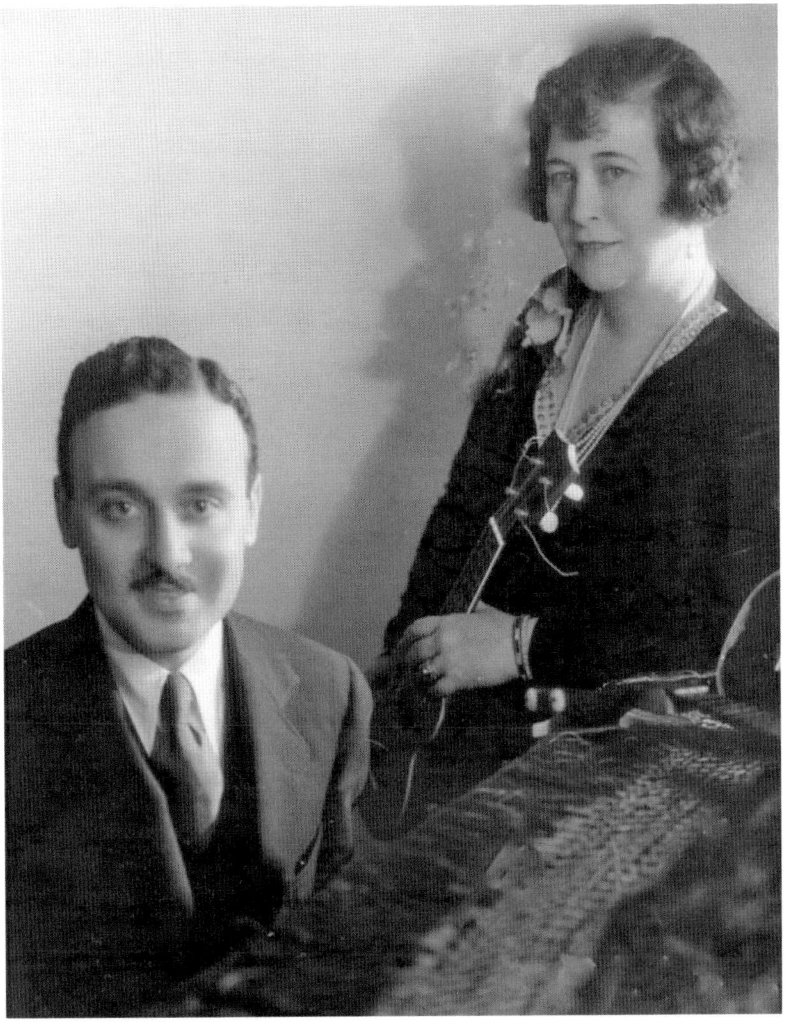

Sweethearts of the Air
He was the Hall of Fame songwriter and pianist whose dozens of hits, including "Wagon Wheels," "Deep Purple," and "It's a Marshmallow World," were recorded by the greats of jazz, pop, country, and early rock and roll. She was "The Ukulele Lady," a performer, arranger, educator, and advocate credited with the instrument's acceptance by the musician's union and major sheet music publishers. Together they were the *Sweethearts of the Air*, the title of their NBC radio show. At the height of their fame, Peter DeRose and May Singhi Breen DeRose were also proud residents of Asbury Park. Their home overlooking Deal Lake was the scene of countless parties and celebrations as well as frequent stays by Babe Ruth. Between 1920 and his final years in the late 1940s, the Babe would make numerous visits to Peter and May, reportedly indulging such recreational pursuits as ukulele playing and competitive scallion eating. The De Roses would entertain at Ruth's 1929 wedding to Claire Hodgson ("Deep Purple" being a particular favorite of the slugger), and even after the Bambino's death in 1948, the couple would remain active in the Babe Ruth Foundation, his charity for underprivileged children. Peter's compositions continued racking up royalties and Grammy awards long after his 1953 passing, and May, who died in 1970, became the only woman ever elected to the Ukulele Hall of Fame, in 2000. The sweethearts were interred together in upstate New York, and their Asbury home on Eighth Avenue can still be recognized by the iron wagon wheels built into the front porch steps. (Courtesy of Sherrie Hoyer.)

Holy Clown Prince Coincidence!

Indeed, what are the odds that two of the actors who took on the role of the Joker shared an Asbury Park connection? For Cesar Romero, the perennially mustachioed Latin lover who would play Batman's arch-nemesis in the 1960s television series and feature film, the connection was his two years at Asbury Park High School, an institution that would later employ one of his sisters as a faculty member. Before going Hollywood with breakout parts in *The Thin Man*, Shirley Temple's *Wee Willie Winkie*, and a starring turn as the Cisco Kid, the resident of nearby Bradley Beach, who famously continued to sport his signature mustache beneath the Joker's ghastly greasepaint, worked briefly in a Cookman Avenue sporting goods emporium.

Another neighboring town, Neptune City, was the early home of one Jack Nicholson, an aspiring thespian who became a shining star at Manasquan High School before heading West to appear in, among other things, Tim Burton's *Batman*, the 1989 feature that reignited the phenomenon of the modern superhero film.

Nicholson was already an established star in

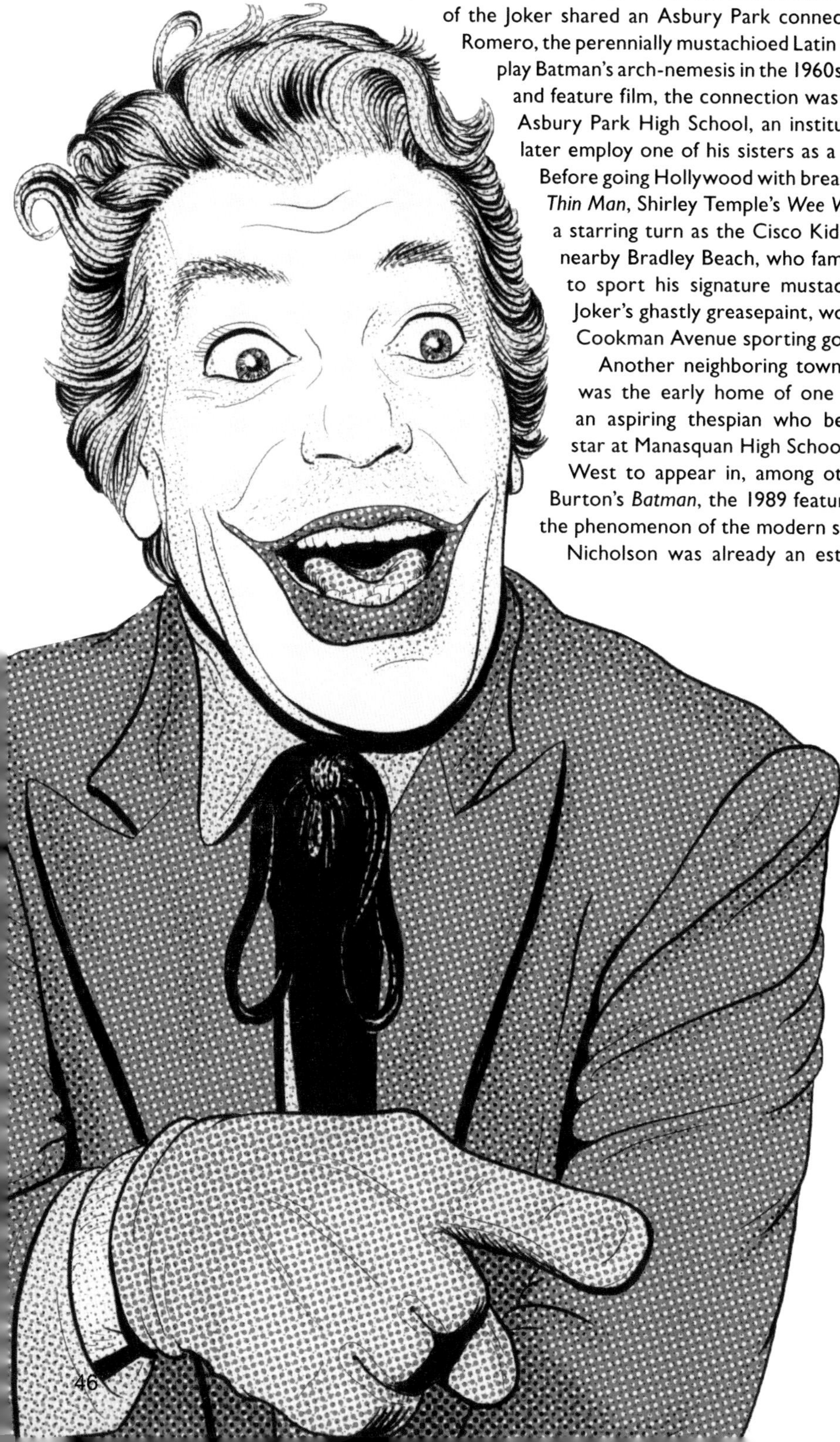

1974 when he learned (via a reporter from the *Asbury Park Press*, no less) that the maternal figure he had known all his life as "Mud" was in fact his grandmother and that "older sister" June Nicholson was actually his mother, having given birth to the boy under mysterious circumstances in 1937. The beautiful young chorus girl had done a tap act at Asbury's Monterey Hotel, performed with Earl Carroll's Vanities, and danced locally with Jersey Shore–area vaudevillians Donald Rose and Eddie King, both of whom were rumored at various times to have been the father of the Nicholson boy. It was King who was often seen bringing young Jack along on errands about Asbury Park, a place to which the Oscar-winning screen legend has returned for impromptu, low-profile visits in recent years.

It was the late Heath Ledger who spirited away the Oscar gold as Gotham City's Clown Prince of Crime, but not before Asbury's own Danny De Vito played the Penguin in *Batman Returns*. The film was produced by Michael Uslan, a native of nearby Ocean Township who has steered every Bat-film in the modern franchise (and who hosted a day-long Batfest on the Asbury boardwalk in 2011). (Copyright and courtesy of Jason Robinson.)

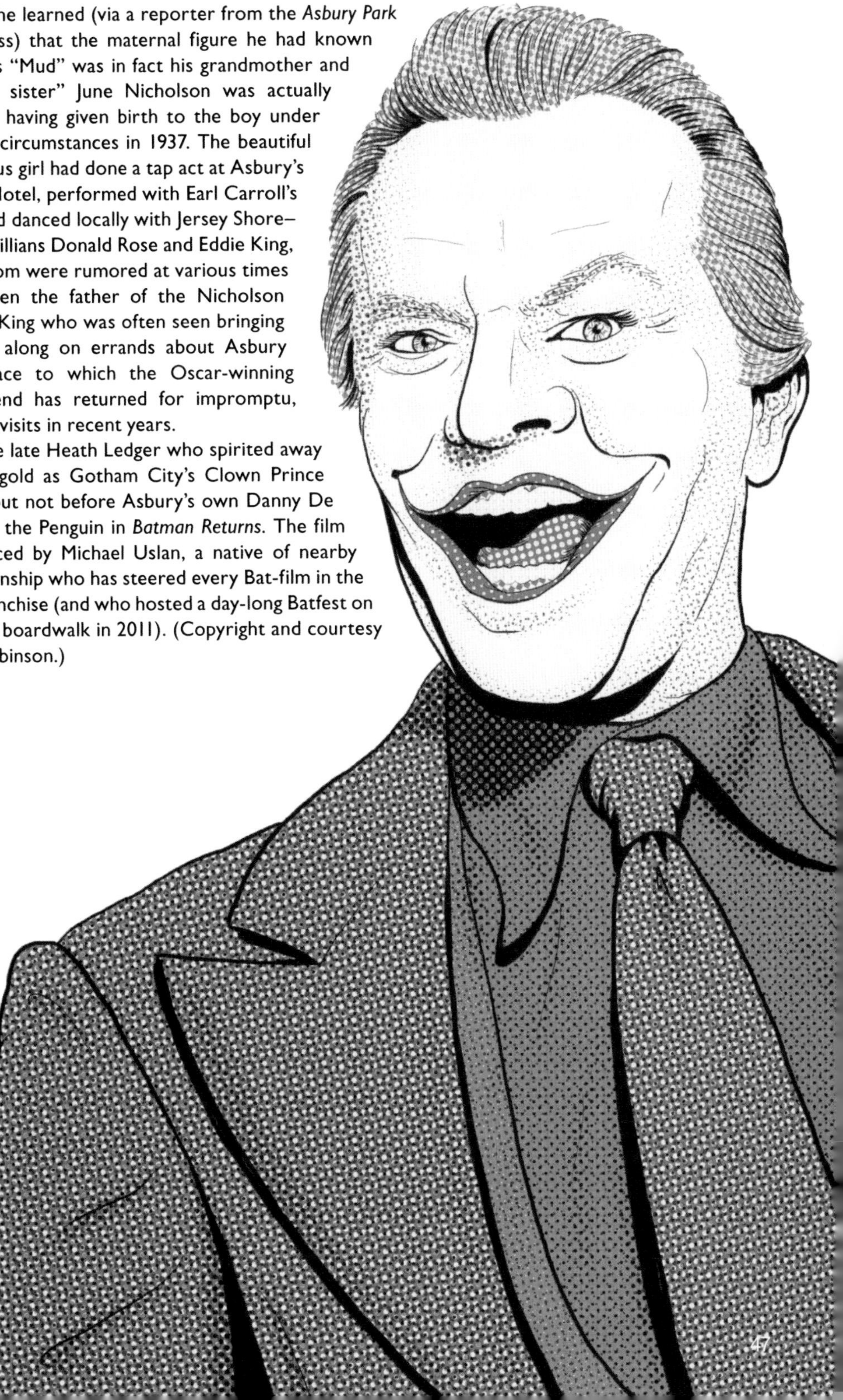

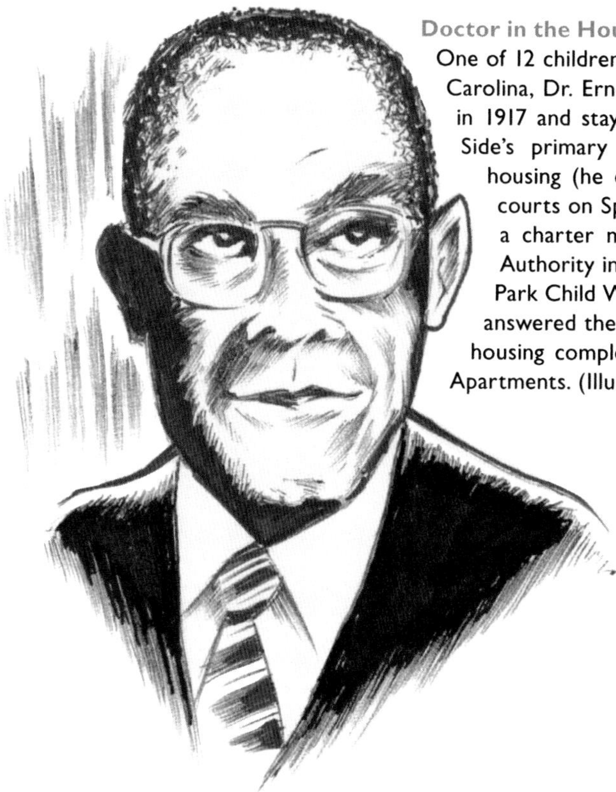

Doctor in the House

One of 12 children born to former slaves in rural North Carolina, Dr. Ernest A. Robinson came to Asbury Park in 1917 and stayed for 50 years, as one of the West Side's primary physicians. An advocate for public housing (he even built a set of community tennis courts on Springwood Avenue), Robinson became a charter member of the Asbury Park Housing Authority in 1938 and helped establish the Asbury Park Child Welfare Clinic in the 1920s. The doctor answered the final call in 1968, after which a public housing complex was christened Dr. E.A. Robinson Apartments. (Illustration by the author.)

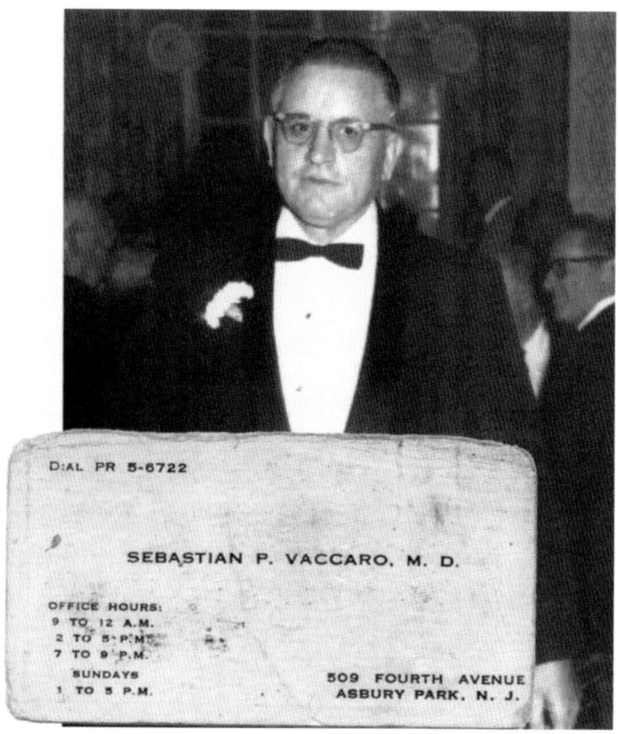

Doctor On Duty

For 25 years, Dr. Sebastian P. Vaccaro served a cross-section of city residents, not just the Italian-American community, but the West Side neighborhoods to which he and his wife and nurse, Rosemarie, paid special attention. It was not unusual for the doctor to cover the cost of prescriptions, vaccines, and even heating oil for his patients. His seven-days-a-week schedule was extended by remaining on call constantly. In October 1959, Vaccaro attended a Berkeley-Carteret banquet given in his honor, after which the tuxedo-clad doctor made house calls until after midnight. He died in his sleep the next night, aged 51. (Courtesy of Henry Vaccaro Jr.)

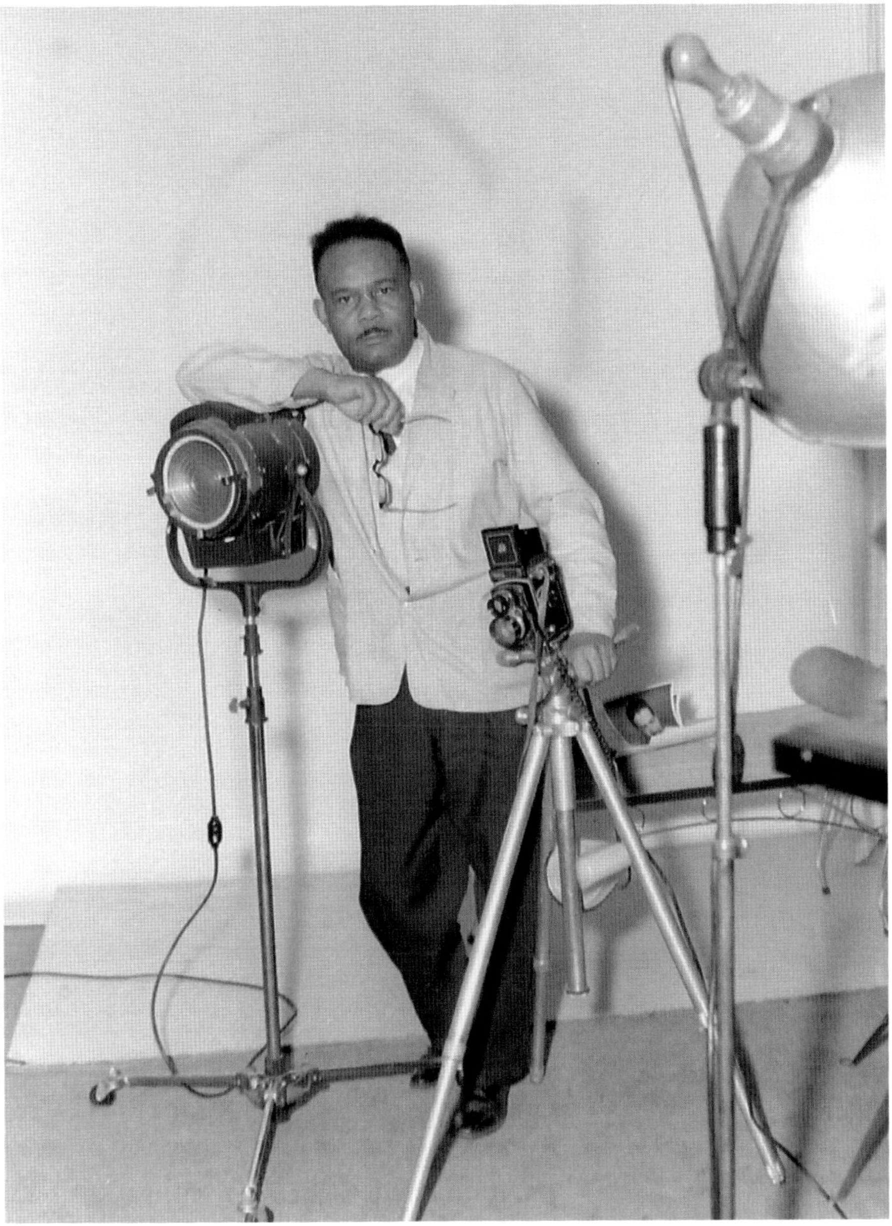

Negatives and Positives

For 40 years, Joseph A. "Joe" Carter Sr. captured the rich pageant of day-to-day city life, not just in his West Side base of operations, but all around the sidewalks, storefronts, schools, and sands of a complex and multihued community. His bulky Speed Graphic was there at cotillions and couture shows, church socials and children's birthdays, dance recitals and days at the beach. His Kodak negatives from the Springwood Avenue clubs would reveal Lionel Hampton and Billie Holiday sharing stages with Sam Pugh and other locals. Springsteen rehearsed in his basement alongside Joe's son (and "Born to Run" drummer) Ernest "Boom" Carter. A quiet chronicler of a city in trouble and transition, Joe retired in 1980. His daughter Madonna published two volumes of priceless images from her father's files as *Asbury Park: A West Side Story*. (Photograph by Joseph A. Carter Sr., courtesy of Madonna Carter Jackson.)

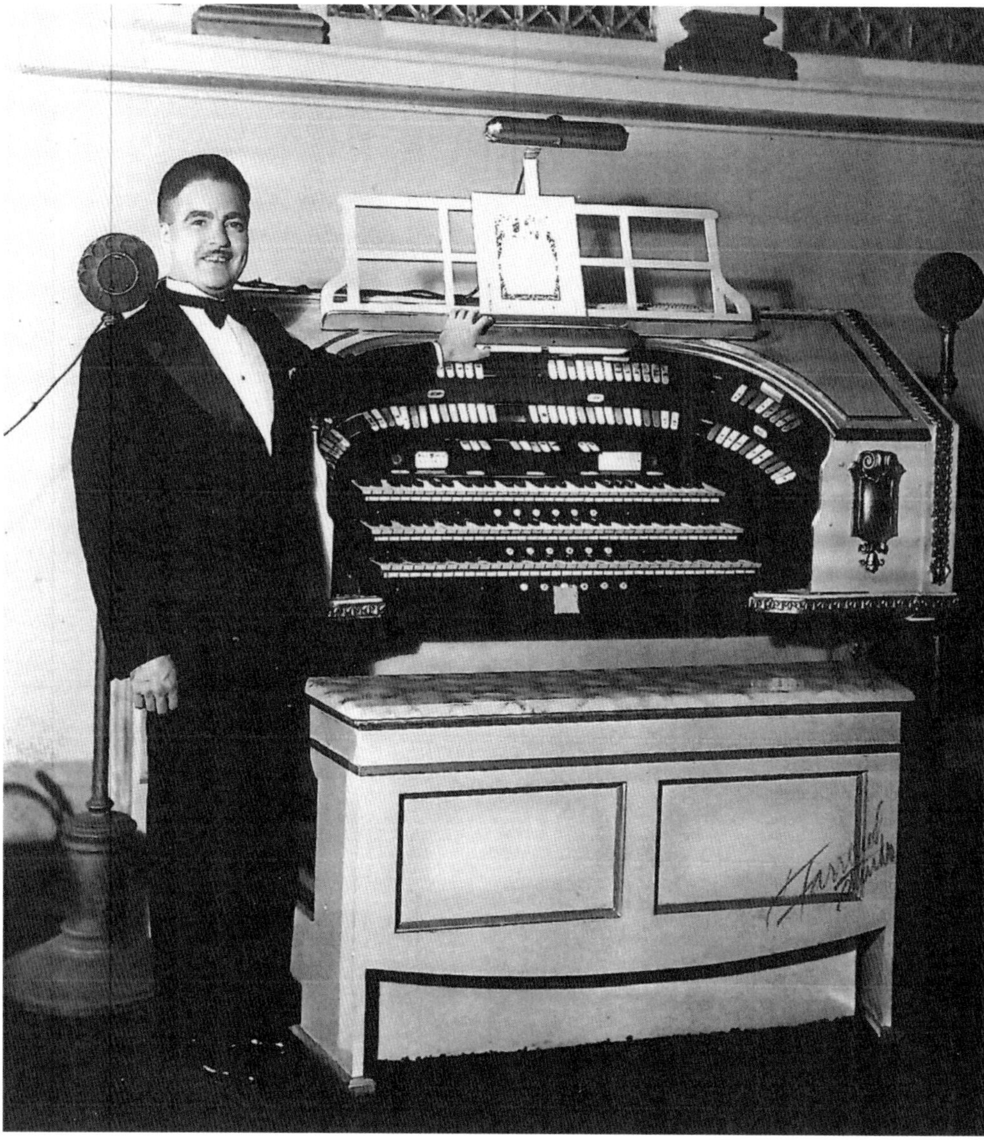

Keeper of the Keys

From 1930 until his 1958 passing, Asbury Park's own official municipal organist performed free concerts at Convention Hall for boardwalk visitors throughout the summer season. An in-demand theater accompanist, composer, and choral conductor, George (G. Howard) Scott would reportedly play more than 5,000 performances on the three-manual Kilgen, many of them broadcast by local station WCAP from its studio inside the Convention Hall complex (MacDowell's "To the Sea" was theme song for his programs, which often featured Arthur Pryor's "The Whistler and His Dog"). Scott, who also played the $40,000 pipe organ at Walter Reade's grand Mayfair movie palace (and who is credited as the first "music colorist" to use color-keyed synchronized lights), would go on to found the Asbury Park Civic Oratorio Society, and serve for many years as musical director at the First Methodist Church of Asbury Park. He was remembered by many of the servicemen who were stationed at the Hall during the Second World War—and noted for his participation in a 1938 experiment that determined classical music to be better sonic bait for pierside fishing than jazz. (Courtesy of George and Tom Scott.)

CHAPTER FOUR

Ebb Tide

1950s–1960s

First the tide rushes in/ plants a kiss on the shore /
then rolls out to sea / and the sea is very still once more.

—Carl Sigman

So wrote Carl Sigman in his lyric to "Ebb Tide," a hit composition by Robert Maxwell that spawned vocal versions by everyone from Frank Sinatra to Jerry Colonna before surfing nearly to the top of the charts in a 1965 take by the Righteous Brothers.

The tide had definitely come in for a young West Side crooner named Lenny Welch when he had his turn with the dreamily dramatic ballad in 1962. Even if his one big hit lay elsewhere, his "Ebb Tide" was a romantic walk on the beach that, according to his first album, "earned him a spot on Merv Griffin's *Talent Scouts* show on CBS in September 1963."

Visitors to Asbury Park might have sensed that a tide of prosperity had washed in a wave of newly mobile families and increasingly independent young people. Whether shopping at Steinbach's Mammoth Department Store, taking in a movie at the Mayfair or a concert at Convention Hall, thrilling to the rides and arcades, or exploring scenes that were not touted in the proverbial family newspaper, Asbury Park was the place to be, even if much of it closed down after Labor Day.

Asbury was more than just a summer love, of course. It was a functioning city, albeit one constructed on the shifting sands of a service economy. It was a place where people lived year-round, attended a high school they were proud of, and worshipped at a panorama of places on the weekend. As the outside world would eventually find out, it was also a place with big-city tensions—the kind that would soon enough alter the public perception of the town for a generation.

There were other forces at work that forever changed the character of city life. The opening of the Garden State Parkway, a toll road that would later get its own space-age concert venue, the Garden State Arts Center, allowed potential visitors to bypass Asbury Park altogether on their way to points even further south. The emergent highway shopping center landscape sounded a death knell for downtowns all over the map, and the growth of the suburbs meant new schools for the old sending districts, a riptide that decimated the diversity of Asbury's student body.

At the same time, the newly supercharged car culture would birth the phenomenon known as the Circuit, that cruise-able course that looped past the bars, eateries, arcades, motels, and amusements of Ocean Avenue and Kingsley Street. It would have been understandable for a visitor on a summer's night in the early- to mid-1960s to take in the lights, the music, and the motion of the boardwalk cavalcade and declare this to be an all-new golden age. Another observer might have stood staring out at the dark expanse of sea and sensed that the tide was beginning to steal away from shore.

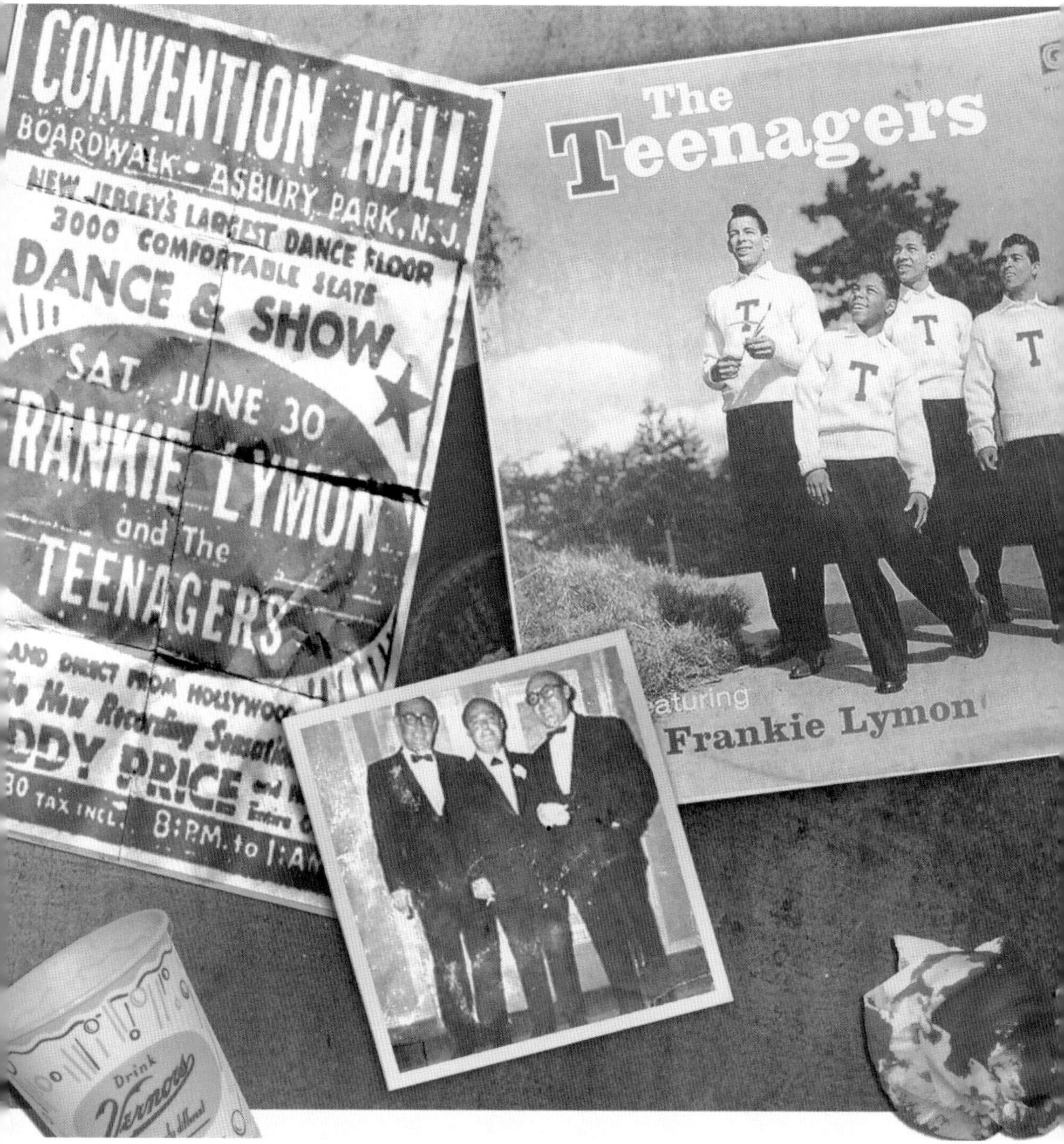

(I'm Not a) Juvenile Delinquent

"The whole place erupted," recalled concessionaire (and future Superior Court of New Jersey judge) Ira Kreizman of that hot night in June 1956, when a wounded stabbing victim asked him for a napkin. Convention Hall's first-ever rock-and-roll show spawned a racially charged riot that spilled onto the Circuit and into the downtown business district, causing Asbury Park to ban rock music outright. At center stage were Frankie Lymon and the Teenagers, the seemingly nonthreatening performers of "Why Do Fools Fall in Love," and behind the curtain were Joe, Willie, and Al Rediker, the brothers who booked Bill Haley and the Comets into the Casino in 1955. The owners of Reeds Jewelers would stick with jazz thereafter. In 2014, the Redikers' relative Ira Kreizman accepted the honor when the brothers were memorialized as Asbury Angels. (Author's collection.)

Moe Town

To the Broadway theater world, he was the producer who matched Pacino with Shakespeare and put younger, more diverse audiences in the seats with shows like *Bubblin' Brown Sugar* and an all-black *Guys and Dolls*. In Philadelphia, he is recalled as the founder of the Philly Pops, but to anyone who spent a chunk of his or her wonder years on the boardwalk, the name Moe Septee stood for the Summer of Stars concert series at Convention Hall. Beginning in the early 1960s, the Newark-based, Polish-born promoter partnered with Felix Gerstmann in Asbury Park, and it was there that he discovered a concert industry that was increasingly being driven by teenaged ticket buyers. Shows by veteran acts like Ella Fitzgerald would soon give way to folk (Peter, Paul and Mary), soul (James Brown, Otis Redding), Motown (the Supremes, the Temptations), and a British invasion that brought the Who, the Dave Clark Five, and the Rolling Stones to the seaside city. Before long, founder James Bradley's statue would stand within earshot of sets by Jimi Hendrix, Janis Joplin, the Doors, and Led Zeppelin, who opted to play Asbury on August 16, 1969, rather than make the trip up to the muddy and chaotic Woodstock Festival. Working from his summer home in nearby Deal, Septee would continue booking some of rock's biggest acts at the 3,500-seat venue before handing the keys to John Scher following the summer of 1974. (Courtesy of Eileen Chapman.)

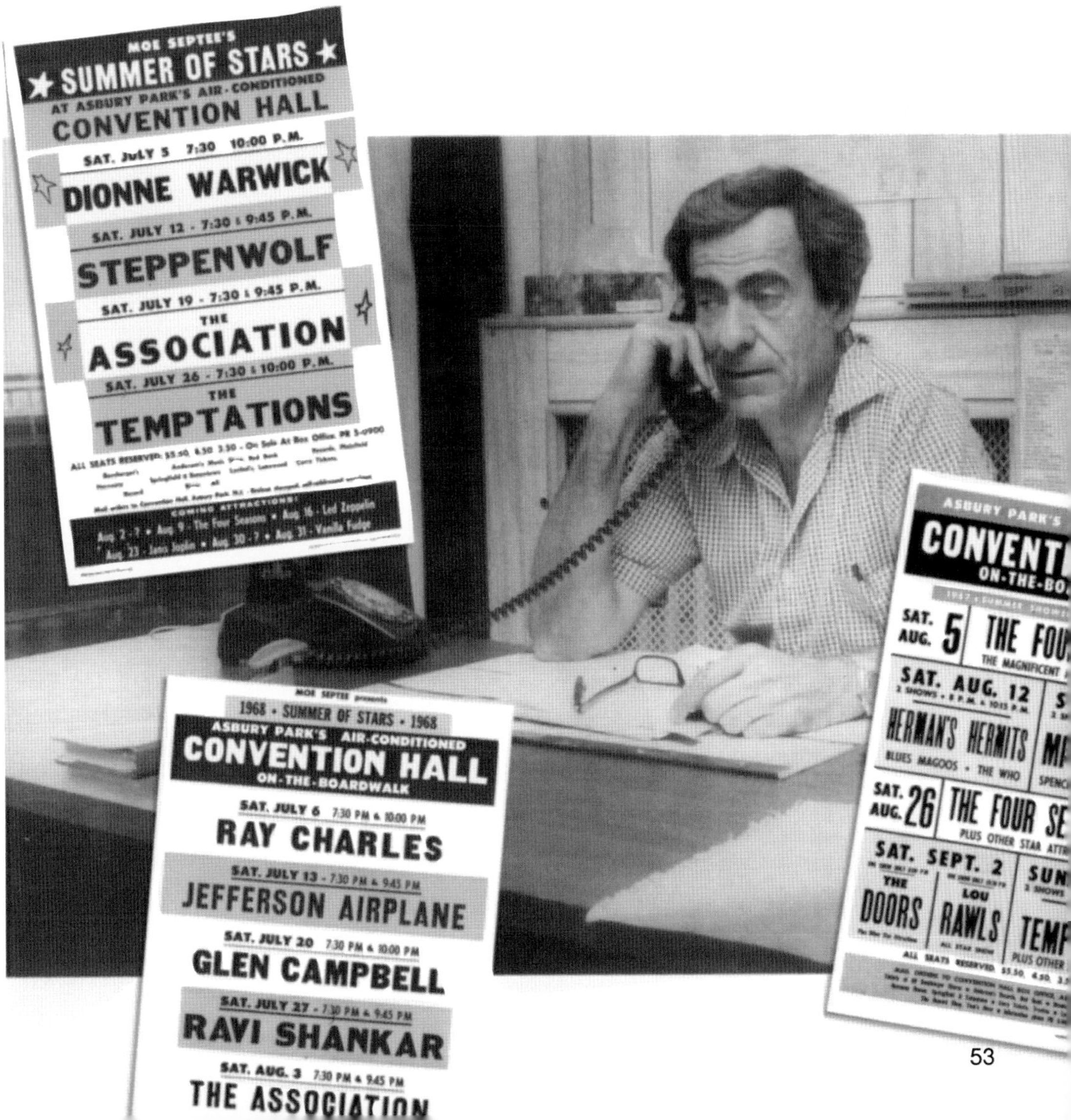

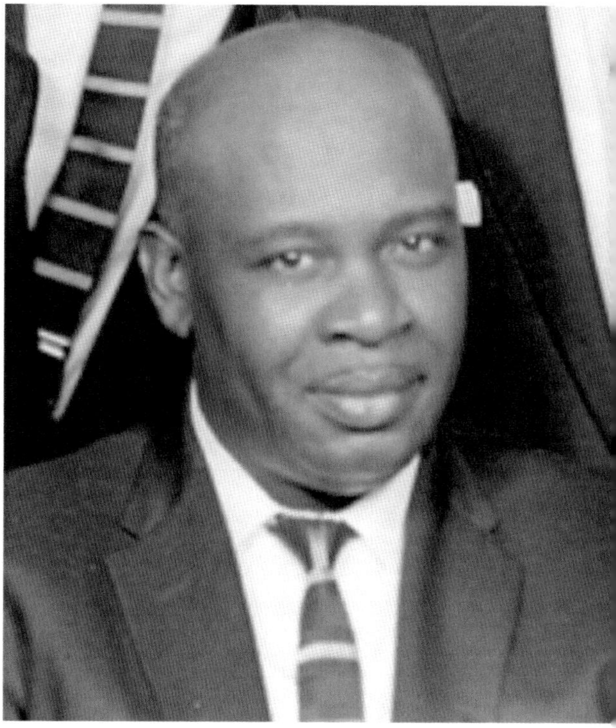

The Gospel Train

As unofficial "Mayor of the West Side," former migrant worker Arthur Morris was one of those Asbury figures that straddled the worlds of music and civic life. The lead singer of the locally legendary Golden Harmonaires served as liaison to visiting black speakers like Jackie Robinson and Dr. Martin Luther King Jr., and as a deejay for WCAP. His *Gospel Train* program nurtured a new generation of vocal groups, while the "mayor" brought gospel superstars to the National Guard Armory and secular acts to once-segregated Convention Hall. He was honored among the inaugural class of Asbury Angels. (Photograph by Joseph A. Carter Sr., courtesy of Charlie and Pam Horner.)

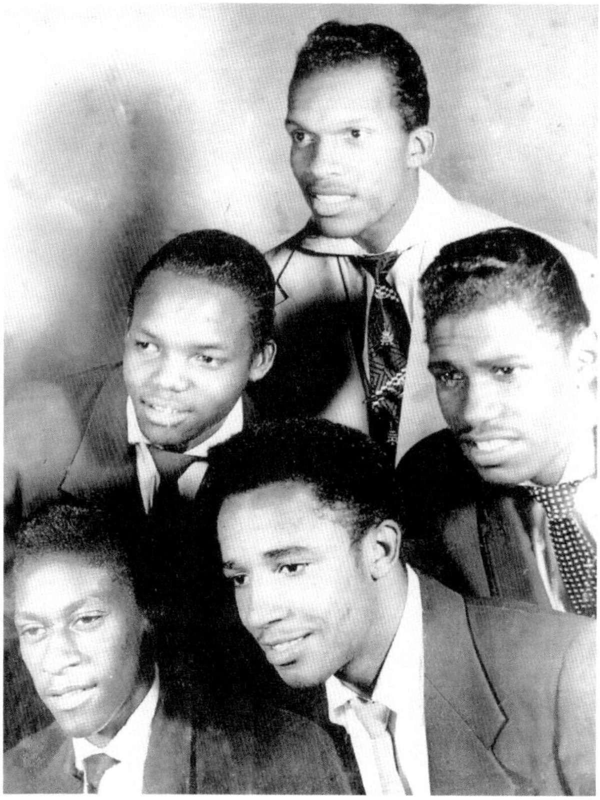

My Heart

A West Sider whose soaring tenor—inspired by Sonny Till and the Orioles—was at the heart of numerous group configurations, Bobby Thomas is pictured up top with the 1954 lineup of the Vibranaires. He also joined Lenny Welch in the Vibes and formed the V-Eights (whose "My Heart" on "Gus" Tillman's local Vibro label received nationwide distribution by ABC). In 1966, Thomas and his Vibranaires received an offer they could not refuse: Sonny Till requested their services as the new Orioles. Bobby performed alongside his hero through 1974 and fielded his own Orioles following Till's death. (Courtesy of Charlie and Pam Horner.)

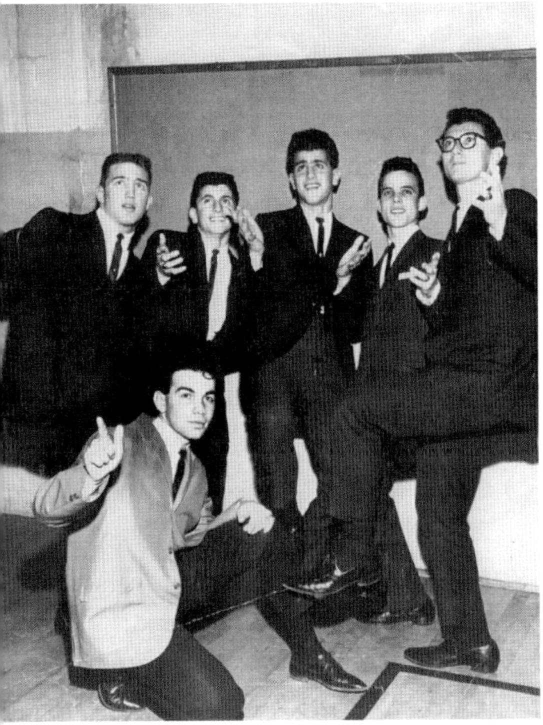

There Will Always Be
Asbury's West Side, where blacks and Italians lived in close proximity for generations, was a musical melting pot, and the Darchaes connected the 1950s Springwood scene with the 1960s sound of Asbury Park. Brothers Sam and Patsy Siciliano recorded with cousin Sal Capolongo, then with Ray Dahrouge, before teaming with "honorary West Side singer" Nicky Addeo (pictured) for several sides, both band-backed and a cappella. Dahrouge would pen songs for Tom Jones, the Manhattans, and the Moments, and the Sicilianos were honored on the Creators of SOAP monument outside Convention Hall. (Courtesy of Charlie and Pam Horner.)

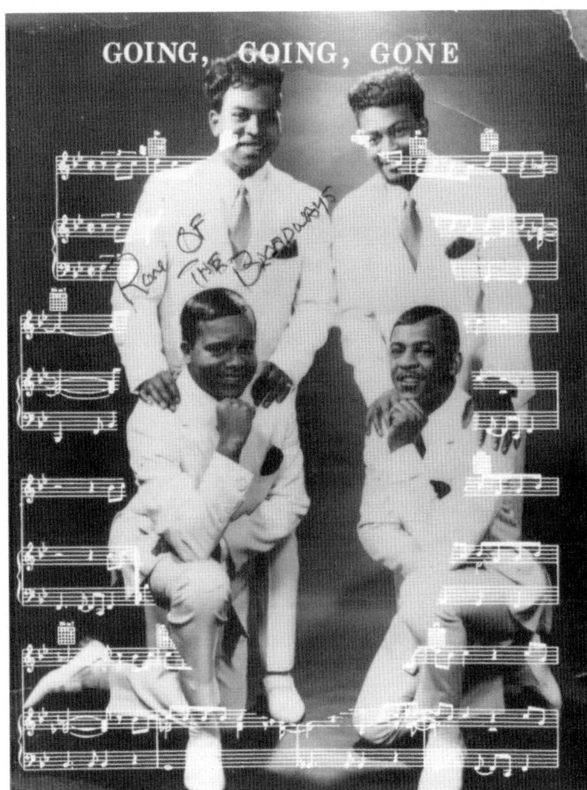

Going Going Gone
The Broadways originated as the Trennels from Neptune High and became the Zircons when Asbury's Leon Trent joined. Adding Billy Brown made them the Uniques, and they recorded with producer Norman Seldin under that name (minus Brown, but with Italian American fill-in Nicky Addeo). The group went nationwide for two singles on MGM as the Broadways. Brown went on to top the charts with the Moments while Trent formed the "kick ass funky horn band" Waterfront in the 1970s. The Broadways, sans Trent, performed for the first time in 40 years during a 2011 concert at the Paramount. (Courtesy of the Billy Smith Collection.)

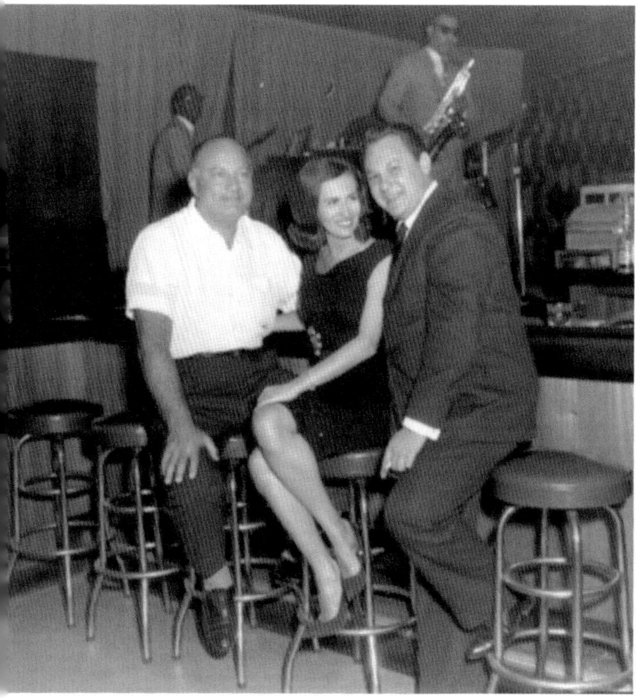

Leo's Turf

He was called "irascible . . . a tough businessman." Leo Karp's Turf Club on Springwood Avenue was a joint where local-regional combos like Al Griffin's Gents of Jazz or Eddie and the Four Cousins ("featuring Mr. Jellybelly") filled dance floors and dispensed hot-and-cool sounds. National acts like Lionel Hampton upped the ante, and hotel lounge band musicians made Leo's a favorite after-hours jam locale. Cashing out prior to the 1970 riots, Leo (left) passed away in obscurity in 1996 but earned his wings and halo with the Asbury Angels class of 2013. (Photograph by Joseph A. Carter Sr., courtesy of Madonna Carter Jackson.)

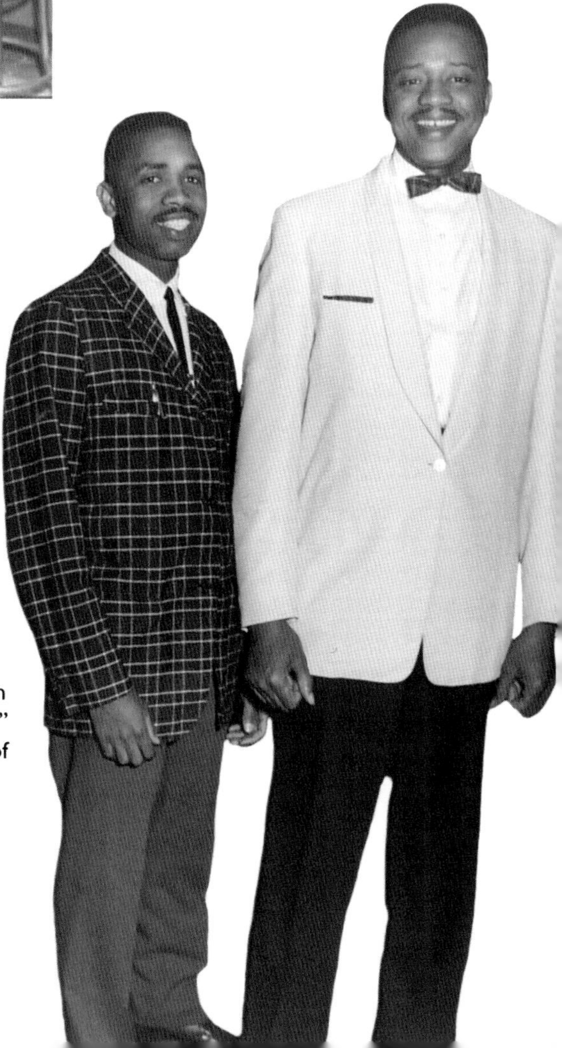

Big Bill's Pussycats

The Springwood Avenue club scene received a late addition in the early 1960s when Andy and Bill Sanders turned the Hampton Inn, a package-goods pit stop bought from bail bondsman-political player Phil Konvitz, into the sophisticated nightspot Big Bill's. With keyboardist Sam Pugh's trio as house band and a live music schedule that favored jazz classics (with occasional room for acts like "Screaming Jason"), Bill's was a jacket-required environment that eventually turned to go-go dancers as a draw, albeit a classier spin on the formula that saw Bill's "Pussycats" advertised on airplane banners and "handled like the Rockettes." (Photograph by Joseph A. Carter Sr., courtesy of Madonna Carter Jackson.)

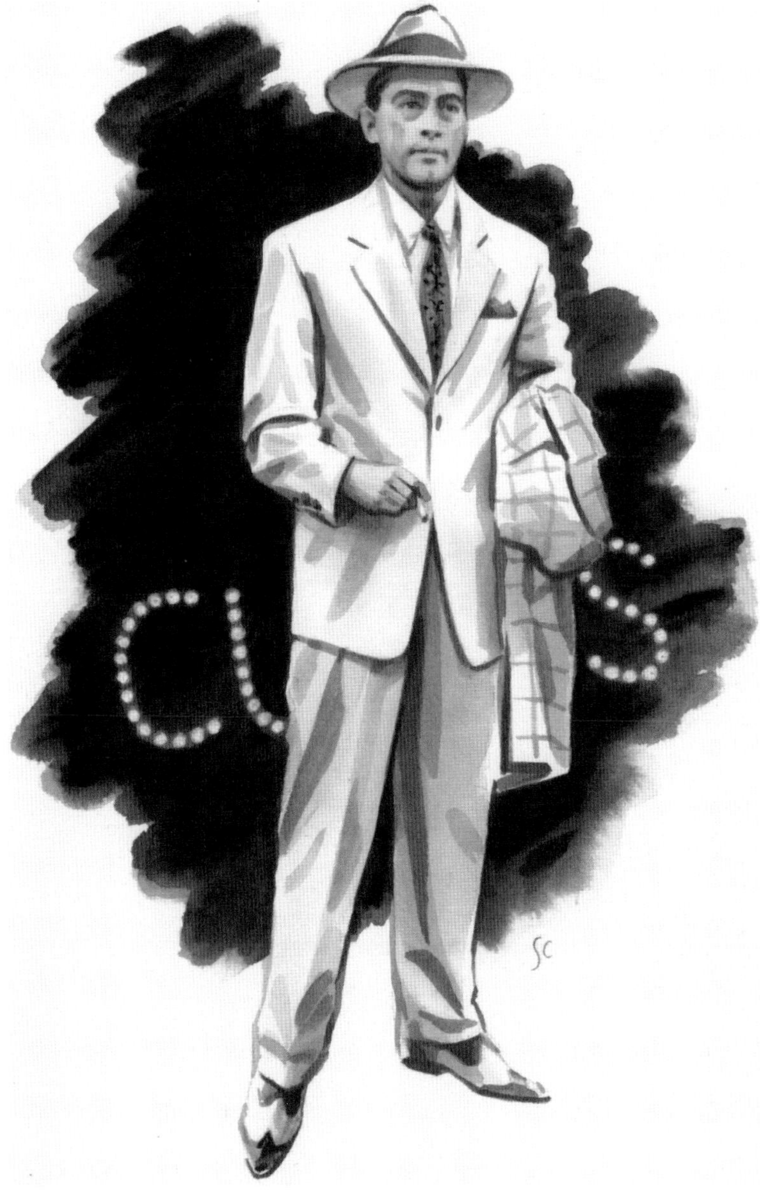

Cuba's Revolution

Suave, dapper Henry "Cuba" Lopez (despite the nickname, a native of Puerto Rico) and his Italian-American wife, Minnie, were West Side merchants who operated a candy and stationery store, but it was Cuba's Spanish Tavern that was the stuff of local legend. Post-Prohibition, Cuba's staked an identity as an establishment with a largely white clientele, "The Finest Floor Show on the Jersey Coast," and headliners that ranged from 1940s singing stars (Billie Holiday, The Ink Spots), to 1950s rock and rollers (Little Richard) and 1960s soul acts (Ike and Tina Turner Revue, the Four Tops). The Washington *Afro-American* described Cuba's as "the glittering jewel of Springwood . . . where the lights are copies of beer mugs, the waitresses are garbed like Spanish peasants, and where Barrington Guy sings nightly and thrills rich white women and prosperous colored with his dramatic voice." (Copyright and courtesy of Susan Culbert.)

A Taste of Honey

Bruce Springsteen's first Top Five single ("Hungry Heart") was still years away when Asbury Park produced its only breakout recording artist since Arthur Pryor. It would be a smooth crooner by the name of Leon "Lenny" Welch who took the 1940s songbook standard "Since I Fell For You" all the way to Number Four on the nationwide pop charts in 1963, one year ahead of the Beatles' reshuffling of the deck and a few months ahead of a bluesy reading of that same song by Doris Day. A product of the West Side clubs and a veteran of the Mar-Keys and the Vibes, the singer entered the 1960s with a style that was more supper club than Springwood Avenue, the 1961 novelty "Changa Rock" notwithstanding. Sad, romantic ballads like the country crossover "You Don't Know Me" would prove to be the forte of the elegant vocalist, and while he never enjoyed another trip to the top of the charts, he exerted an influence on his fellow music makers: introducing the Fab Four (and the world) to the vocal version of "A Taste of Honey" and recording a radical rethink of "Breaking Up Is Hard to Do" that would similarly inspire the song's original composer Neil Sedaka. Making few concessions to the shifting musical tides of the Aquarian age, Welch would put in a handful of television appearances before settling into a long and consistent career as a casino, cruise ship, and oldies-circuit act. He performs continuously, voice, looks, and dignity intact, to this day. (Courtesy of Charlie and Pam Horner.)

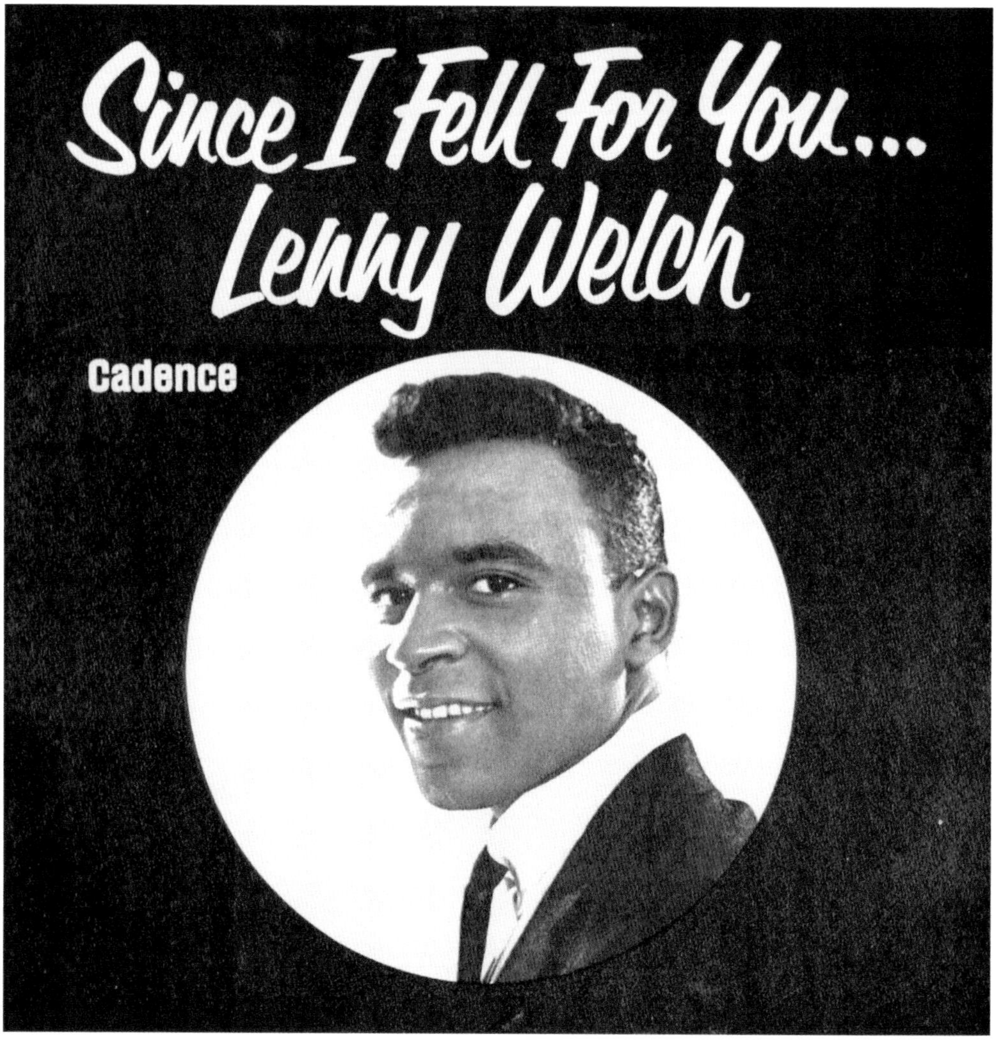

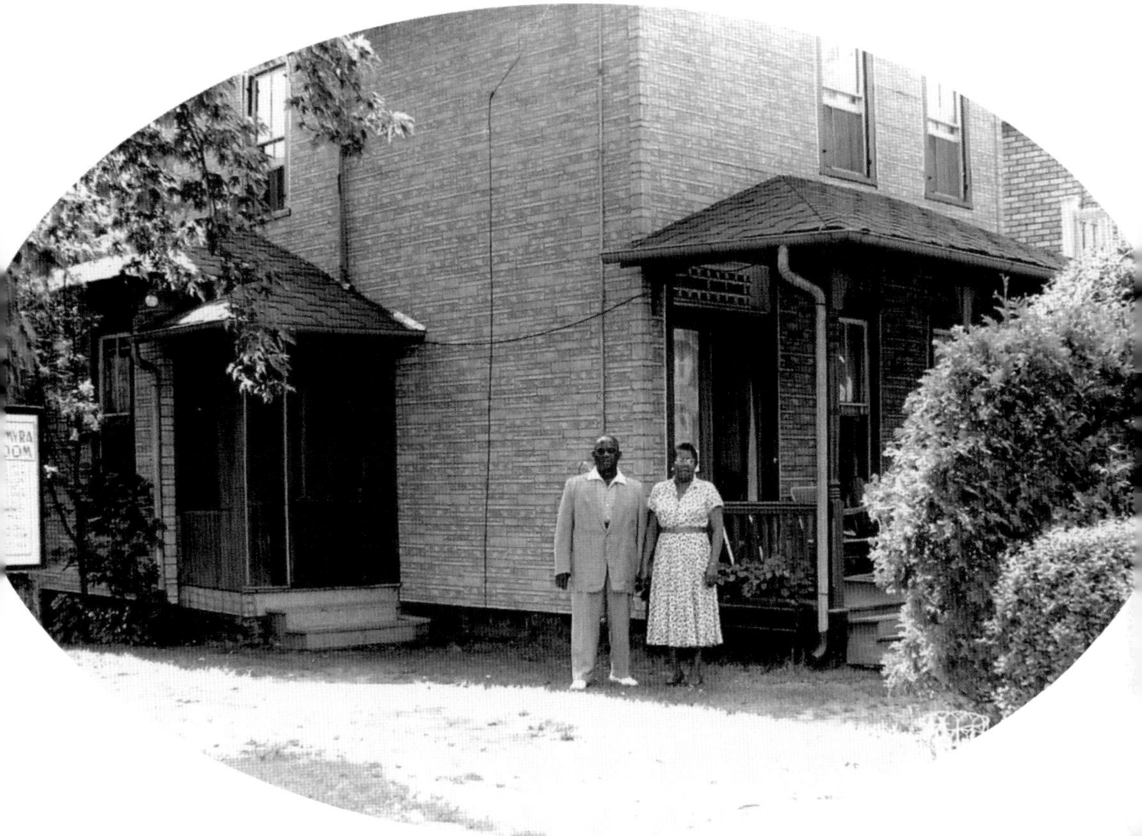

The Parreott Principle
Police officers and public schoolteachers; civil rights activists and city councilpersons; labor leaders and local commissioners; merchants, ministers, and makers of sweet, sweet music are all woven into the fabric of community life and are all represented within one extraordinary family. A member of the Asbury Park Police for 25 years (and, as a detective with a specialty in youth affairs, a crucial voice of reason during the interval surrounding the 1970 riots), David Parreott Sr. would bear witness to a pivotal era of local history, and his marriage to Esther Fauntleroy Parreott connected him to a family history with deep ties to the West Side's Methodist, Baptist, and Pentecostal churches. In the 1950s, the Parreotts would operate the Almyra Tea Room on Mattison Avenue (a site that would make way for the Frederick Douglass Apartments), and together they raised seven children, three of whom remained well known people around Asbury. David Jr. would follow his father to a stint on the police force, later serving on the city's zoning board and becoming an associate Baptist minister. He also had a brief tenure as a musician, a conga player (joining brother Dorian Parreott on sax) in a mambo-combo known as the Cu-Bops. Dorian would stick with music as a career; he became the band director and music teacher at Asbury Park High School, a musician's union president, and professional multi-instrumentalist who would continue gigging with his jazz ensemble well into his eighth decade. Daughter Rovena Parreott Sanders worked for the Walter Reade Organization and became a proud parent to one of Asbury's many musician-politicians: jazz-drumming mayor Kevin Sanders. (Photograph by Joseph A. Carter Sr., courtesy of Madonna Carter Jackson.)

Renaissance Man

He was an All-State basketball player and sprinter for Asbury Park High School's class of 1942, and team captain for the Dartmouth hoops squad. His college career in law studies was interrupted by two years as a World War II Army bombardier. He served as an Asbury Park city councilman from 1957 to 1965, followed by three terms in the New Jersey General Assembly. He spent five years as Monmouth County prosecutor in the 1970s and subsequently served on the county's superior court bench for much of the 1980s. That might have been more than enough for one résumé, but even after hanging up his robe from the juvenile and domestic relations court, there was a sense that James M. "Chippy" Coleman Jr. was just getting warmed up. The retiree would go on to serve 10 years as an advisor on the joint legislative committee on ethical standards and, with his wife, Judith Stanley Coleman (APHS class of 1952), would take a prominent role as a tireless advocate for open-space preservation in Monmouth, a stance that often led to skirmishes with many of his fellow Republicans. Frequently credited as a founding father of the New Jersey State Lottery, a genuine local legend in the fields of politics and philanthropy, Coleman, who passed away in 2014, garnered a rare respect from both sides of the aisle and all aspects of public life. And, when asked to nominate potential legendary locals in the fields of sports, public service, and community activism, then-councilman John Moor did not hesitate to answer, "Chippy Coleman . . . Chippy Coleman . . . Chippy Coleman." (Courtesy of Michael Booth and the *Coaster.*)

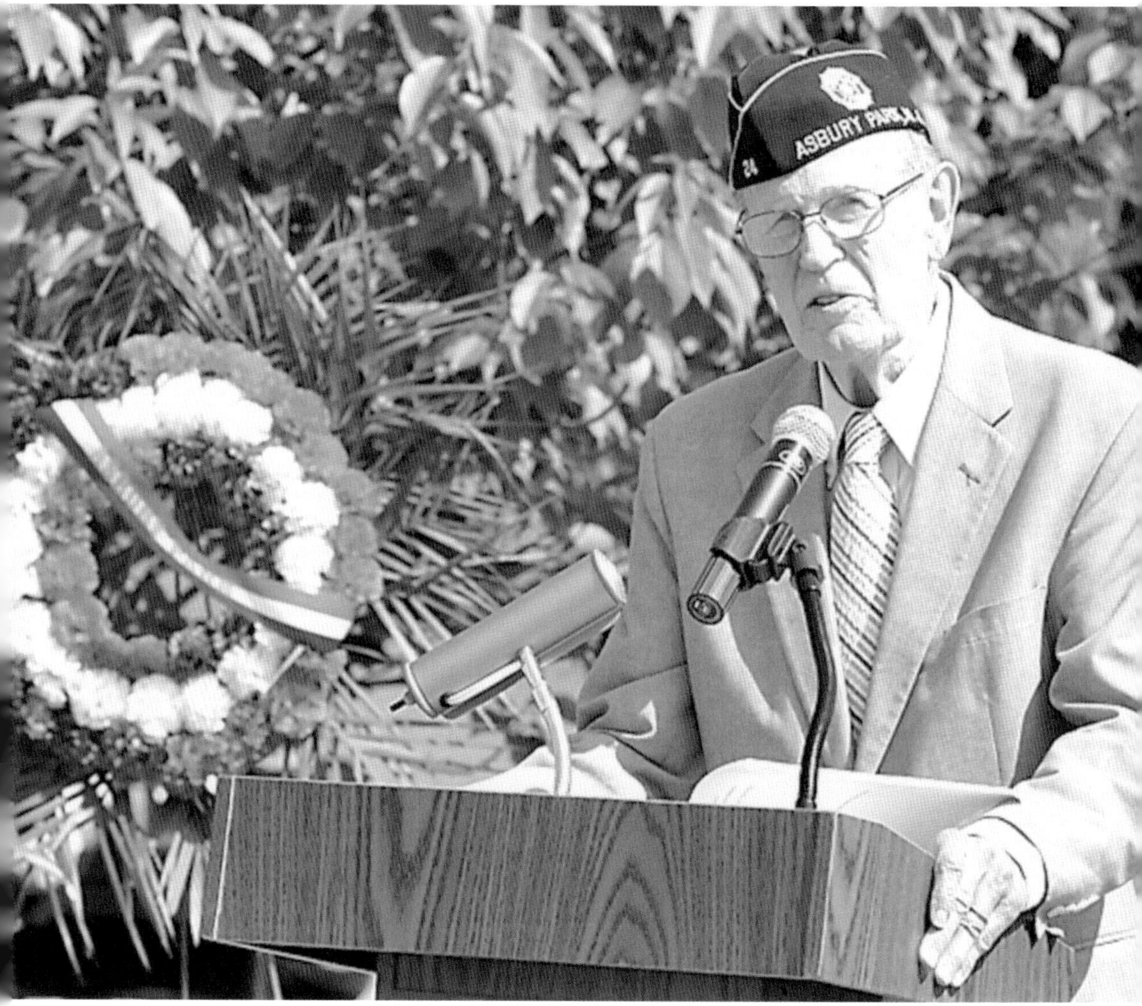

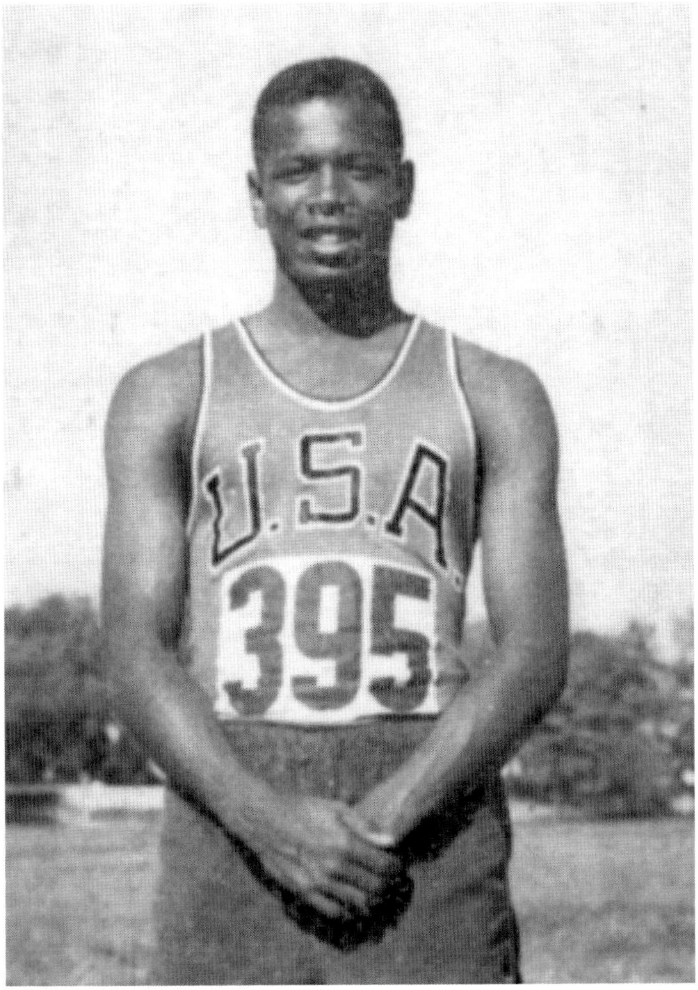

The Fastest Man on Earth

As a child in a West Side public housing project, he battled polio with the help of his mother's homemade remedies. As a junior varsity baseball hopeful, his skin color would reportedly deny him a place on the roster. Still, for a shining moment in the early 1960s, Frank Budd was the World's Fastest Human—a record-setting sprinter, former Olympian, and future NFL wide receiver who would come to be named the *Asbury Park Press* Athlete of the Century. An All-State footballer at Asbury Park High School, the quiet multisport star (football, track, basketball) would go to the 1960 Olympics in Rome, Italy, as a member of the US track team, placing fifth in a very tight 100-meter field. It was in 1961, however, that Budd would enter the record books for the ages. The Villanova University junior had already sprinted to victory in both the 100- and 220-yard events at the NCAA event when, competing in the 100-yard dash at that year's National AAU track meet, the speedster would overcome a leg injury to clock a time of 9.2 seconds, breaking a long-standing record by a tenth of a second. Turning his career aspirations toward the gridiron in 1962, Budd would go on to play two seasons with the Philadelphia Eagles and Washington Redskins (as well as three years with the CFL's Calgary Stampeders) before returning to New Jersey and a long but largely anonymous working life with the New Jersey Department of Corrections and an Atlantic City casino. Confined to a wheelchair in later years, the onetime Fastest Man on Earth would see his hometown high school honor him with the annual Frank Budd Track Meet, an event that continues on after Budd's 2014 passing at the age of 74. (Courtesy of the Billy Smith Collection.)

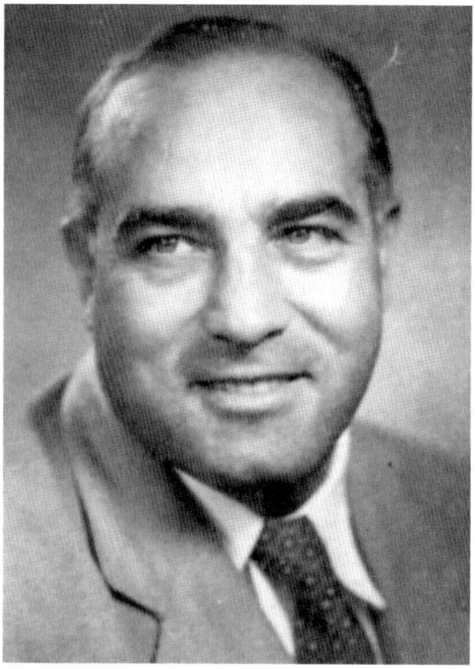

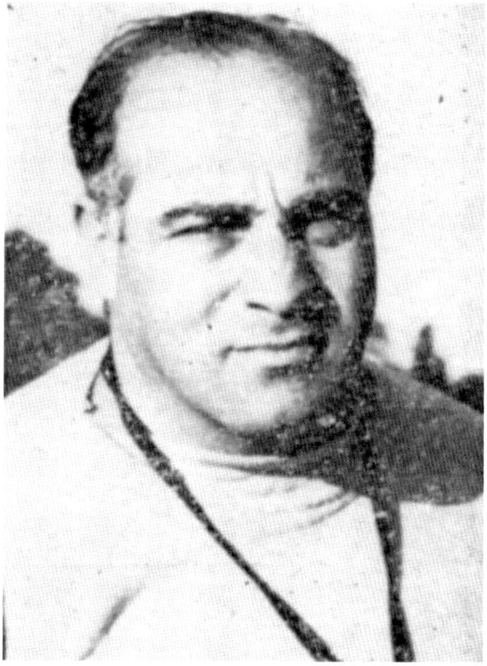

The Undefeated
The only APHS athlete to win four varsity letters for four consecutive years, Bill "Butch" Bruno returned to lead the Blue Bishops football squads in a 20-year run (1946–1966) that included an undefeated 1953 season and three regional Group IV titles on his way to a 114-50-13 record. Married to fellow faculty member Pat Bruno, he fathered two school athletic directors, Bill Jr. and Pete, while his son Jimmy and daughter Mary Pat served council terms in Asbury and Ocean respectively. The city's summertime recreation director was named to the NJSIAA's Hall of Fame following his 1981 passing, and the city dedicated William (Butch) Bruno Stadium at APHS in 2012. (Courtesy of the Billy Smith Collection.)

Knuckles Electric
One of the West Side's most successful businessmen, electrical contractor William Knuckles (left) took an active hand in civic life as far back as 1935, when he ran (unsuccessfully) for council. A longtime supporter of institutions like the Boys Club, he is pictured here in the late 1950s donating funds to the West Side Community Center, an entity established in 1945 at the onetime DeWitt Avenue home of a local doctor. The WSCC continues into the new century, but Knuckles' Springwood Avenue electrical and appliance shop was burned out of existence during the July 1970 uprising. (Photograph by Joseph A. Carter Sr., courtesy of Madonna Carter Jackson.)

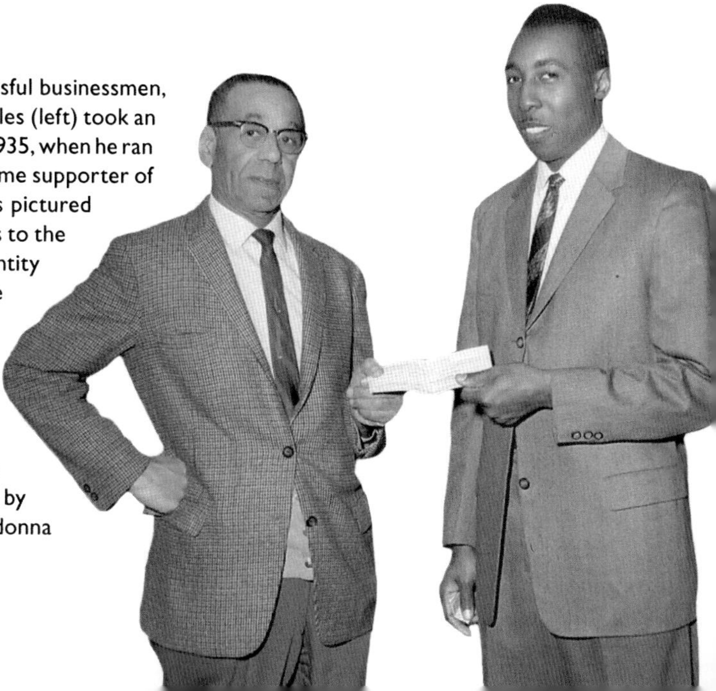

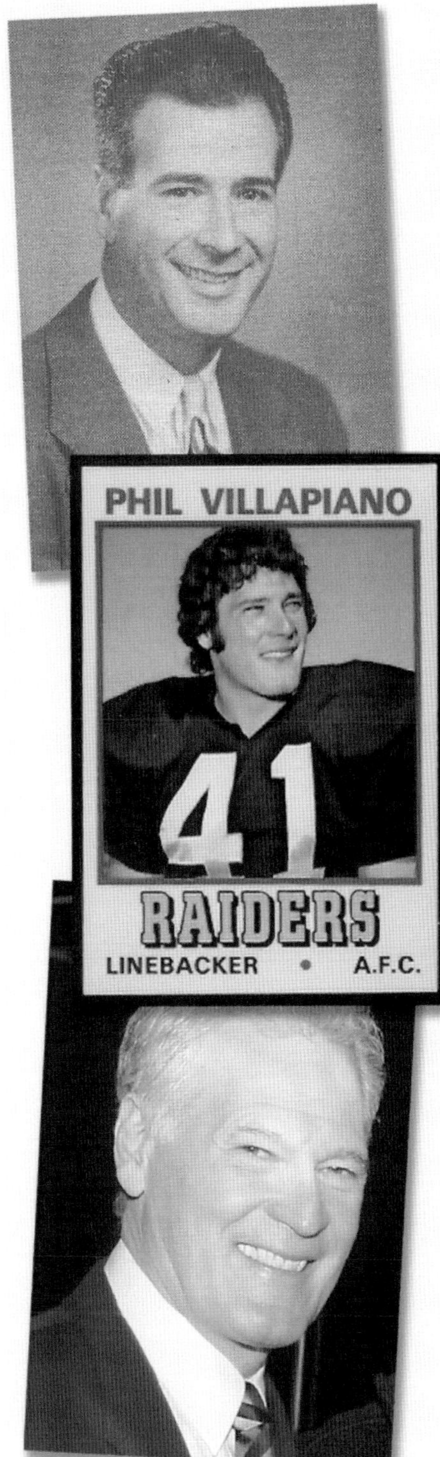

Put Me in, Coach
Like Butch Bruno, he played on a championship football team at Asbury Park High, and he returned to coach. In his case, he led the basketball and track programs at a school about which his son Phil told Helen Pike, "Asbury was big . . . almost like a college . . . we all thought we were the cream of the crop." Augustus "Gus" Villapiano served as APHS athletic director during the glory days of intense local rivalries and games that necessitated relocation to large public venues like Convention Hall. A summer job with Seashore Day Camp (operating originally at APHS) would culminate in his purchase of the private camp in 1974, moving it to a dedicated complex in Long Branch and instituting a year-round school program.

Phil Villapiano lettered in his sophomore year on the Blue Bishops squad, graduating from the new Ocean Township High School a couple of years later and going on to an illustrious NFL career as a hard-playing linebacker with the Oakland Raiders lineups of the 1970s (including a spectacular showing in Super Bowl XI). "Coach Gus" continued to oversee Seashore Day Camp until his 1984 passing, and the facility continued under the stewardship of a new generation of Villapianos: John (a former state assemblyman), Gus (a retired Asbury Park firefighter), and Carolee (a retired school teacher). (Courtesy of Ocean Township Historical Society and the *Coaster*.)

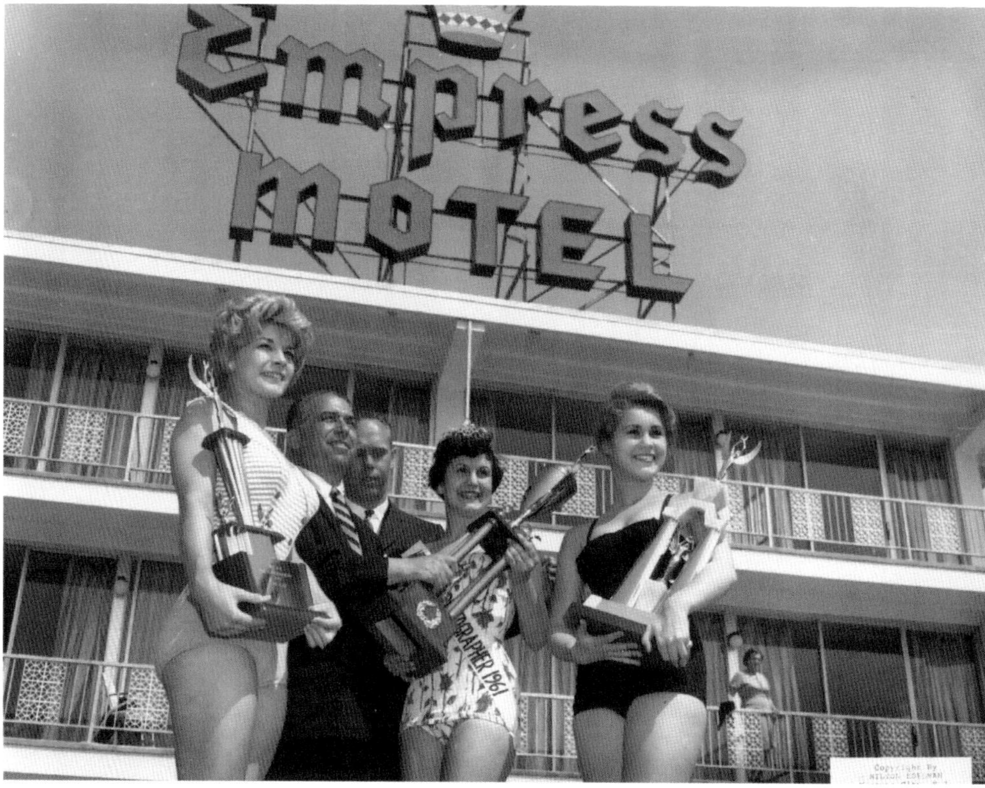

The Putt-Putt Game

The title "Mr. Asbury Park" is not something conferred lightly, and perhaps no one was more deserving of the honor than Anthony Petillo, the police officer, entertainer, and event organizer known for all time as "Putt Putt." The nickname derived from his beat as one of Asbury Park's first motorcycle cops, but it could just as easily have evoked the putt, clack, and bop of the wooden balls in bocce, the clay-court Italian game that has been called an amalgam of bowling, shuffleboard, and marbles. Petillo (second from left in the photograph) would be remembered for many things: as a lounge singer in the Berkeley-Carteret's Grill Room, his signature tune was an adaptation of a Rodgers and Hammerstein standard, "You'll Never Dance Alone," and as the city's special events coordinator, he brought back the Baby Parade and oversaw many other holiday activities and attractions. Still, his greatest legacy rested with the annual Anthony "Putt Putt" Petillo National Bocce Tournament, an event that pitted officials from several local towns against each other in a round of friendly competition that would draw the participation of Asbury-bred celebs Danny DeVito (page 92), Phil Villapiano (page 63), and Bam Bam Bigelow (page 79). The APPD veteran was named honorary bocce commissioner of New Jersey, and Asbury Park, where his first tournament took place in 1977, would be designated the bocce capital of New Jersey by the state legislature in the early 1980s (a state senator would later introduce a bill to make bocce the official state game). Putt Putt passed away suddenly on the eve of the 1987 event, and Petillo's cousin Sal Caliendo took over the tournament, which moved in 1998 to Long Branch, and then to Neptune City in 2006 for its final two editions. (Photograph by Milton Edelman, courtesy of Kay Harris.)

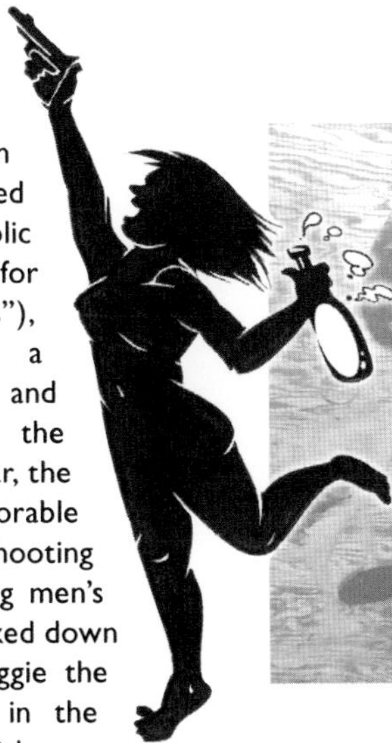

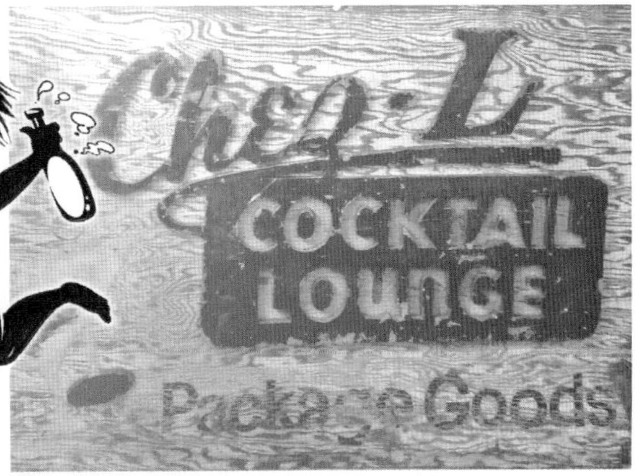

Maggie the Cat

Asbury establishments like Fox's and the Blue Note traditionally welcomed gay men from around the region (and were regularly raided by the state alcoholic beverage commission for "catering to homosexuals"), but Margaret Hogan, a policeman's daughter and former nun, founded the city's vanguard lesbian bar, the Chez-L Lounge. A memorable character given to shooting guns at the ceiling, using men's urinals, and streaking naked down Cookman Avenue, "Maggie the Cat" would reemerge in the 1970s as owner of the Odyssey. (Illustration by the author.)

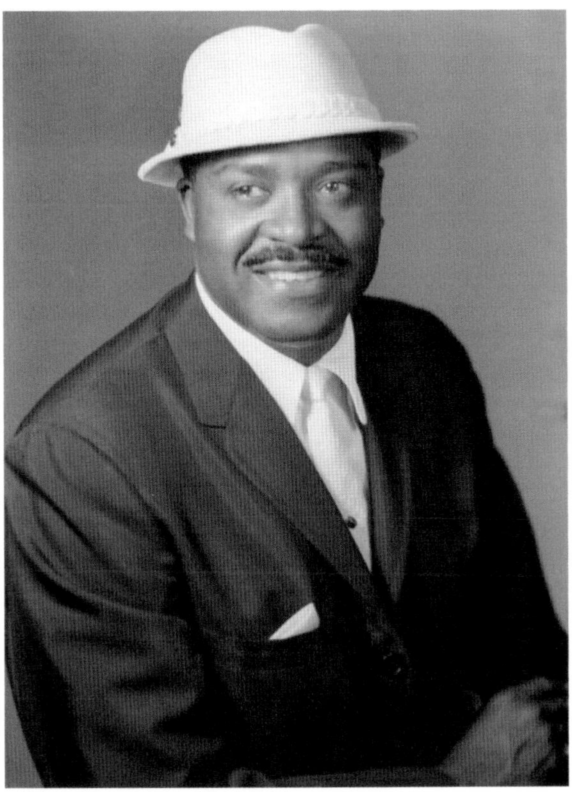

Odyssey's Orchid

When an Asbury Park policeman named Odyssey Moore realized his dream of opening a swanky jazz club, the Orchid Lounge quickly staked a place on a crowded scene. In addition to showcasing up-and-comers like guitarist George Benson and drawing a nattily-dressed African American clientele (many of whom likely shopped at the nearby men's shop co-owned by Moore), the establishment at Springwood Avenue and Memorial Drive featured big-time blues (B.B. King) and Memphis soul (Al Green) before the decade dissolved into devastation. The building was eventually demolished, and Moore passed in 2004, becoming an Asbury Angel a decade later. (Photograph by Joseph A. Carter, courtesy of George McMorrow.)

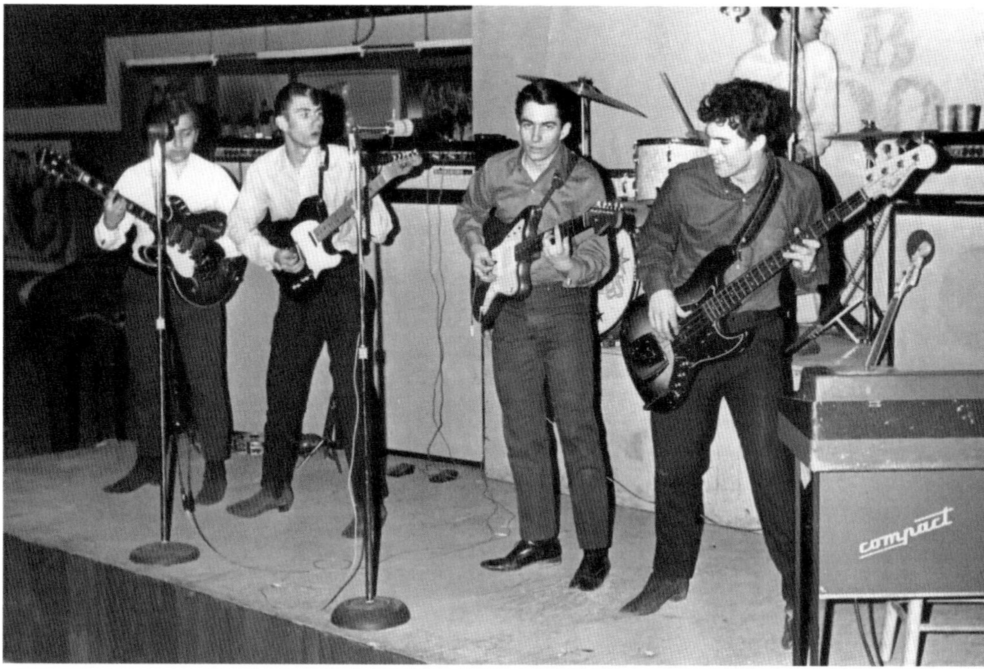

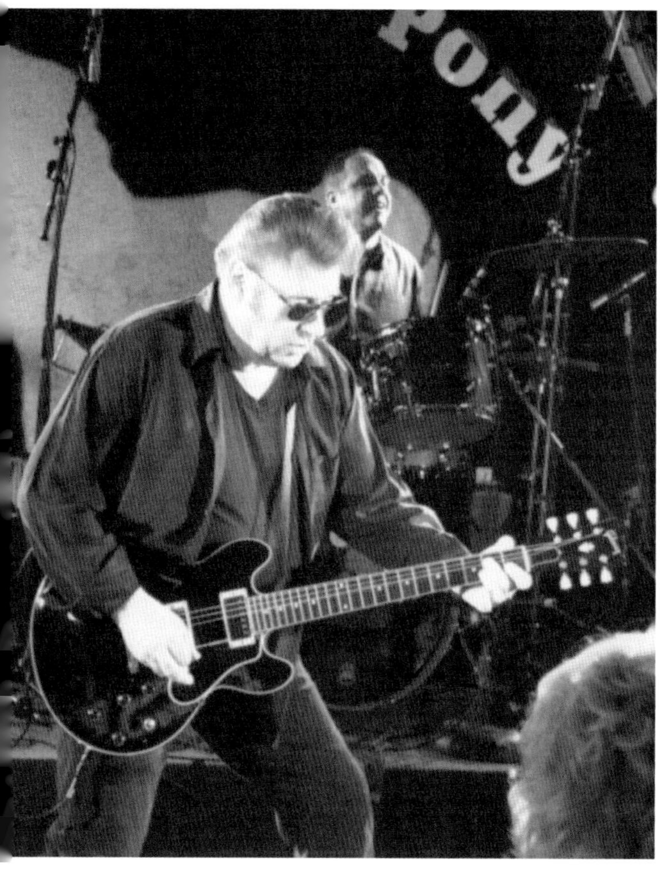

When Sonny Gets Blue

He was there on the ground floor—playing the Asbury Hullabaloo in 1960s combo the Starfires; opening for Jerry Lee Lewis, Soupy Sales or J. Fred Muggs—and 50 years on, Sonny Kenn is still going strong as the city's pioneer guitar-slinger rock star. Whether joining Johnny Lyon in the power trio Maelstrom, or fronting the 1980s-era Wild Ideas, Kenn was all about the blues; stripping the big-band SOAP sound down to its atomic core, and cutting a sartorially splendid figure (in carefully coiffed sideburns, ice cream blazers, and sunglasses after dark) while his contemporaries sported shaggy beards and beat-up jeans. Navigating decades of bar-band rapids by his own blue star, this son of a Western "song wrangler" can be seen and heard these days anywhere from a neighborhood watering hole to an art gallery, where his sought-after paintings write an all-new chapter in the Sonny saga. (Above photograph courtesy of Sonny Kenn; left photograph courtesy of Dave Christopher.)

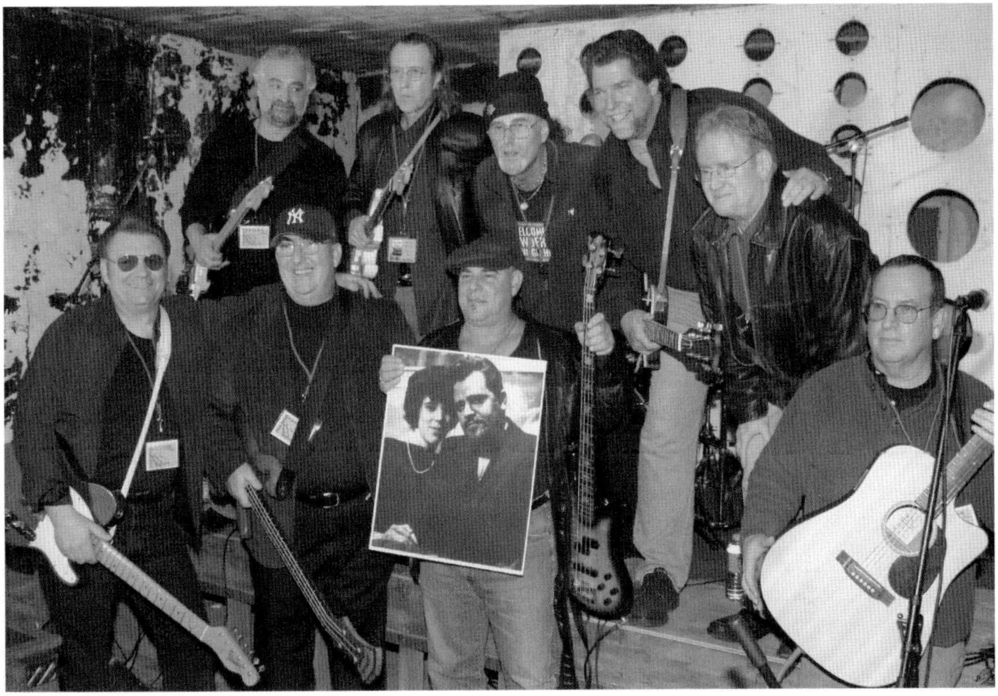

Three Stories High

Given the significance accorded its place in rock history, one would think that the Upstage might have lasted more than three years. But Tom Potter and Margaret Romeo Potter never danced to anything but the different drumbeat of the music lover. Hairdressers by trade and hosts by night of a party never before seen on either side of the tracks, they set a tone that was exploratory, improvisatory, and anticipatory of all that could happen in the oddball after hours. What *did* happen there was that an ambitious young man named Bruce connected with those likeminded souls who helped him crystallize his sound and vision—men named Van Zandt, Lyon, Lopez, Tallent, and Sancious.

Birthed from house parties at the Potters' Ocean Grove home, the windowless space two flights above a Thom McAn shoestore was not a bar or even a folkie coffeehouse (that would have been the Green Mermaid, the middle-floor buffer zone between workaday Cookman and the weirdness up top). The distinction between the Mermaid and the Upstage was as clear as the cool reception that Springsteen got from the second-story crowd, and the star power that crackled around him when he plugged into the house sound system on the third floor. By 1968, the Freehold guitarist was already a veteran of the Castilles (featuring scene stalwart George Theiss) with a yen to explore something heavier. He found his venue at the Upstage, and a vibe that shared little with the cover-band bars of the Circuit or the segregated scenes out on Springwood Avenue. Running on its own liquor-free logic, the club hosted an early session for teens (often with Margaret's own Distractions as house band), then closed for an hour, reconvening at 1:00 a.m. for the late-night jam that lasted until the morning sun. Organized by Tom, those sessions possessed the building-block ingredients of new life; it was up to the musicians to cause something truly evolutionary to emerge from the primordial blues-ooze.

Never a license to print money, the Upstage faded into folklore by late 1971 and the Potters went their separate ways, as Tom relocated to Florida and Margaret resumed her Romeo's salon gig. They passed away within a few years of each other in the 1990s, and in 2006, a group of alumni assembled at the former Upstage space for a last jam in their honor. (Copyright and courtesy of John Cavanaugh and the Asbury Park Musical Heritage Society.)

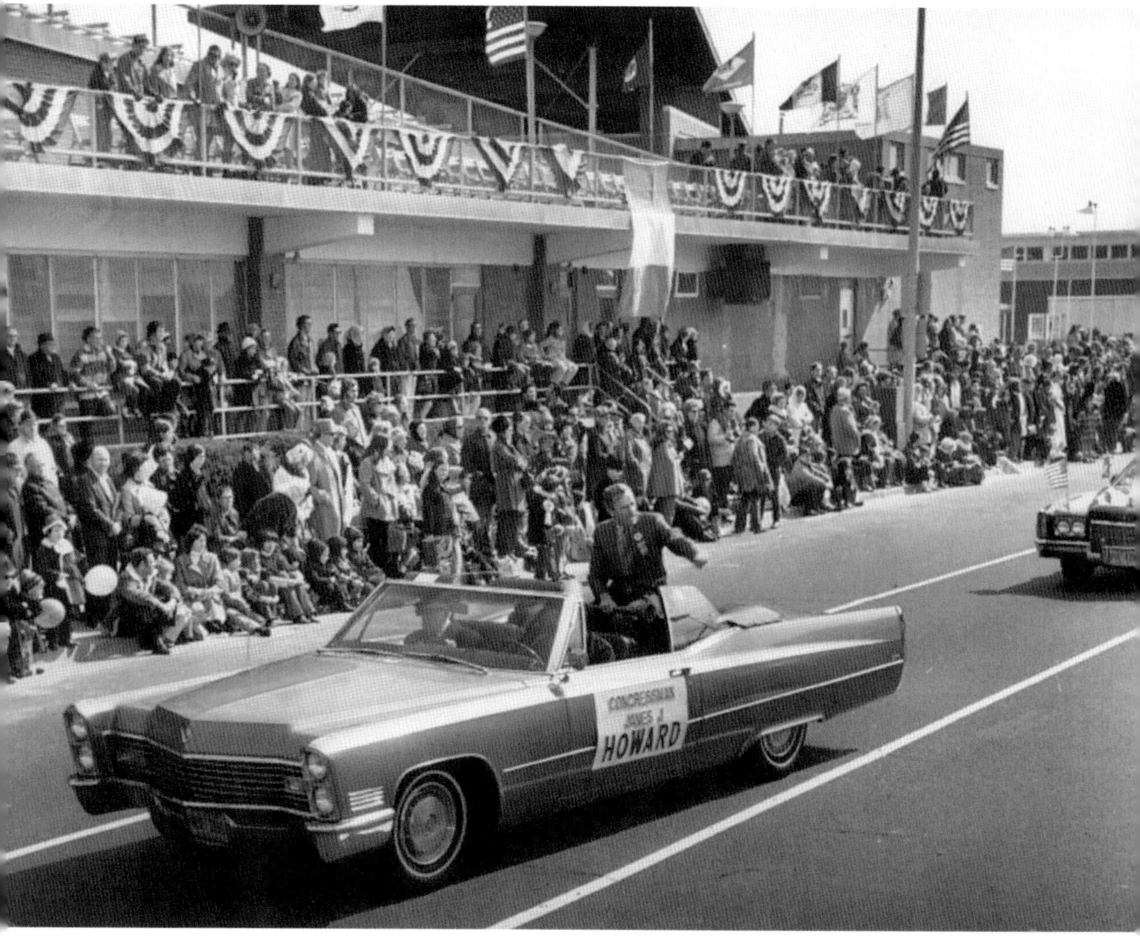

I (Can) Drive 55

The protestations of Sammy Hagar notwithstanding, anyone who has ever enjoyed a cruise-controlled, speed limited ride on our nation's highways can thank Rep. James J. Howard. The Democratic congressman from New Jersey's old Third District was also behind the child car seat law, the National Driver's Register, the raising of the drinking age to 21, and many more acts governing the ways in which goods and people get from one place to another—as well as the infrastructure that they all travel over, under, and through. As the influential chairman of the House Committee on Public Works and Transportation, he made passenger safety, fuel efficiency, and driver responsibility his rallying cries during more than 20 years in office, making few friends among the Circuit cruisers and bar owners, perhaps, but crafting a legacy of legislative action that seemed unimaginable in subsequent Congresses. A former elementary school principal and a 1947 graduate of Asbury Park High School, Howard presided over an era of local history that would see outlying suburbs expand and explode in population, as older cities like Asbury Park hemorrhaged residents. An advocate for environmental causes, he remained a staunch opponent of ocean dumping at a time when the Jersey Shore's lifeblood beaches were threatened by the practice. Following his fatal heart attack in 1988 (on a Maryland golf course, at the age of 60), he would be honored with the construction of a major Marine Sciences Laboratory on the Sandy Hook peninsula. In Asbury Park, an ambitious transportation center consolidating train, bus, and taxi depots would come to bear his name. However, New Jersey Transit's lack of electrified rail service to the city would long keep station stop Asbury a relative backwater to its bedroom-community neighbors up the track. (Photograph by Milton Edelman, courtesy of Kay Harris.)

CHAPTER FIVE

Memorial Drive

1970s–1990s

This town almost burned right down to the ground, on a red-hot 4th of July / Squad cars and fire trucks closed off the highway / And everyone stared and acted surprised / And when the verdict came down the solution was simple / Stay on your side and I'll stay on mine / Till we all come crashing together again, down on Memorial Drive

—George Wirth

Folksinger George Wirth did not get around to recording the epic "Memorial Drive" until 2011, but one can believe him when he says it is a song that took him 40 years to write. Singing with a seasoned rasp, Wirth takes a slow tour through some of the darkest decades in recent Asbury Park history. Where Springsteen's "My City in Ruins" was a skeletal framework, pressed into service as universal rallying anthem for disaster victims everywhere, "Drive" is a detailed mural painted over a boarded-up wreck, that track-scarred gateway to the onetime heart of a community that burned in anger and frustration during the overheated summer of 1970.

The Asbury riots drove a stake into a town already suffering the ravages of poverty, neglect, and suburban sprawl. As the century staggered to its finish, the city was dealt little more than black eyes and bruises, with institutions from Steinbach's to the *Press* departing for highway headquarters and psychiatric hospitals placing discharged patients in the old "summer hotel" boardinghouses.

New suburban schools effectively redrew segregated boundaries between the neighboring communities. An out-of-state developer's bankruptcy and drawn-out litigation tied up the waterfront's most cherished assets for an entire lost decade. A serial killer lured victims from the boardwalk and buried bodies behind a nearby Burger King. A massive real estate scam involved fraudulent mortgages, and county-wide beach closings were traced to contamination from Asbury's antiquated sewage treatment plant. City officials would be nabbed on federal bribery charges; one mayor was caught buying cocaine right across the street from City Hall.

To the tourists it once depended upon, Asbury seemed dirty, desperate, and dangerous, a haven for bikers and burnouts, criminals and crazies. But while the music played on for a good while, thanks to a certain scruffy standard bearer with the goods to make it in the big world beyond, Asbury Park would hit rock bottom at the tail end of the millennium. Blocks of vacant businesses and deteriorating housing left the city in no condition to sustain itself, and over on the waterfront—where even a brilliant summer's day would often see not a soul on the beach or boardwalk—the soundtrack had turned to silence.

Through those less-than-glorious days, however, a core group of city residents soldiered on, opening for business each morning, preparing a lesson plan or a sermon, and protecting that pilot-light ember in the trust that it would illuminate the way once more. They were the true believers, and they occupy a special place in the history of Asbury Park.

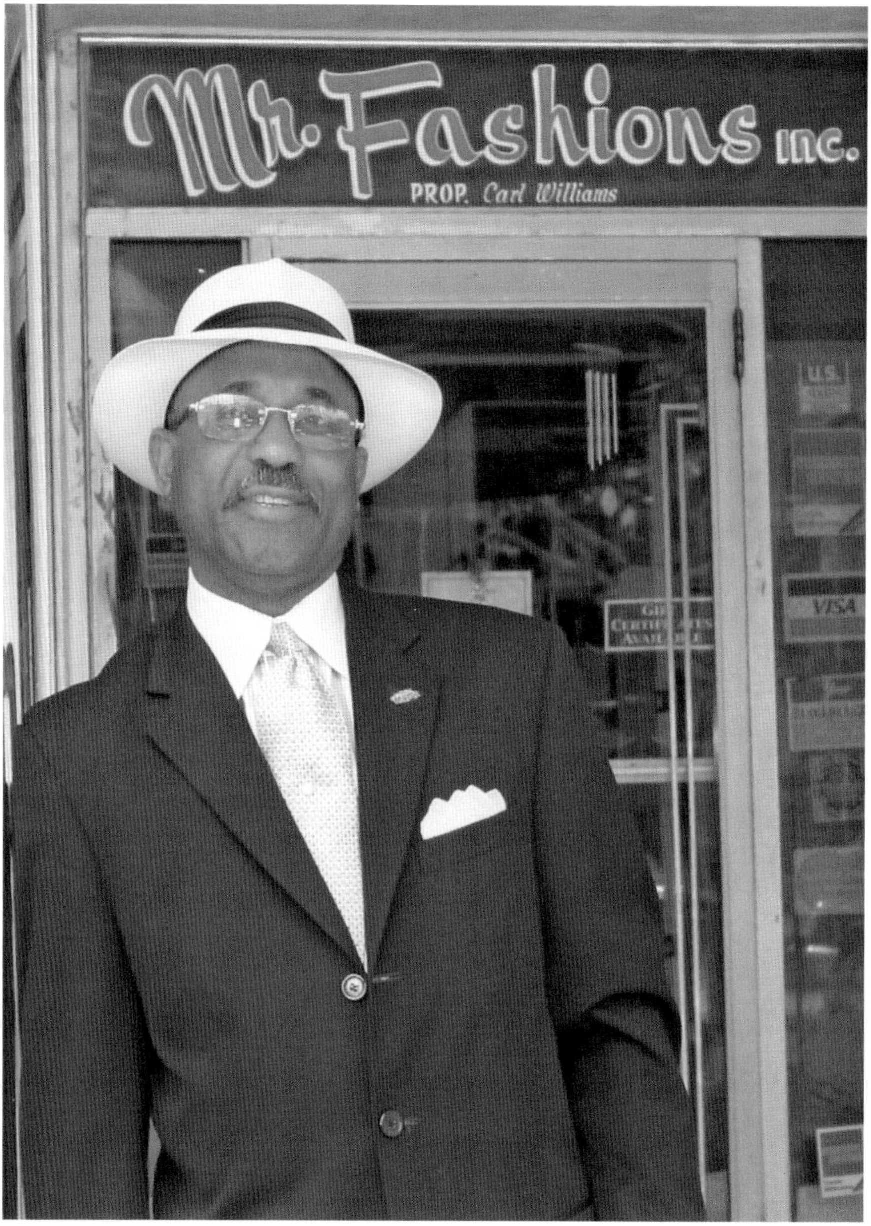

The Man Who Cares

"Carl Williams represents all that is good in Asbury Park," states his biography for the Asbury Park High School Hall of Fame, a project that the longtime merchant helped spearhead. Formerly of Fisch's, the West Side emporium that burned in the July 1970 uprising, Williams opened Mr. Fashions ("For the Man Who Cares") across from Steinbach's in 1971. Purveying a peacock-proud selection of debonair menswear amid the squalor of a dying downtown and storefront-ministering to his neighborhood flock, Williams remained long after the demise of the Mammoth Department Store and kept a light in the window until his retirement some 27 years later. He was elected to city council in 1993 and became mayor in 1996. During Williams' tenure, he was invited to the White House, and he gifted President Clinton with a Mr. Fashions necktie. (Courtesy of Michael Booth and the *Coaster.*)

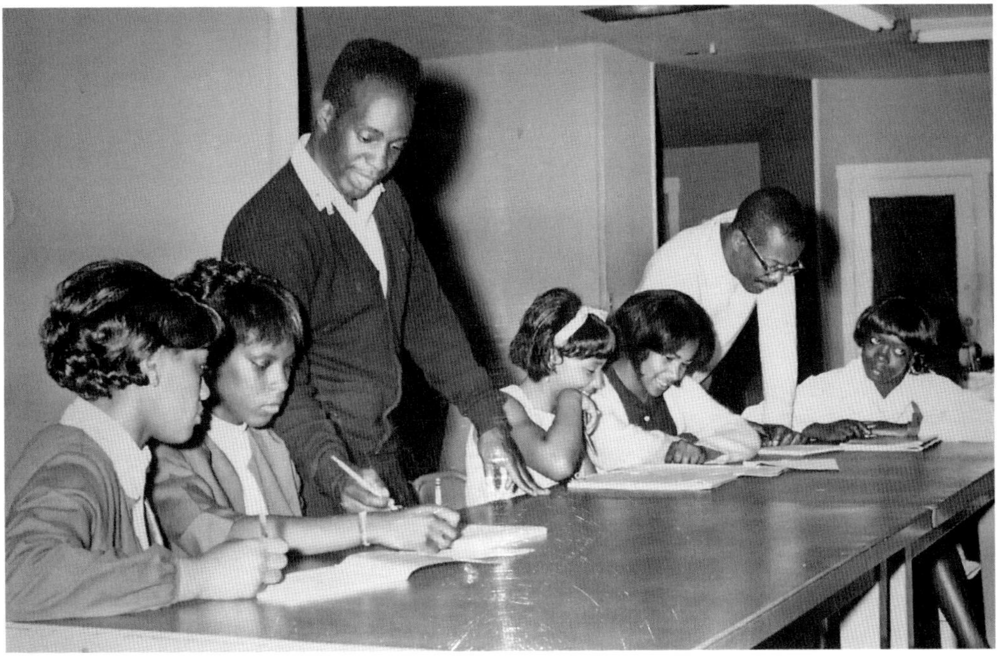

Donald's Dynasty

He was usually "the short one" in the room when coaching his AAU championship basketball teams, but Donald Hammary Sr. (standing at left in this photograph) towered over decades as an advocate for West Side youth. An active force in the NAACP, Boys Club, and Westside Community Center, the city recreation director, APHS coach, and teacher stood tall as a community spokesman during the powder-keg summer of 1970. His sons DiTeko (SportzFarm Foundation) and Darryl (Charity Kings) carry on his legacy in youth-oriented endeavors, and the Community Courts on Prospect Avenue were named for Hammary Sr. following his 2007 passing. (Courtesy of DiTeko Hammary.)

Body and Soul

Is it a church, as the sign says? Or is it a doctor's office, day spa, holistic retreat, or restaurant? Hidden in plain sight (and "steps to the ocean") on Third Avenue, Abunda Life Center is or has been all those things over the course of 30 years, reflecting the diverse energies and mission of Dr. Robert H. Sorge, ND, PhD. A consultant on matters both naturopathic and spiritual (and a former Mr. North America), Sorge and his wife, Gloria, have "coached tens of thousands of men and women to HIGH LEVEL WELLNESS" from the former Hotel Powhatan, a huge, rambling seashore manse that stands as one of Asbury's enigmatic best-kept secrets. (Courtesy of Michael Booth and the *Coaster*.)

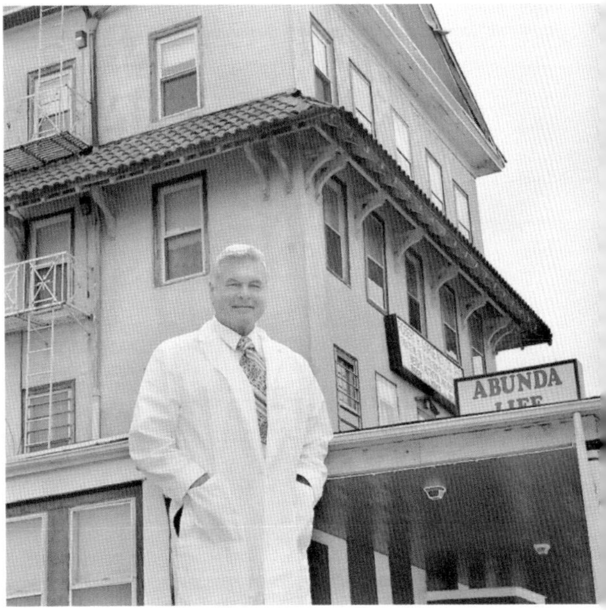

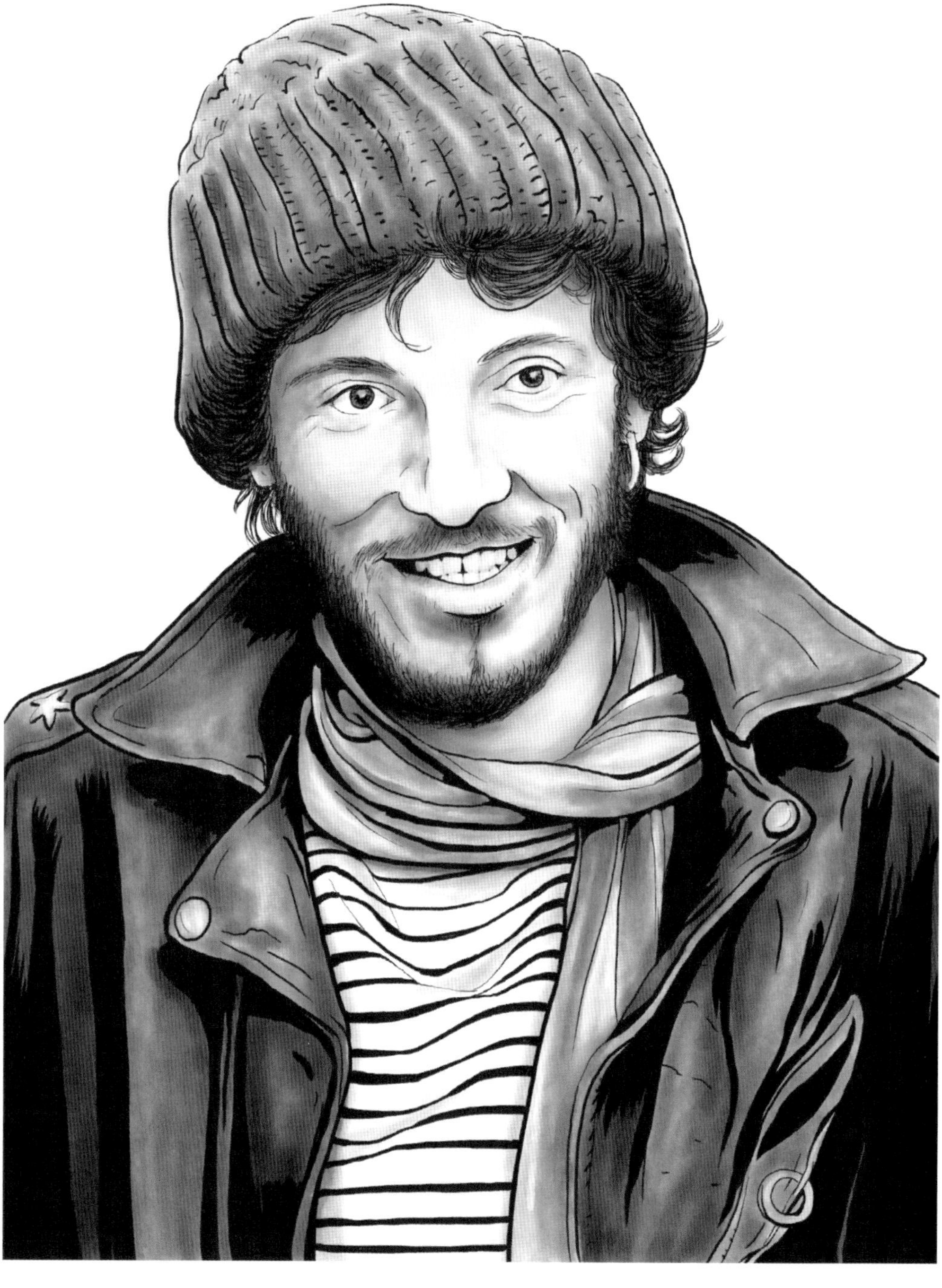

Out on the Kokomo (OPPOSITE PAGE AND BELOW)
In Long Branch, there is a bungalow branded the "Born to Run House." A Cookman Avenue apartment reportedly served as songwriting studio for his first album. But if one had to pinpoint a workshop for what would become the "most Asbury" song of Bruce Springsteen's prodigious catalog, "4th of July Asbury Park (Sandy)," it would be the entire Circuit of the early 1970s.

Even if he spent that superheated 1970 summer in Neptune watching the flames from the water tower above Carl "Tinker" West's surfboard shop, Asbury Park's most legendary non-local did his time in his adopted homeland. When he titled his debut *Greetings from Asbury Park*, it was clear that this was no carpetbagger-come-lately. Having dipped into the 1960s Asbury music scene with his teen band the Castilles, Springsteen would, by decade's turn, create pure poetry and crazy commerce from every aspect of its basic bar band template. He stayed with friends, rehearsed in basements, and slipped out of the downtown Sands Hotel leaving his driver's license and underwear (the owner threw them out).

Projects like Steel Mill, Earth, Child, and Dr. Zoom built the buzz at venues like the Student Prince. All-nighters at the Upstage served as experimental mad laboratory, and by the time that the big, biracial, bolt-tight Bruce Springsteen Band made its bow, so did a Unified Field Theory that strove to unite east and west sides of town—the "future of rock and roll" with the splintered vinyl of all that came before. Still, the artist who recorded *The Wild, the Innocent, and the E Street Shuffle* was a man for whom "this boardwalk life is through"—and by the game-changing *Born to Run*, it was evident that sad, dying Asbury Park needed to release its shining stepson to the wider world and open road.

Springsteen never really left Asbury, of course. Playing the benevolent deity, he made dependable "surprise" appearances with virtually every act to hit local stages, augmented by multi-night concert stands for local charities, Convention Hall tour rehearsals, Light of Day shows and video shoots, and squiring the cast of NBC's *Today* around town in 2002. By that time, he had penned another Asbury song, "My City in Ruins"—with its redemptive rise-up chorus, and a between-the-lines feeling that the destinies of man and city remained forever intertwined. (Opposite page, copyright and courtesy of Jason Robinson; below, courtesy of Michael Booth and the *Coaster*.)

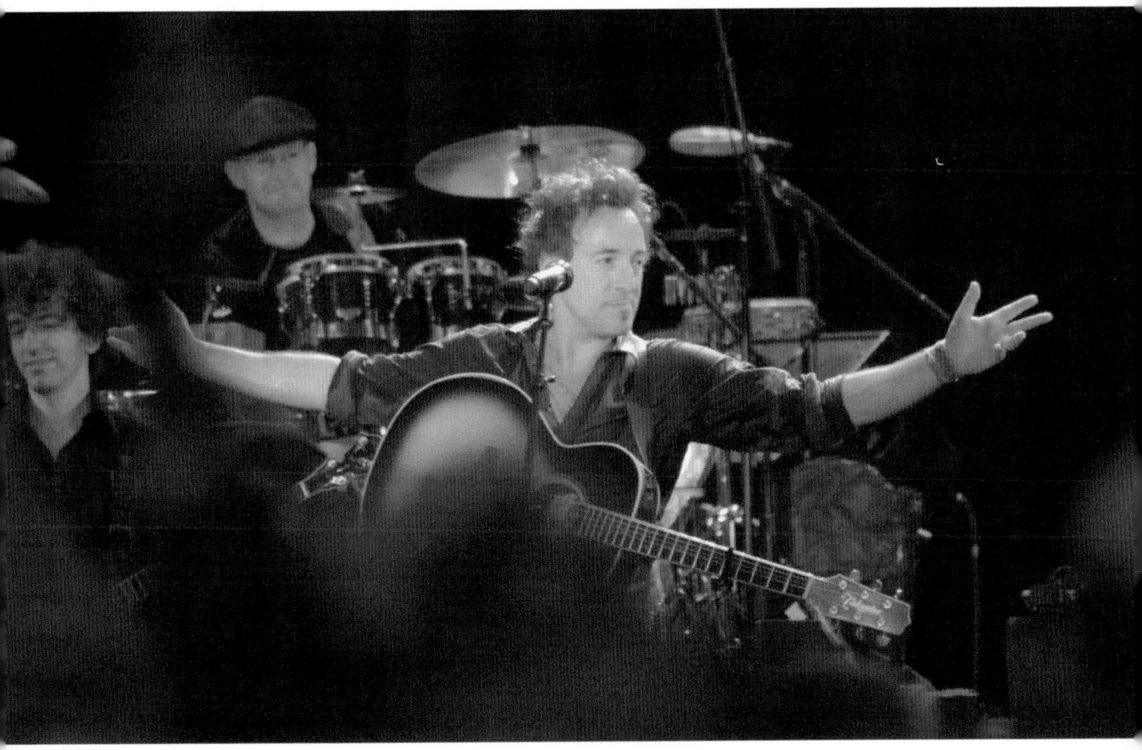

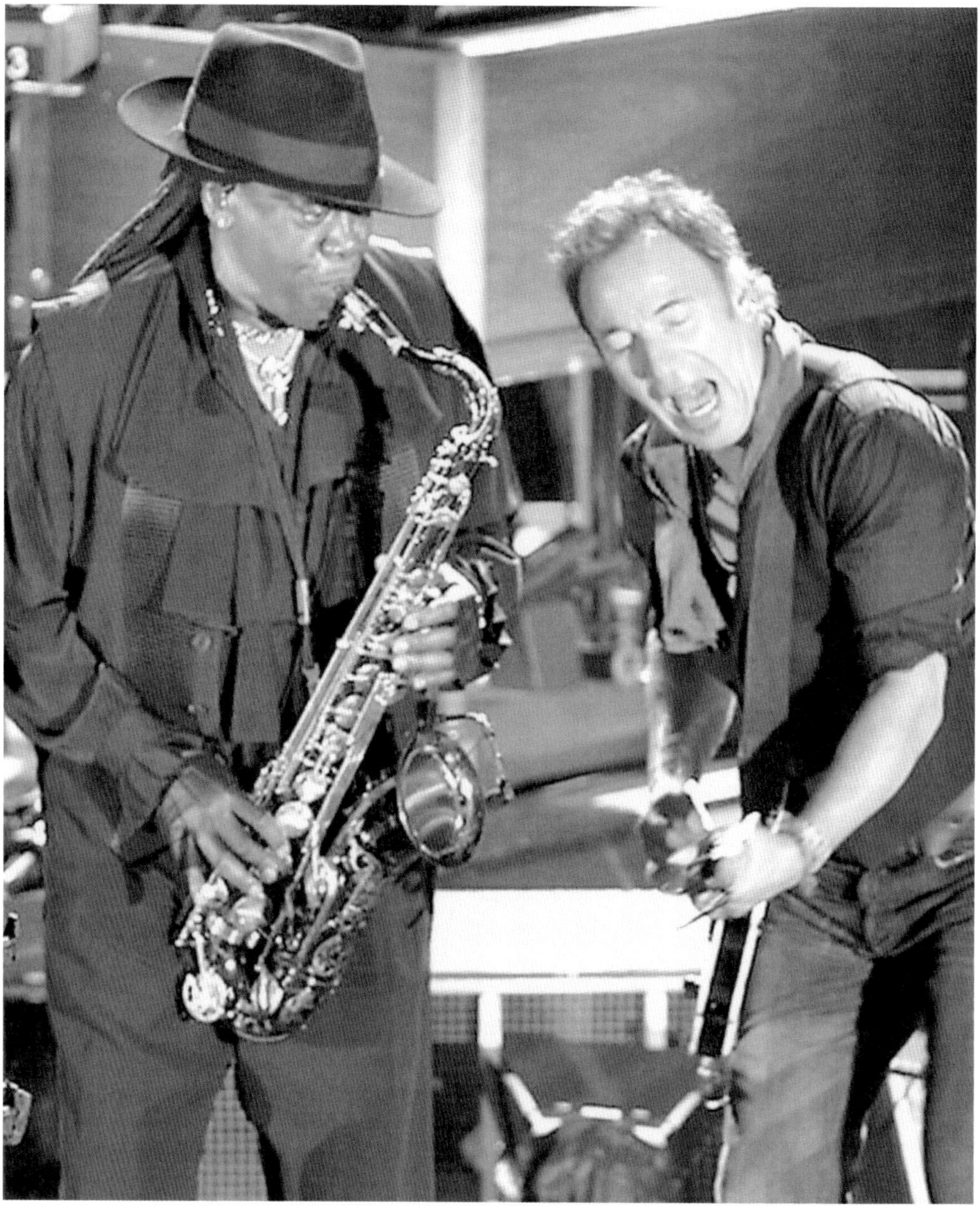

Friend of Mine

The legend of how Clarence Clemons came to play with Bruce Springsteen, complete with a dark and stormy night and a flying door, has been told so many times that it rings of epiphanic truth. Virginia-born "CC" played with Norman Seldin's Joyful Noyze before destiny led him to the Student Prince that night, and casual jams led to appearances on the Boss's first album, full band membership on the second, and a front-cover image for the ages on *Born to Run*. Clemons catalyzed the sound and vision of the E Street Band, scored solo success, appeared with the greats, and briefly hosted Big Man's West in Red Bank, New Jersey. His final releases with the Temple of Soul were recorded at the Stone Pony, and his 2011 death from stroke complications spurred the launch of the Asbury Angels project. For more on CC's early career, see Eileen Moon's *Legendary Locals of Red Bank*. (Courtesy of Mike Jones Photography.)

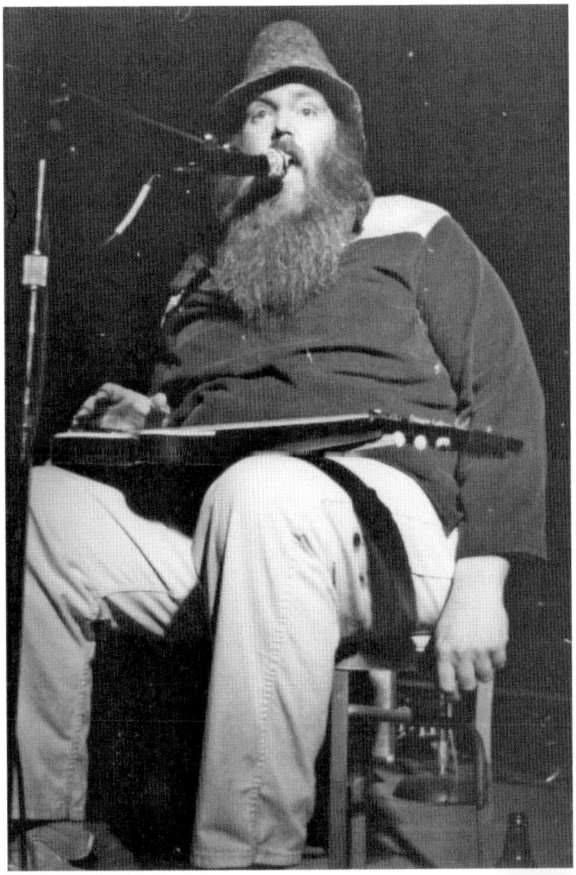

The Other Big Man

His credentials are impeccable: bouncer at the Upstage, roadie (and roommate) for the Boss, BBQ purveyor to the stars, and member of Bruce's barely contained Dr. Zoom and the Sonic Boom, to which he contributed backing vocals, tapped tambourine, and played Monopoly on stage (though he claimed it was craps). At six-foot six-inches tall and "72 stones," Big Danny Gallagher would have been a presence without even trying, but the red-bearded Hagrid of the Asbury soundscape would find his spotlight fronting authoritative organizations like the Boppers and Renegade Blues. The beloved "gentle giant" passed away in Colorado in 2007. (Courtesy of George McMorrow.)

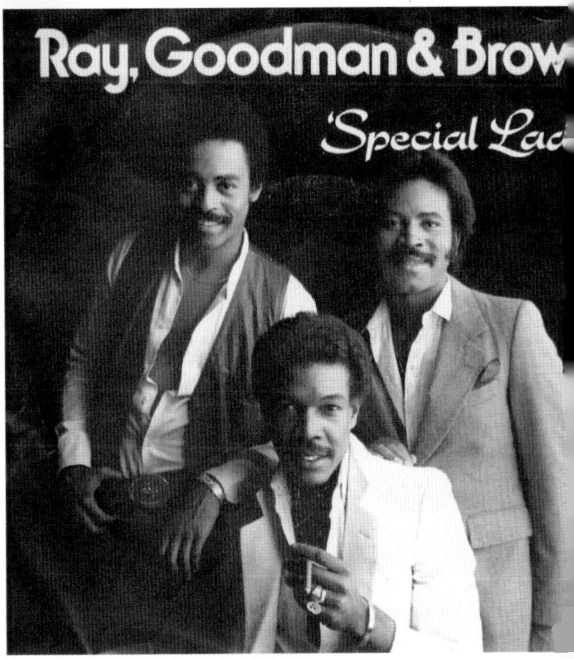

Three Way Street

While the 1970s found Springsteen generating monumental buzz, another Asbury-spawned act regularly topped the charts. Billy Brown (formerly of the Broadways; page 55) joined the Moments in 1969, helping the realigned trio take "Love on a Two-Way Street" to the number-one spot on the billboards. When Long Branch's Harry Ray joined Brown and Al Goodman, more hits ("Look at Me" and "Special Lady") and a name change (to Ray, Goodman, and Brown) ensued. Following numerous regroupings (and the deaths of Ray and Goodman), Brown, who reunited with the Broadways at Asbury's Paramount in 2011, continues working under the Moments brand. (Courtesy of Charlie and Pam Horner.)

Dig a Pony

The consensus said the golden age of Asbury rock clubs had peaked by the time Robert "Butch" Pielka (top left) and Jack Roig opened the Stone Pony in 1974. Relying on out-of-town cover combos at first, the partners found a comfort zone with "Miami" Steve Van Zandt and Johnny Lyon's Blackberry Booze Band, and it was not long before the party atmosphere saw Columbia recording artist Bruce finding his way to the jam-friendly stage. The house band that became the Jukes helped define the Asbury sound, and, with an assist from DJ-spokesman-spirit guide Lee Mrowicki, the Pony poured it on in the 1980s with a mix of national names, cover band kings (the Nines, Cats, TT Quick), honorary Shorecats (John Eddie, Beaver Brown), and surprises like the secret kickoff to Springsteen's "Born in the USA" tour. (Courtesy of the Billy Smith Collection.)

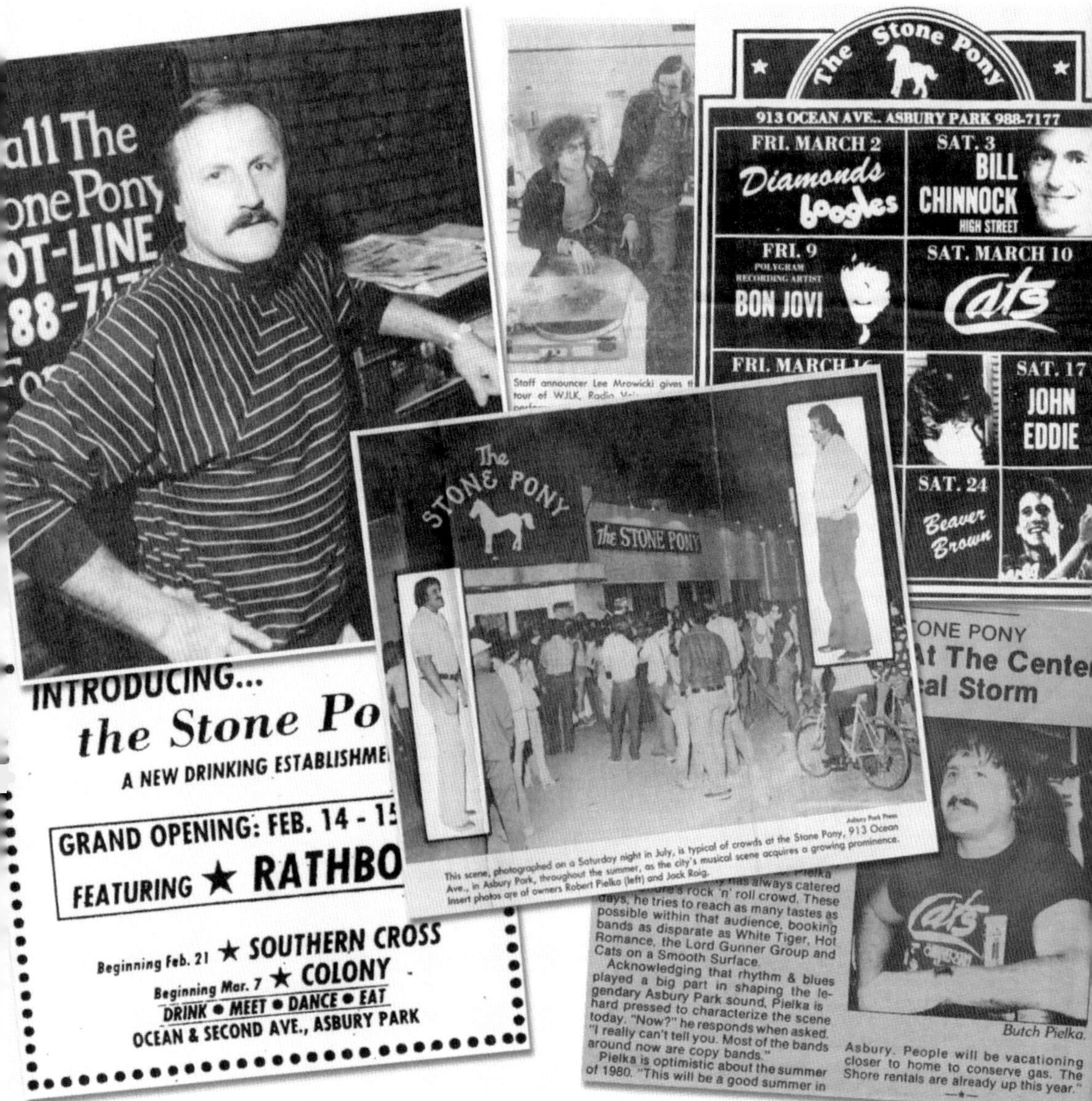

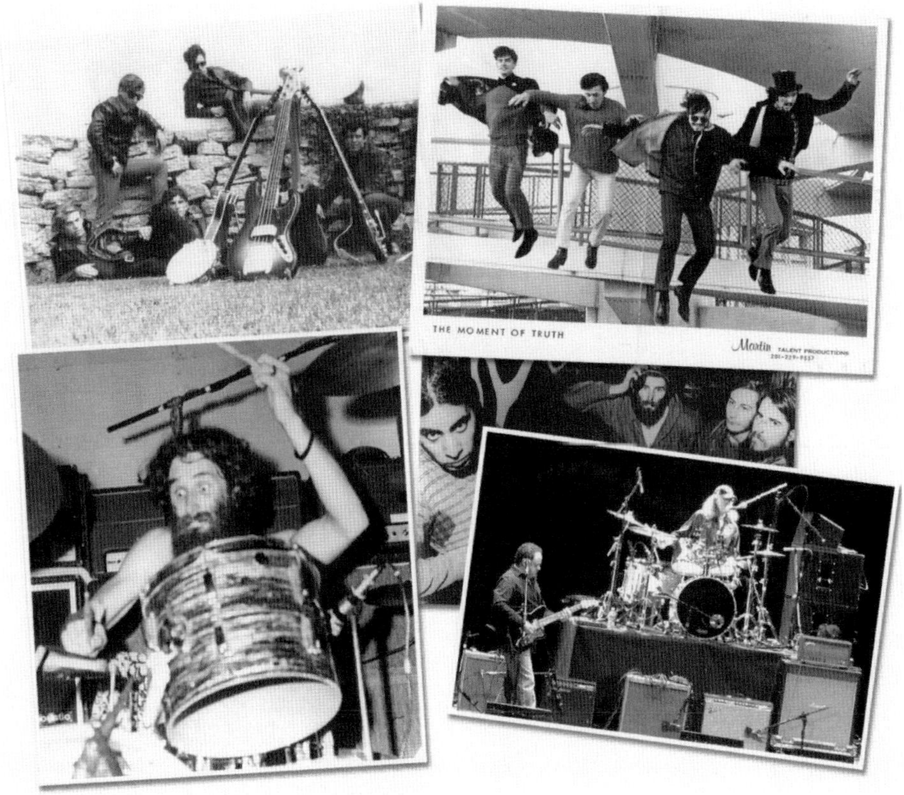

Whatever Happened to Asbury Park?

"In the beginning, there was Mad Dog Vini Lopez" intoned Bruce Springsteen, as the surviving E Street Band members were inducted into the Rock and Roll Hall of Fame in 2014. The veteran drummer's old Boss could have been speaking for the entire timeline of the Asbury Park Sound, a family tree that would not flourish and branch without the crucial cross-pollinating presence of the man whose rabidly rocking nickname was supposedly bestowed by beyond-legendary record man Clive Davis. The New Jersey State Golf Association, meanwhile, placed the ceremony in proper context, when they reported that "Caddie and drummer Vini Lopez" was going into the hall.

Long before he paid his bills on the links, Lopez paid a lifetime of dues gigging with Sonny Kenn's Starfires (top left) in the Jersey Shore's first great guitar band, hooking up with Danny Federici, Garry Tallent, and Bill Chinnock in Downtown Tangiers, and leaping from the old north boardwalk ramp with Tallent and Ricky DeSarno in the Moment of Truth (top right). He birthed Child (later Steel Mill) with Springsteen and joined Steve Van Zandt, Southside, and Tallent in the Sundance Blues Band (center right). He reteamed with Bruce in the pre–E Street lineup that found him steering the fire truck on those standalone early albums. He was fired in 1974 (and missed the "Born to Run" gravy boat), following an incident with Springsteen manager Mike Appel.

Those 40 years since have seen Lopez remain a man-of-a-thousand-bands mainstay of the Jersey Shore music scene: Chinnock's band, Cold Blast and Steel, Whistler and the Wheels, Acme Boogie Company, the Shakes, and unsigned legends Lord Gunner, to name but a few, and the new century would see him seek Springsteen's blessing to revive those early songs in Steel Mill Retro. Any Asbury night of the year, one could find Lopez jamming with the likes of Stringbean or Billy Hector, reuniting with Paul Whistler as Dawg Whistle, and bringing hall-of-fame credentials and attitude to those bar-pie and boardwalk sessions from whence all life originated. (Courtesy of Sonny Kenn, the Billy Smith Collection, and Dave Christopher.)

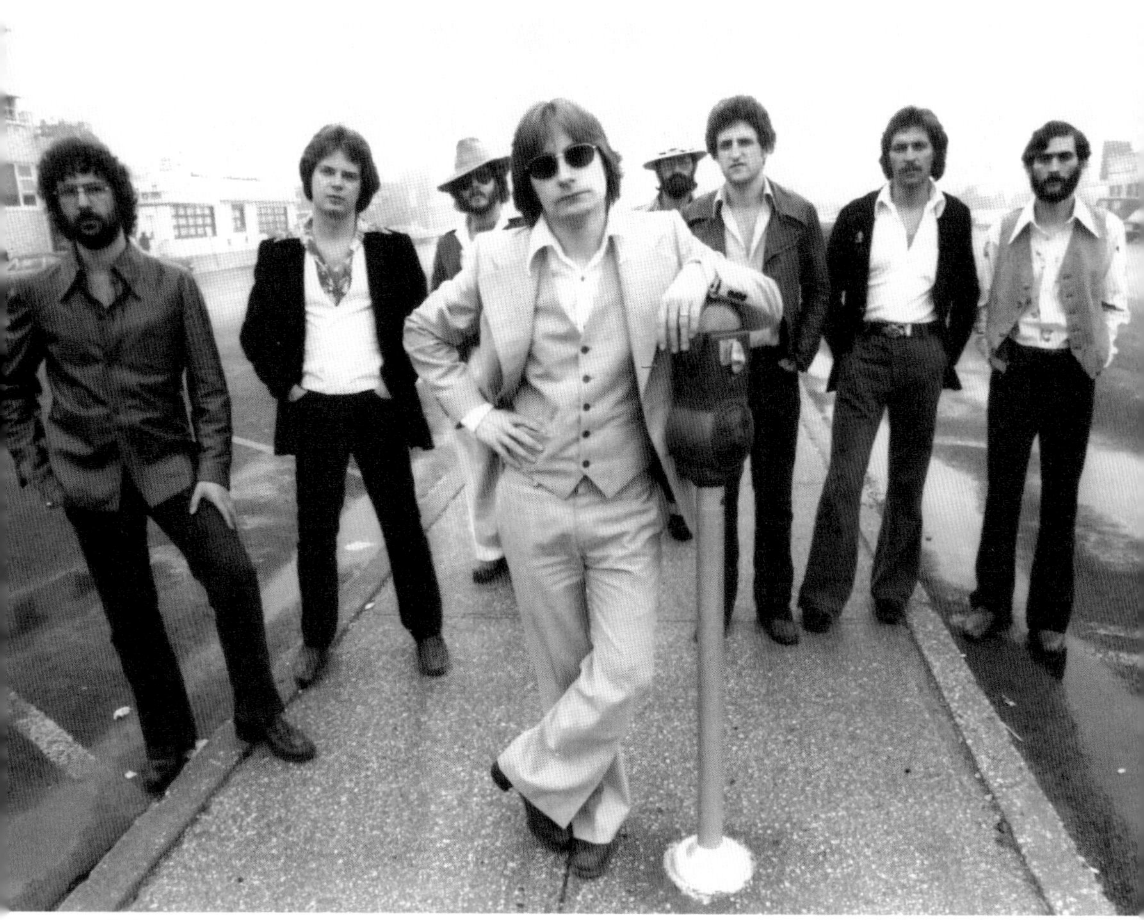

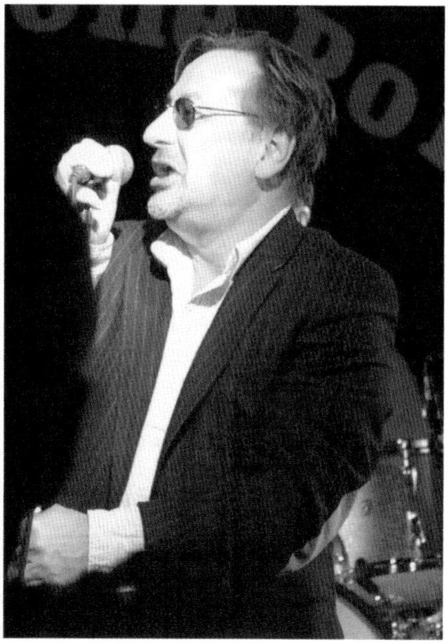

The Fever

Growing up in provincial Ocean Grove, "Southside" Johnny Lyon haunted West Side record shops, played bass in a power trio, and joined Steve Van Zandt in Sundance Blues before finding his front man calling with the Asbury Jukes (née Blackberry Booze Band). Pictured here around spring 1976, the Jukes formed a symbiosis with the fledgling Stone Pony, parlaying their house-band status and Springsteen synergy into some fine LPs and a justly hailed live show. While they never set the charts afire, those first two albums (packed with guest cameos, Boss liner notes, and solid songs by Van Zandt and Bruce) are a savvy snapshot of the 1970s SOAP scene. Lyon's annual Independence Day gigs with the Jukes remain a highlight of the SummerStage season, and his Poor Fools sideline is an engaging look into his musicologist's soul. (Above, photograph by David Gahr, courtesy of Tony Pallagrosi; left, photograph copyright and courtesy of Dave Christopher.)

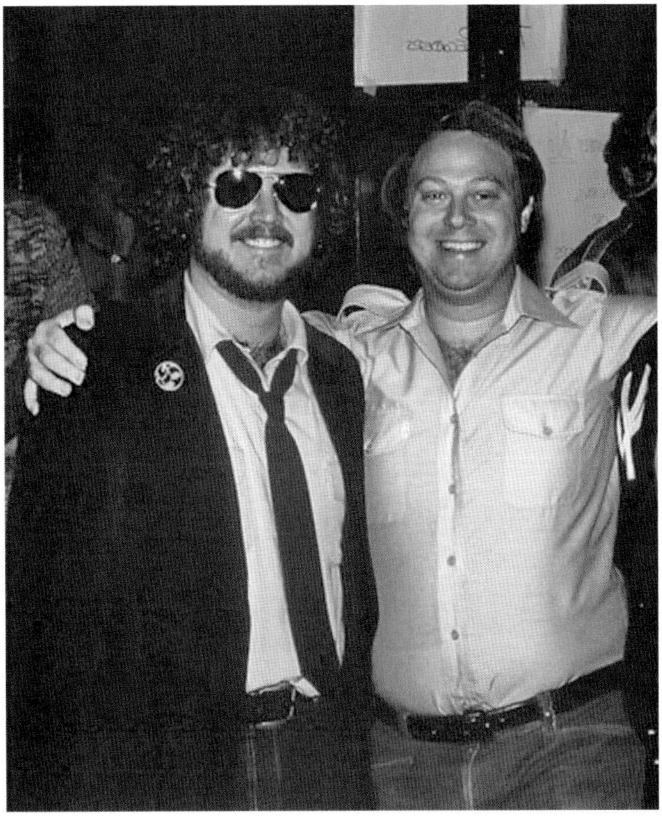

On the Boardwalk
He rode the rock concert era to success at venues from Passaic's Capitol Theatre to Giants Stadium, and his legacy encompasses everything from the Dead at Raceway Park to the flame-out that was Woodstock 1999. For 10 years, John Scher (right, with late Jukes keyboardist Kevin Kavanaugh) was a major player in Asbury, promoting shows at the much-missed rock garage the Sunshine In and the boardwalk Casino Arena. Taking over Convention Hall bookings from Moe Septee, Scher packed the "concrete bathtub" with muddy-sounding but memorable shows by classic rockers and new wavers from Jerry Garcia to the Clash. (Courtesy of Billy Smith Collection.)

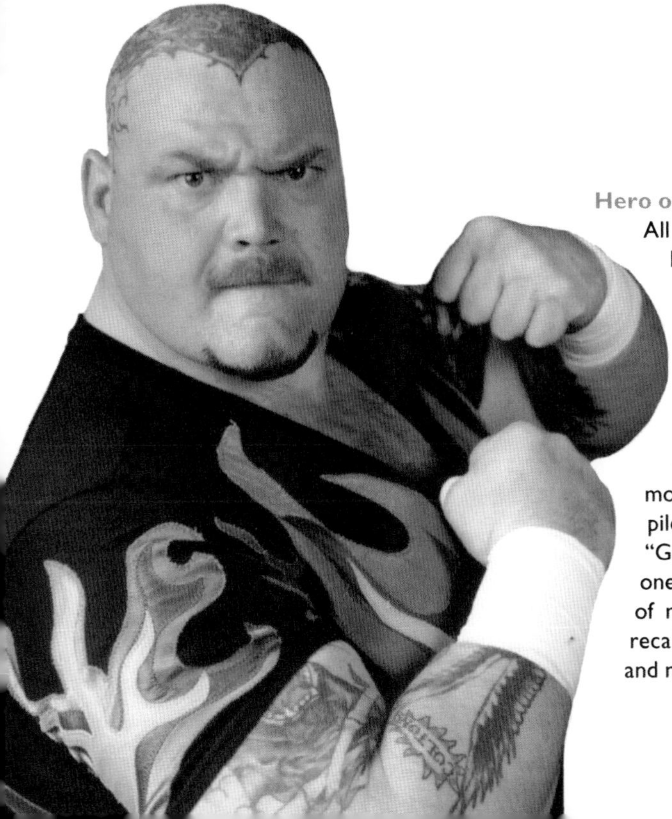

Hero or Heel?
All who recall "Diamond Dallas Page" Falkinburg when he managed Club Xanadu know Asbury's a wrestling town, and in the late Scott "Bam Bam" Bigelow, Asbury claimed its own native-son superstar. A hero and heel in a 20-year career with the WWF, WCW, and others, the nearly 400-pound grappler was called "the most agile big man" of his era. His reverse-piledriver finishing move was branded "Greetings from Asbury Park," and the onetime Pony bouncer remains the subject of many memorable stories, and a fondly recalled favorite among townies, ring fans, and music scenesters. (Author's collection.)

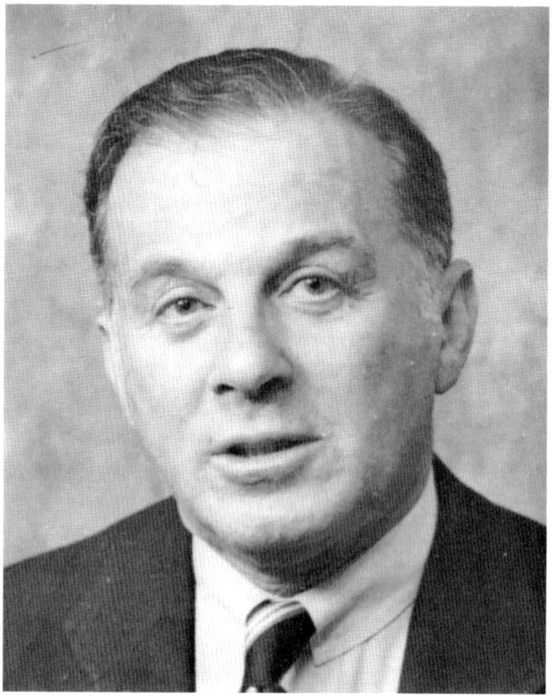

Famous Ray

He was not mayor during 1970's fiery summer, but Ray Kramer occupied city hall's hot seat as Asbury entered a steep decline in the new decade. An APHS grad and veteran councilman, Kramer became the last of the city's long-term executives to date, serving into the mid-1980s and surviving a recall. A proponent of failed bids to bring casino gambling and a new convention center to town, the Democrat also served three non-consecutive terms as a county freeholder. Congressman Frank Pallone honored Kramer on the floor of the US House of Representatives just weeks before his 1992 passing, and Jack Nicholson thanked him when accepting his 1997 Academy Award as Best Actor, for reasons that must remain clear only to Nicholson. (Courtesy of Peter Lucia.)

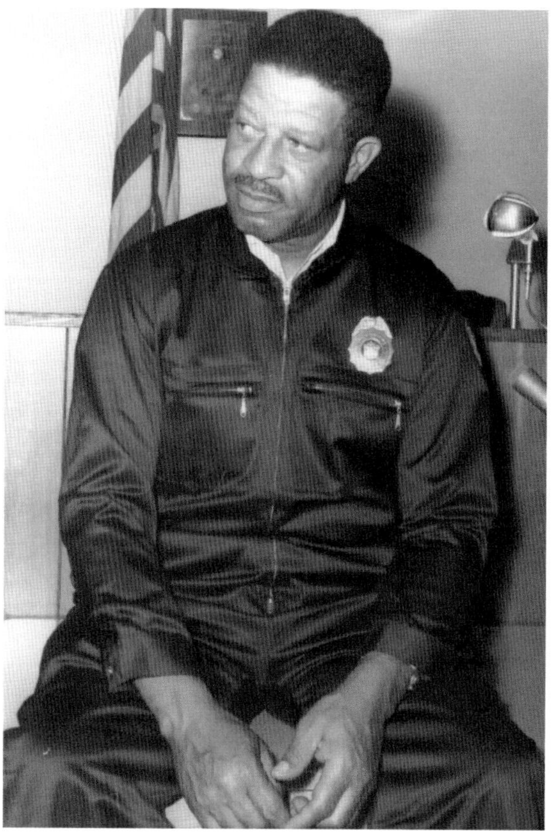

The Chief

Asbury's first African American mayor was also its first black police chief, appointed in an acting capacity in the late 1960s. He was also one of its first black officers, attaining detective captain's rank before becoming full-time chief. After retiring from the force, Thomas Smith was elected councilman in 1985 and served as mayor from 1989 to 1993, an interval marked by dashed dreams of redevelopment. The World War II veteran and Howard University graduate capped his career with 10 years as assemblyman for the 11th district, serving until his 2002 death. The state office building on Bangs Avenue is named in his memory. (Courtesy of Werner Baumgartner.)

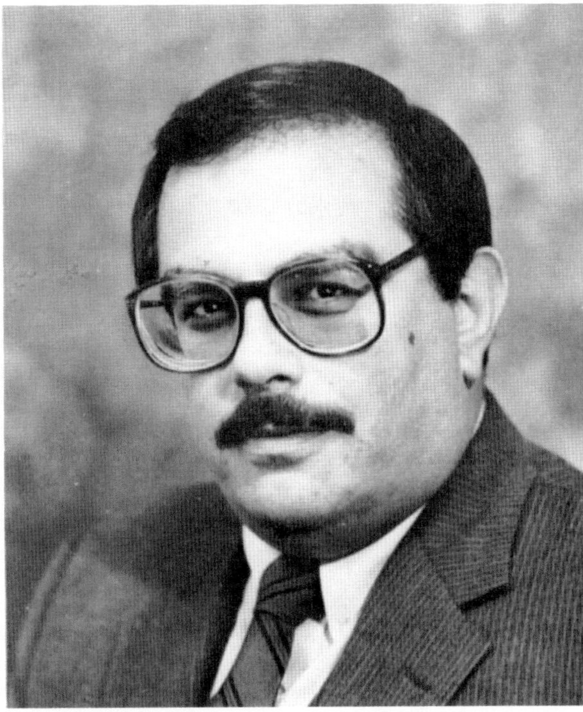

Sam's Club
With the authority to hire and fire most anyone in the municipal government, Asbury Park's city manager is an exceptionally powerful position, and Sam Addeo held it for an exceptionally long stretch, between 1980 and 1993. That his tenure fell within the city's rock-bottom era has not detracted from the esteem in which Addeo was held by those who knew him. When he told the *Times* in 1986 that "things are looking up," he tempered it with a realistic "we've still got a long way to go." In 2012, the published poet and scuba enthusiast passed away in Georgia. (Courtesy of Peter Lucia.)

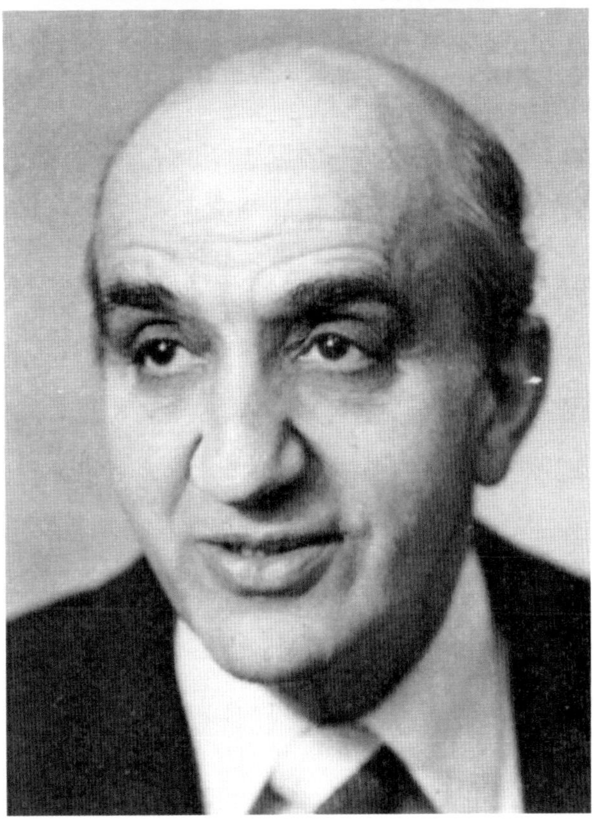

Frankie-isms
Witty, sarcastic, and sometimes downright combative: that is how Frank Fiorentino described himself in a 1989 *Press* profile. His colleagues in city government recalled him as "a good man who loved Asbury Park," and one whose "Frankie-isms" and trademark hat made him a larger-than-life mayor in a 1982–1989 interval of greatly reduced circumstances (and a big Ocean Mile debacle) for the city. The lifelong Asbury resident and longtime councilman hung up his hat on the cusp of the 1990s, ushering in an era of city government that the *Press* called "something like chaos." He died in 2007. (Courtesy of Peter Lucia.)

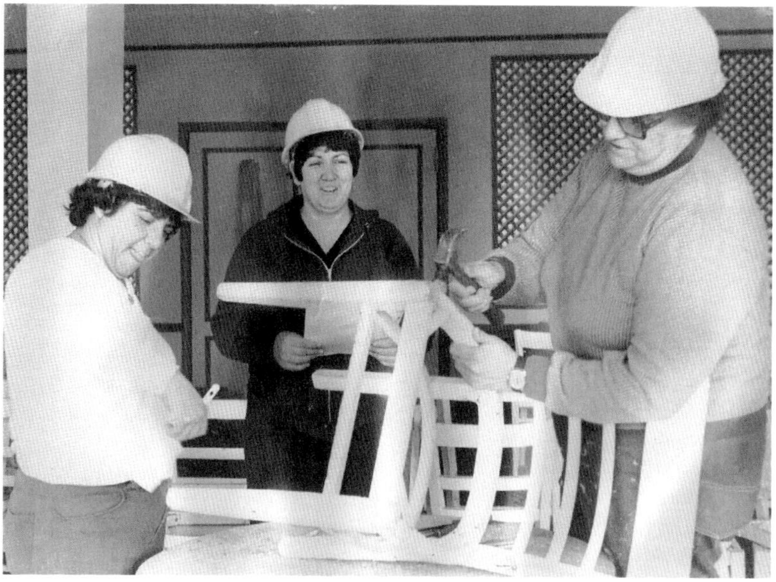

Key to the City

"We had no money, no experience running a hotel," recalls Carol Torre. "But this was a time in Asbury when you did what you had to do." Carol (center), Camille Neto, and Kay SanFillippo operated Main Street's Owl and the Pussycat lesbian bar, when in 1980 they purchased the derelict oceanfront Albion Hotel from Paul Wisnewski. Bartering rooms for construction work (and performing much of the work themselves), the partners got most of the Albion's units back on line. They opened the Key West nightclub on the ground floor and eventually restored the elegant Rainbow Room. A genuine authority on the era's thriving gay club scene, Torre made an aborted run for city council (with Odyssey owner Ray Palazzo) in 1983 and moved on to Wisnewski's equally legendary M&K (in the Charms Building) by the 1990s. The Albion met the wrecking ball in the new century, but in 2012 Torre joined Mayor Johnson and other dignitaries to rededicate the restored Rainbow Room sign in its James J. Howard Transportation Center berth. It is a reminder of a place that offered a challenging but welcoming home to those who once lived in the shadows, and of an extended family who kept the lights burning and the music playing, in those darkest hours. (Above photograph, courtesy of Carol Torre; below photograph, courtesy of Michael Booth and the *Coaster*.)

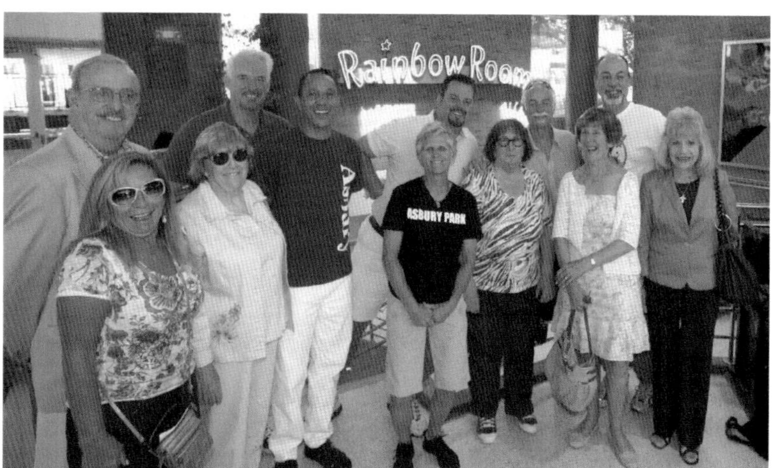

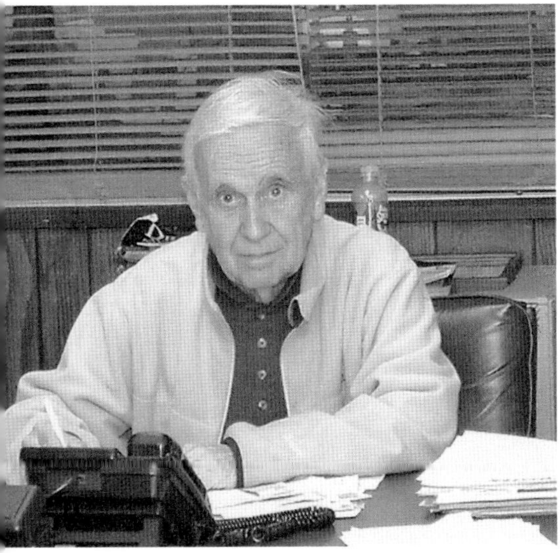

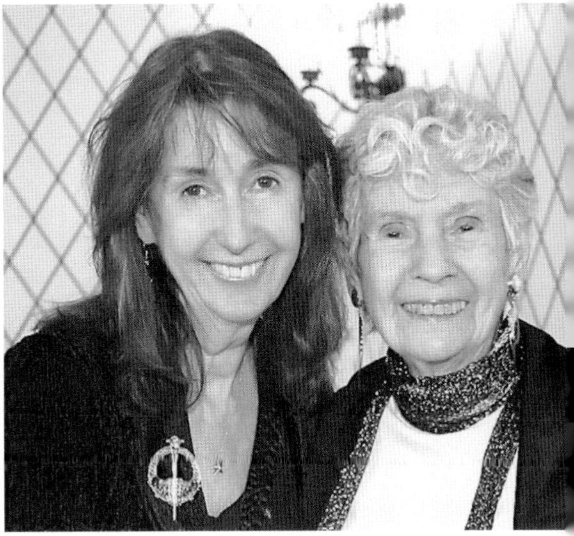

Rollercoaster History

In 1983, Asbury Park might have seemed neither the time nor the place to start a newspaper, but when Bob and Doris Carroll founded the *Coaster* at their Sunset Avenue home, they were in it for the duration. More than 30 years of continuous publication later, the greater Asbury area has a weekly to take pride in. A veteran of the *New York Daily News*, Bob (who passed away in 2011) sensed an opening for street-level, hyper-local reporting when the city's established daily skewed toward a suburban readership, moving his operation into an unglamorous but industrious Main Street office, where it has held down the fort ever since. Their daughter Ellen Carroll left the *Asbury Park Press* to lend her savvy editorial instincts to the family business, and the *Coaster* married into another local weekly dynasty when it partnered with publisher Michael Booth (founder of the original *Atlanticville* in Long Branch) in the new millennium. Adhering to a strategy of intensive shoe-leather reporting by Don Stine and others, energetic features (Booth's Facing the Question, John Cavanaugh's Rock Shots, Richard Virgilio's engaging column The B Plot), and lots of great people photographs, the *Coaster* has covered real-world Asbury Park and surrounding communities with clarity and respect during a tumultuous era of local history. Steven Froias, who inaugurated an online companion edition of the *Coaster* in 2013, said it best when he asserted that the paper's "low-key style puts the emphasis on news rather than relentless self-promotion." (Courtesy of Michael Booth and the *Coaster*.)

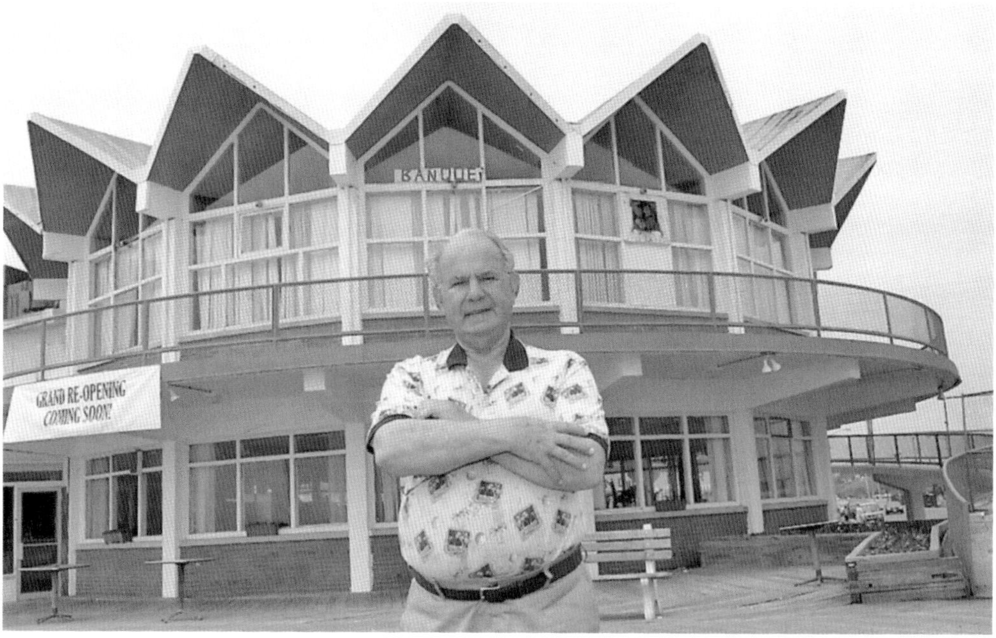

Last Man Standing

When the gleaming Howard Johnson's restaurant opened in a futuristic boardwalk pavilion in 1962, Greek immigrant George Panas and his wife, Helen, were the host franchisees. By the time George threw in the bar towel 44 years later, it was the last HoJo's in Jersey and pretty much the last open business on the boards. It was a time capsule complete with a Panorama Room, vintage signage, few remaining menu items, and even fewer regular paying customers. Panas, by then accepting bartered costume jewelry as payment, sold his liquor license and retired in 2006. (Courtesy of Michael Booth and the *Coaster.*)

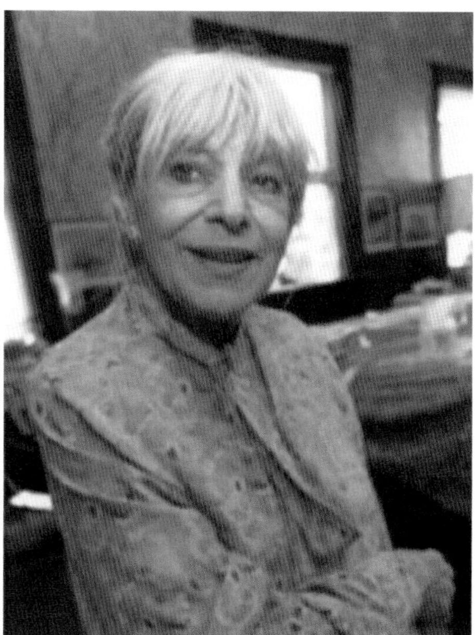

A Grand Era

She was a teacher, friend, and mentor as well as "a charmer and a manipulator extraordinaire." For an astonishing 51 seasons, Madame Era Tognoli and her Metro Lyric Opera Company brought the bel canto to the boardwalk, shaking the Paramount proscenium with professional-quality productions of the operatic canon (featuring conductor Anton Coppola, of the Hollywood Coppolas) and shining a beacon through some of the faded resort's darkest days and nights. The artist who sang with Maria Callas at the Arena di Verona dedicated decades to the nonprofit company and was posthumously given wings as an Asbury Angel. (Courtesy of George McMorrow.)

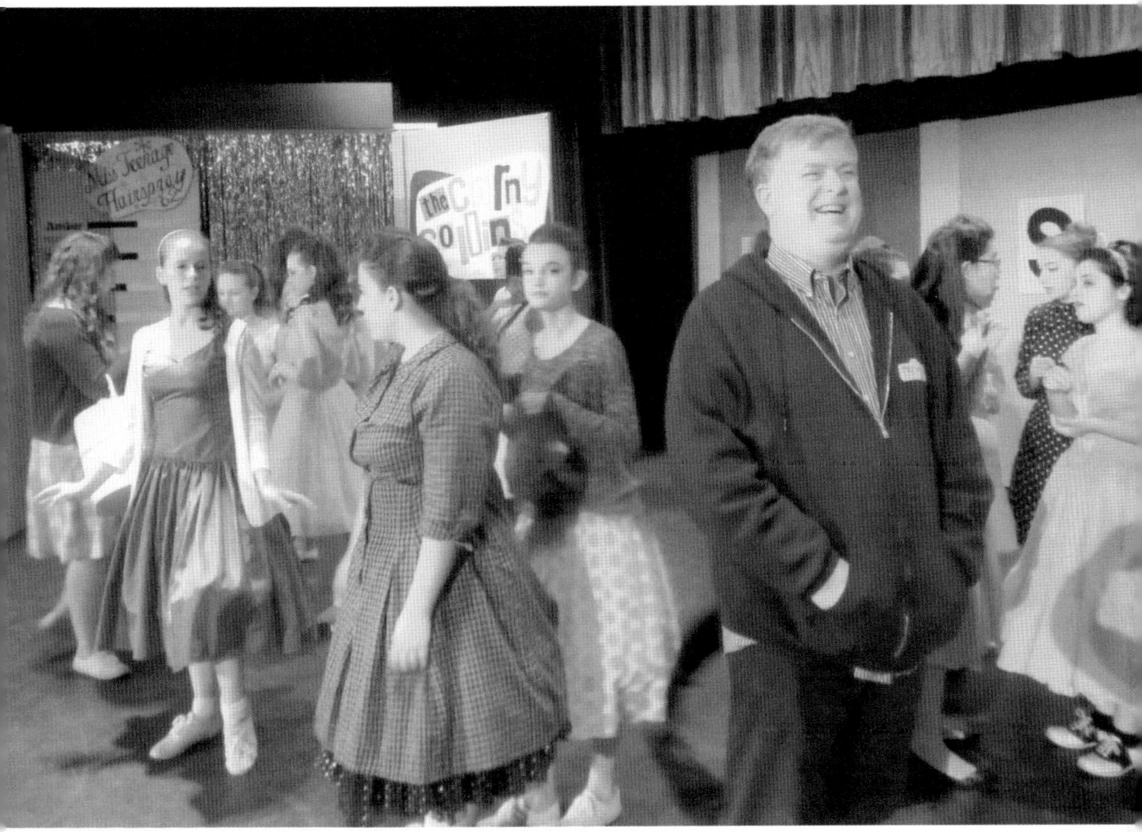

Stage Door Canteen

Ask Mark Fleming about the interlude that he calls Asbury's "plywood and pigeon phase," and you'll hear stories of break-ins and blizzards, bankrupt landlords, busted boardwalks, and the kind of persevering spirit that has seen his nonprofit Premier Theatre Company make a glorious noise since those too-silent nights of the early 1990s. A veteran of several other local theatrical troupes and programs, the producer-director arrived at the Berkeley-Carteret Hotel (and later the Paramount Theatre), armed with a repertoire of tried-and-true musical favorites, limited production budgets, and a whole lot of showman's gumption. Staging shows that ranged from *Sunday in the Park with George* to *Joseph and the Amazing Technicolor Dreamcoat*, the company took it upon themselves to light up their own community Christmas tree during the annual staging of *Scrooge*, performing amid the smell of circus animals housed next door or the sound of cannon fire from Civil War reenactors. A downtown Stage Door Canteen storefront was both an early signifier and early casualty of the Cookman Avenue rebirth, and his actors could stage a Friday night dance number in the street as late as 2004 without blocking any vehicular traffic.

Still the Paramount's resident stage troupe, Fleming and company have renewed their commitment to Asbury Park, refurbishing and repurposing several performance venues around town when not performing on the boardwalk boards. A resident of the city since 2003, the impresario declares "I've always loved Asbury . . . the idea is not just to bring people to town, but to get people 'into' a town . . . and we'll take at least part of the credit for that!" (Courtesy of Premier Theatre Company.)

Working on a Building

He has a pedigree to match any in Asbury Park history: son of Dr. Sebastian Vaccaro (page 48), nephew of the first independent on the city council and a long-serving city clerk. He is the father of the youngest-ever elected councilperson in New Jersey history and a billion-dollar builder of area schools, hospitals, and senior homes. He was the last owner of Palace Amusements to keep the place open and active, and his many adventures as developer and investor included a bizarre and short-lived partnership with Michael Jackson and family. Ask Henry Vaccaro what he is proudest of, however, and he will answer, "the Berkeley-Carteret Hotel . . . I put my heart and soul in there." He also brought to the project a shot of cash—Johnny Cash.

The story of how the Man in Black became co-owner of Arthur Steinbach's brick behemoth is told in engaging detail by Henry Vaccaro in his 2013 memoir *Johnny Cash is a Friend of Mine*. It is a story that begins with Henry's role as a ground-floor partner in (and traveling salesman for) Kramer Guitars, and it is rooted in a long-lasting friendship between the American music giant and the construction guy from Jersey. More than just an investor in a group that included Henry, brother Sam, and New York television news superstar Ernie Anastos, Cash made frequent trips to Asbury Park, performed a milestone concert at the Paramount, and kept a private hotel suite with his wife, June Carter, and son, John Carter Cash.

The friendship was strong enough to outlast the 1980s–1990s collapse of the Vaccaro group's slate of Asbury waterfront projects; an ill-fated, limited partnership with Carabetta Enterprises of Connecticut and an interlude that ended in flames, foreclosure, bankruptcy, bank failures, and the literal implosion (with Henry's young grandson pushing the button) of the never-finished C-8 condo project. "Johnny told me the only thing that went bankrupt was my wallet," says Henry, "and it was Johnny who got me to go back to church."

Henry Vaccaro continues to perform construction and demolition work around town, still sitting on a cache of unreleased Michael Jackson music as part of that headline-making contretemps with the first family of Motown. The Berkeley sold in foreclosure to the Maharishi Mahesh Yogi as a School of Yogic Flying and continues after many ownership transfers, with Johnny Cash Suite intact as Asbury's longest surviving hotel. (Courtesy of Henry Vaccaro Jr.)

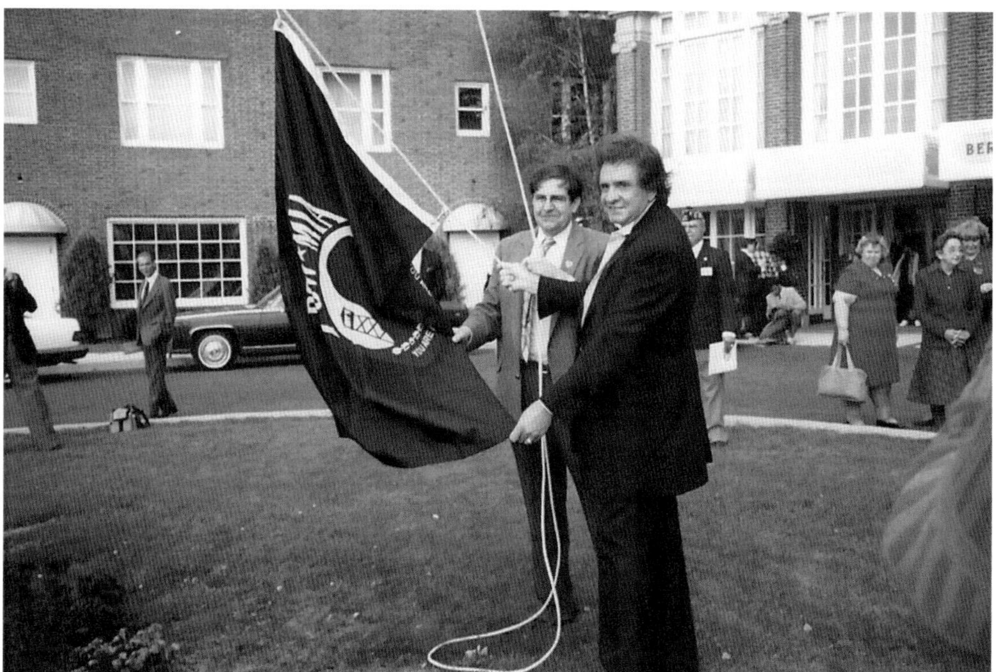

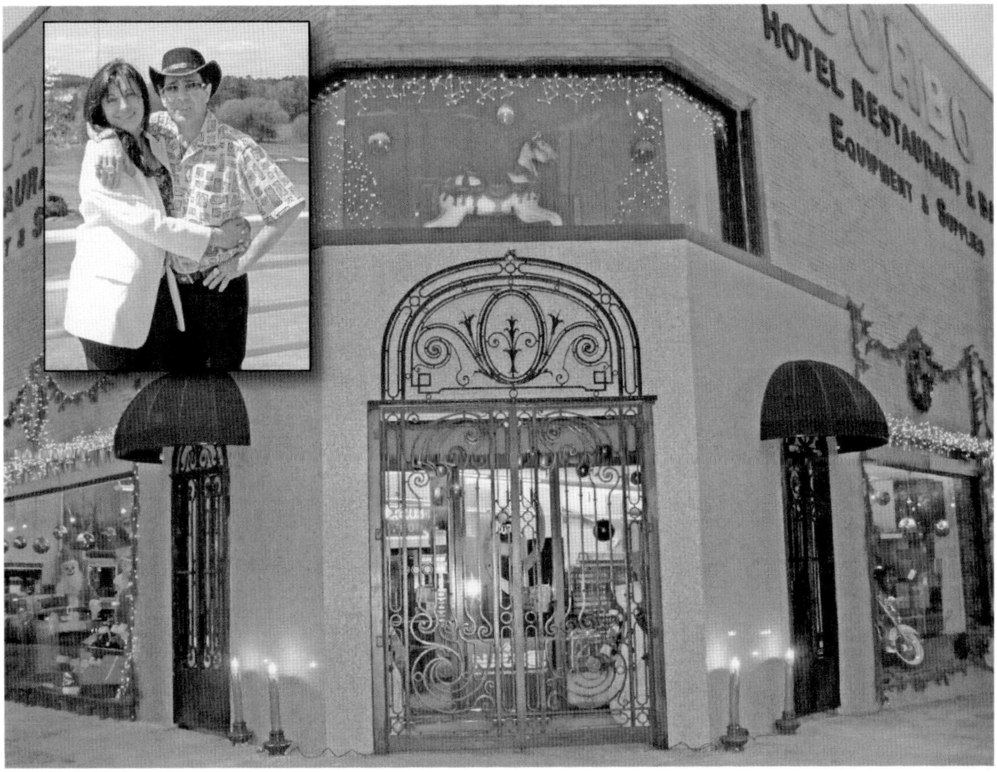

Corbo's Corner

It is not really a walk-in business, but for 30 years the wholesale service-oriented Corbo Restaurant Supply has staked a stylish claim on the corner of Main Street and Lake Avenue. Its street windows are festooned with a collection of bar and restaurant equipment and decorative delights. The museum-quality interior display directly reflects the dashing personal style and old-school business savvy of its equally colorful co-owners, Lester and Myrene Reiff. (Courtesy of Myrene Reiff.)

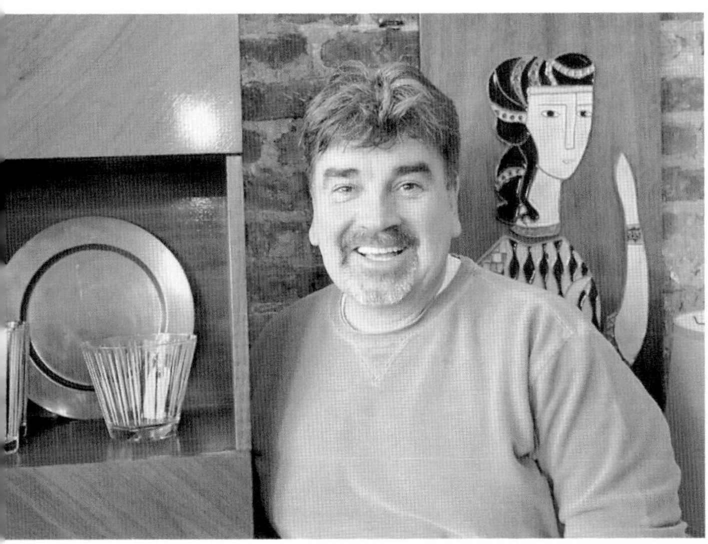

Thoroughly Modern Meisch

Is Billy Meisch a last holdout from the dead-zone days of Cookman Avenue retail, or a pioneer pointing the way toward a more design-conscious downtown? For 30 years, Meisch has purveyed a panorama of mid-century furnishings from his House of Modern Living, in a way that restores the thrill of the hunt to the act of acquisition—a madcap mountain of merchandise that must be explored to be appreciated. (Courtesy of Michael Booth and the *Coaster.*)

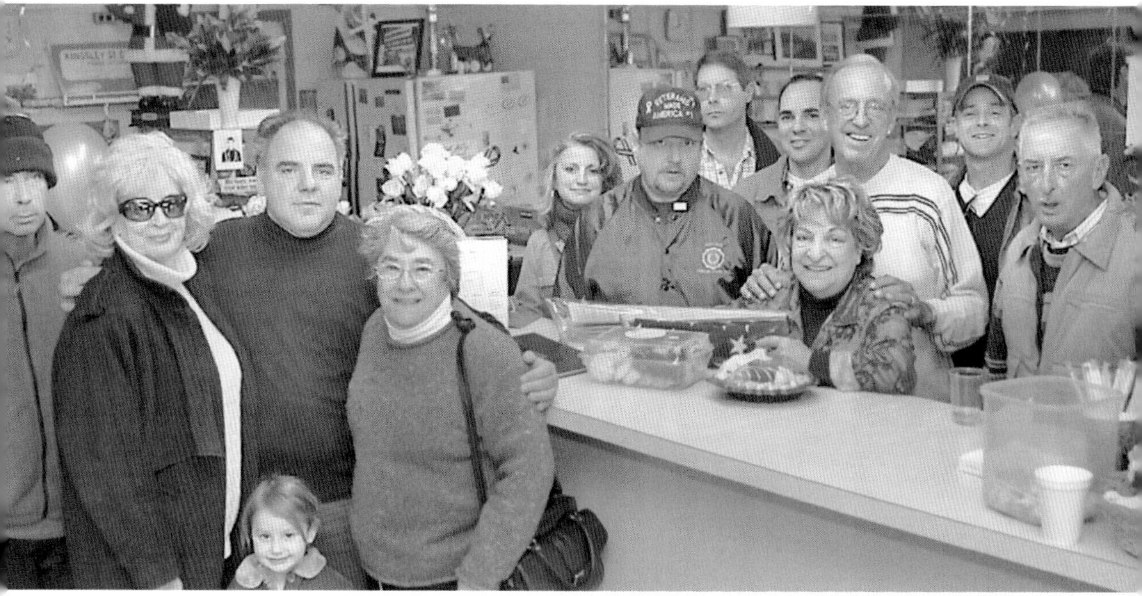

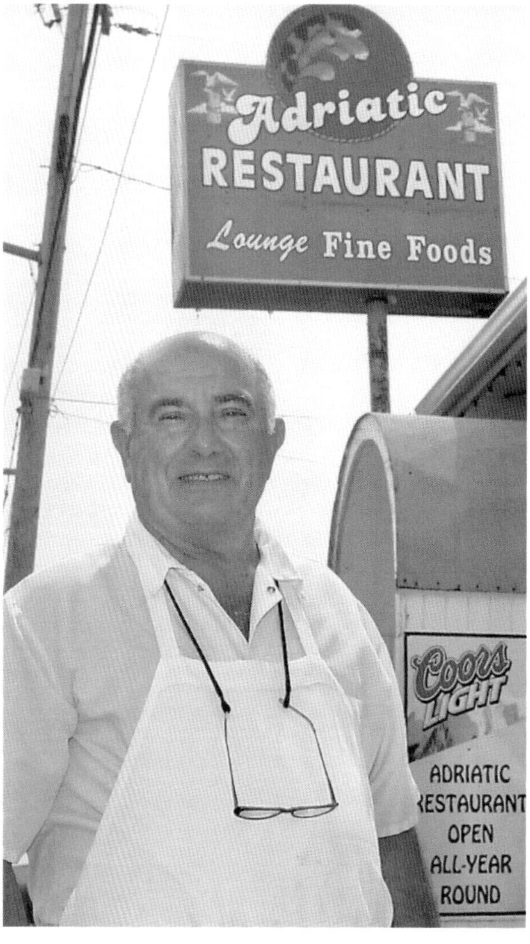

Queen of Kingsley

For over 20 years and in two different storefronts, former city housing commissioner Rita Marano operated the Kingsley Deli as a lively town hall in a dying neighborhood, a place where the coffee and the politically charged conversation flowed nonstop for her Eastsider constituents. Before being claimed by redevelopment-zone eminent domain, the deli served as setting for journalist Maureen Nevin's satirical play *Ocean Mile*. Marano, pictured behind the counter with her regulars on the last day of business in 2009, maintained her voice in community affairs, serving on the Asbury Park Charter Study Commission in 2012. (Courtesy of Michael Booth and the *Coaster*.)

Steak Stanley

It was not hyperbole to suggest that the Adriatic restaurant was "the only reason anybody came to town" during the city's silent years. For three decades, Croatian-born Stan Tokec maintained his isolated Kingsley Street outpost as an engaging, inviting time-capsule taste of the glory days. Stan and his wife, Marie, would retire in 2012, having gained a new generation of hipster habitués. (Courtesy of Michael Booth and the *Coaster*.)

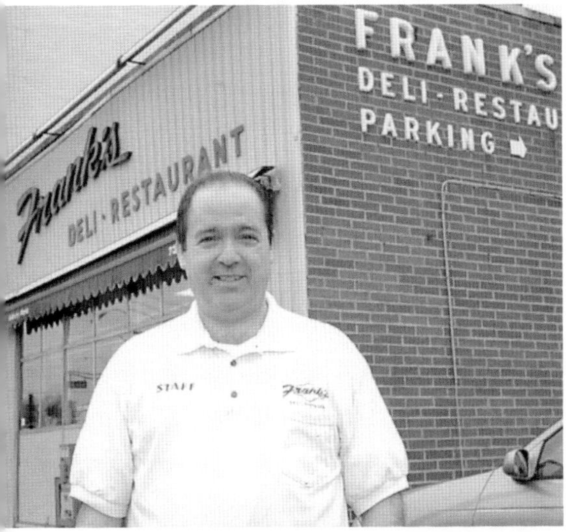

Heart of Town

Anyone on the lookout for that place where everybody goes should follow the locals to Frank's Deli, the unprepossessing Main Street mainstay that has weathered the city's grimmest, most turbulent eras and rocked into the new century on the strength and continuity of its great food and old-school plugged-in vibe. Owner (and son of Frank) Joe Maggio, his family, and crew operate a clean, authentically 1960 institution that is as refreshingly removed from the redevelopment-zone churn as it is packed with those truly in-the-know. (Courtesy of Michael Booth and the *Coaster.*)

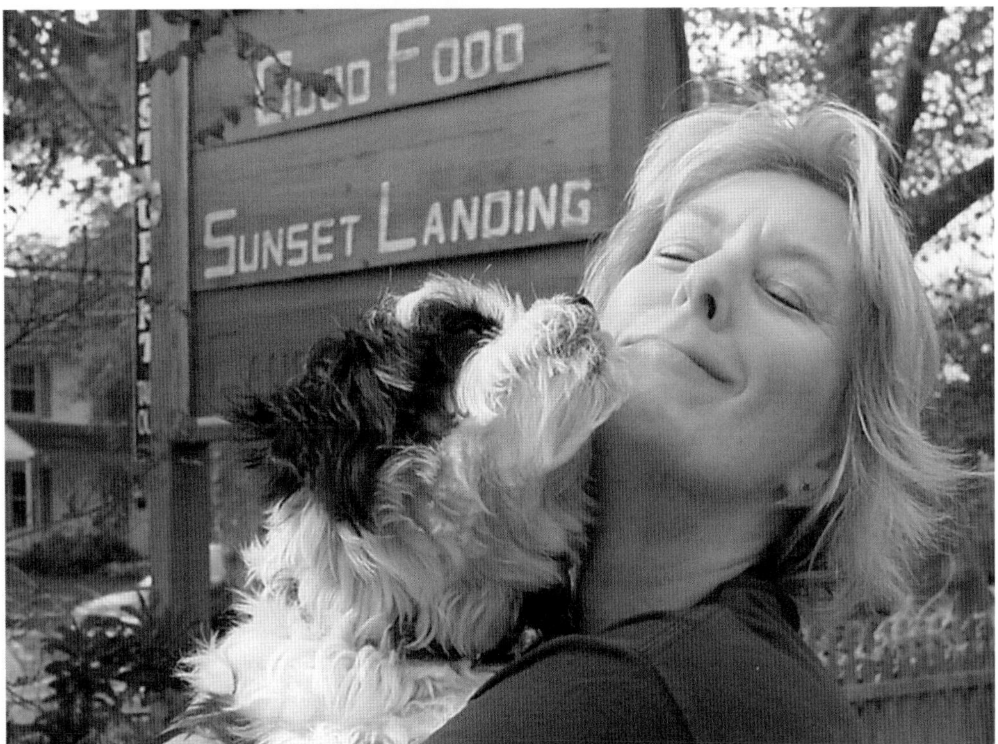

Happy Landings

Existing at both a geographical and a spiritual remove from what most would call the Asbury experience, Sunset Landing has occupied its bucolic waterfront outpost at the border of Ocean Township for more than 50 years. Co-owner Donna Logdon (pictured) took over the little log-cabin luncheonette on Deal Lake from her parents. Her husband, Rob Pruszynski, brought a seasoning of culture and cuisine from his home state of Hawaii—an enjoy-the-view vibe that extends from the coconut pancakes to the vintage surfboards, canoe rentals, "duck zoo," and Aloha décor. (Courtesy of Michael Booth and the *Coaster.*)

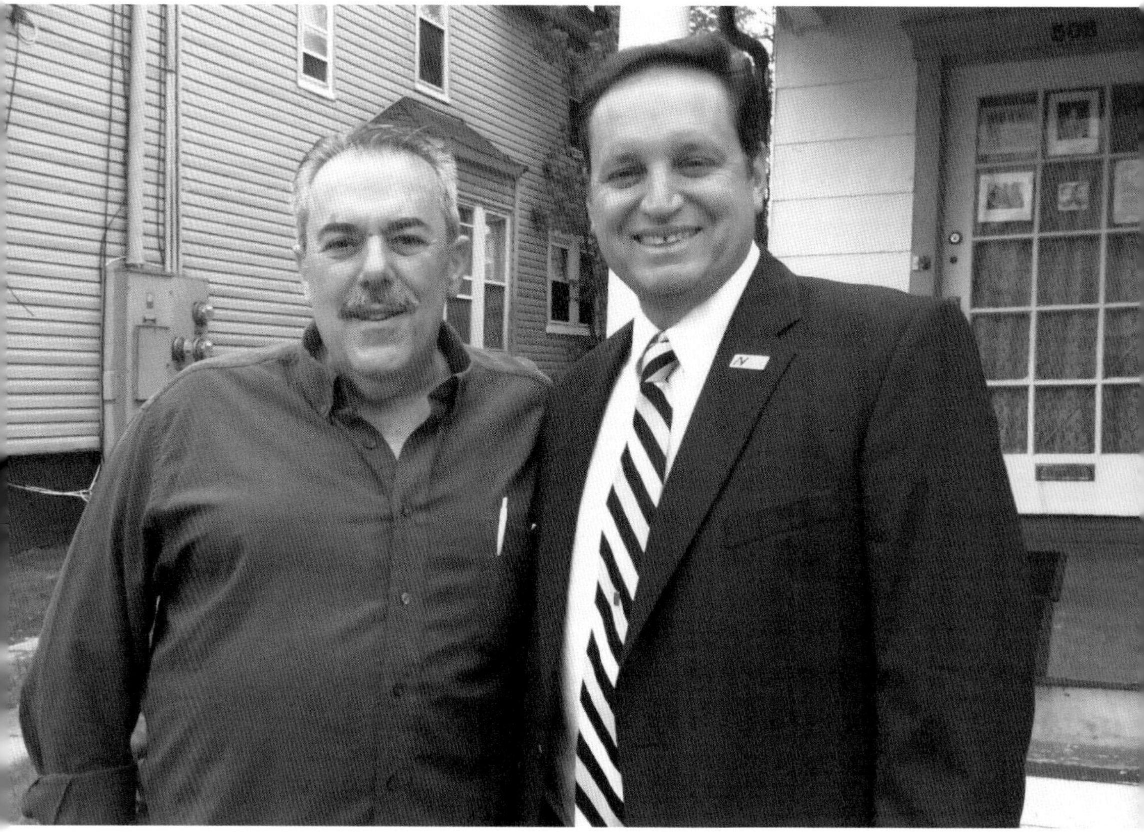

Crane's Crib

They are pictured out front of the former Arbutus Cottage, onetime neighbors and two successive owners and rescuers of the Stephen Crane House. A chance discovery of the cottage's connection to the great American author inspired utilities executive Thomas Hayes (right) to purchase the structures at 508 Fourth Avenue in 1995 when they were boarded up hulks, neglected for years and slated for demolition by the city. It took a major effort by the Hayes family, city historian Werner Baumgartner, and community volunteers to stabilize the main house and ready it as a museum and venue for intimately scaled arts events. When Hayes moved out of the city in 2001, Frank D'Alessandro (left) stepped in as Crane House's owner. The retired schoolteacher and board of education member continued a program of extensive renovations to the 1878 house and its back buildings, while regularly hosting literary-minded film screenings, theatrical presentations, poetry readings, civic meetings, and visitors that have ranged from local schoolchildren to the *Ghost Hunters* television series. With donated hours from local supporters and a generous donation of funds earmarked from Bruce Springsteen's 2001 Asbury Park concerts, the Stephen Crane House remains a welcoming little outpost of culture and community activism that has helped raise funds in turn for charitable causes such as the Asbury Park Little League.

In 2013, the Asbury Park Historical Society, the nonprofit organization of preservationists chaired by journalist and rare-book dealer Don Stine, announced a capital campaign to purchase and continue restoration of the main cottage, with the aim of maintaining it as the city's first historical museum. In 2014, the Stephen Crane House was officially named to the New Jersey Register of Historic Places. (Photograph by the author.)

The History Guy

Asbury Park has had many chroniclers through the years but only one official city historian, the position to which Werner Baumgartner was first appointed in 1999. An engaged presence at municipal meetings, the former Bell Labs researcher spoke for the city's heritage, applying his expertise and advocacy with a zeal that would often swim against the tide of beachfront redevelopment progress, and make him few friends among municipal leaders. With the beachfront since recognized as an endangered national treasure through his efforts, the founder of the AP Historical Society was reinstated to his position in 2014. (Courtesy of Werner Baumgartner.)

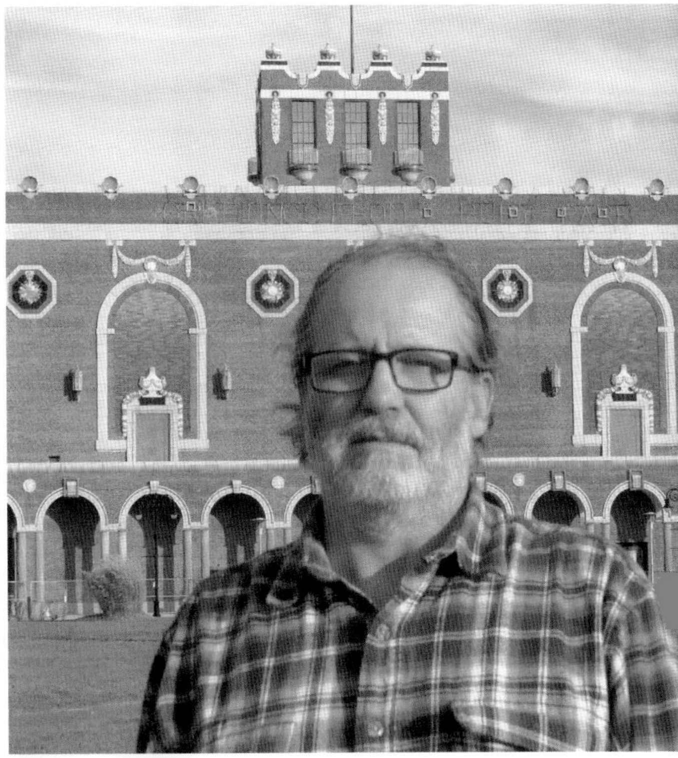

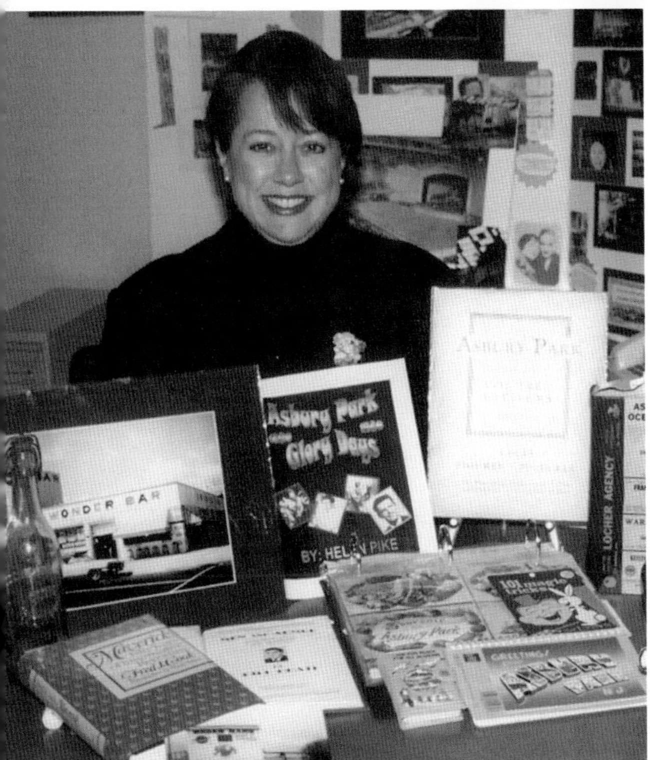

Wish You Were Here

She is a collector of postcards and a chronicler of the passing parade. Helen-Chantal Pike's many books about Asbury Park include an *Images of America* entry, the celebratory anthology *Where Music Lives*, and the essential *Asbury Park's Glory Days*, a work that interweaves its own beautifully detailed spell with the assembled voices of those who rode the front car of the rollercoaster. Recently decamped to Vermont, the journalist-photographer-historian remains a passionate authority on all things Asbury—a storyteller graced with the clear eye of the reporter and the accrued wisdom of the Howard Johnson's waitress she so proudly was. (Courtesy of Pike Archive.)

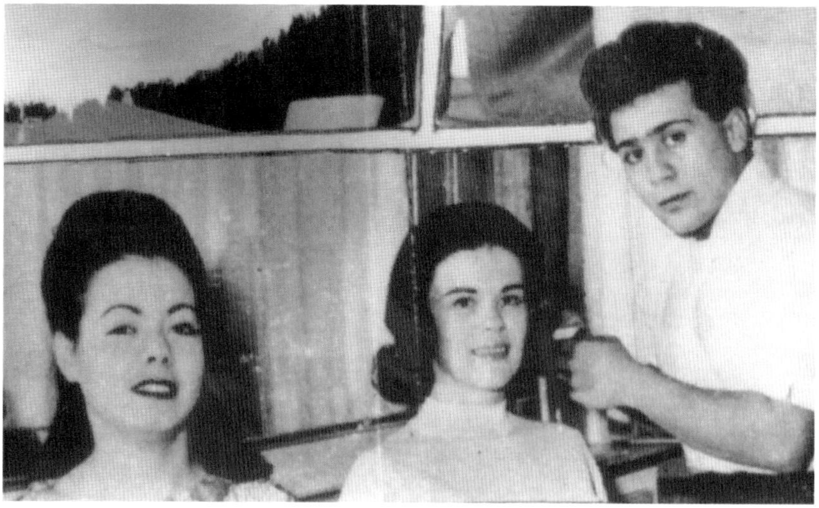

The Big Kahuna

He may stand just five feet solid from the boards, but Danny DeVito is not only Asbury Park's biggest screen star, he also casts a giant profile as an actor (*Romancing the Stone, Tin Men, L.A. Confidential*), director (*War of the Roses, Matilda, Hoffa*) and Oscar-nominated producer (*Erin Brockovich, Pulp Fiction, Man on the Moon*), whose Jersey Films rewrote the Hollywood playbook in the 1990s. The son of a Springwood Avenue storekeep attended Mount Carmel Grammar School, then worked in his sister Angela's hair salon in the early 1960s (above). While a life as a theatrical makeup artist was his goal, the American Academy of Dramatic Arts could only admit him as an actor, and a role in the Off-Broadway production of *One Flew Over the Cuckoo's Nest* started him on a long and remarkably consistent career in film and television (*Taxi, Its Always Sunny in Philadelphia*). DeVito did a decent for his hometown in 1987 when he hosted a premiere for his first major directorial effort, *Throw Momma from the Train*, at the city's down-on-its-luck Paramount Theatre. He is pictured here at that affair with his screen mother Anne Ramsey and real mother Julia. (Courtesy of Peter Lucia.)

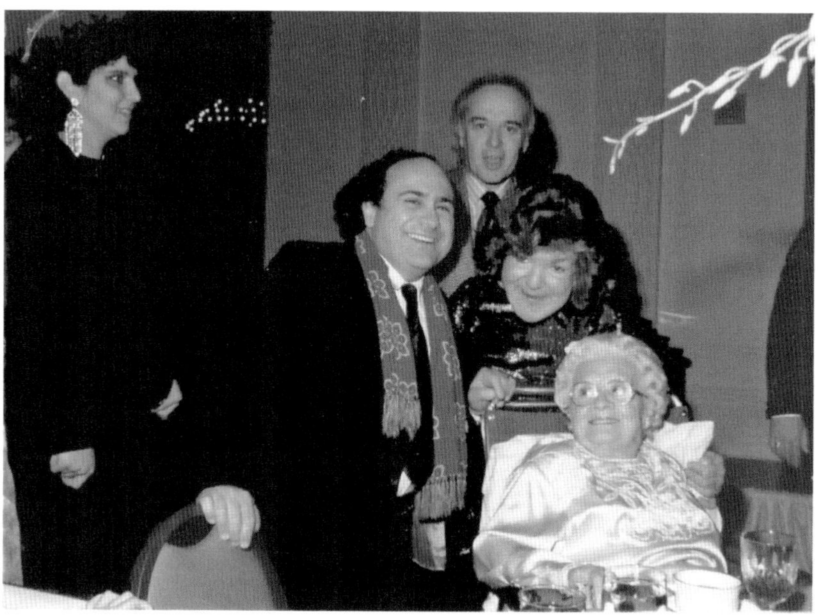

CHAPTER SIX

Asbury Rising

Asbury in the 21st Century

Now when you walk through today, you can see there's a change / Gentrified from the former vibe of memory lane / From the abandoned strip where the pawn shop reigns / Now neighbor to art galleries with four star taste / Where they'd love to forget about the music we make / But when the city failed we were all that remained.

—Christopher Solo Cerchio

The title is not from Bruce, but from a poet-observer no less imprinted by the streets of Asbury Park: the underground rapper Solo For Dolo. A standout cut from his 2012 release *Self Titled*, "Asbury Rising" finds Christopher Solo Cerchio and producer Maker rolling slowly through territory both reassuringly familiar and disarmingly alien. Too young to be one of the glory days' old timers, he is hardly immune to the ways in which Asbury Park gets into the heads of all who breathe it in. He toasts his town, even as he laments the loss of the Kingsley strip clubs, the Moon Rock bar, and the Casino Skate Park. They are forces to be reckoned with, those ghost voices.

Asbury Park's first years of the 21st century seem almost a hundred-year timeline in itself, originating when the decade-long legal logjam on the oceanfront was broken in 2001. It looked like the more bothersome ghosts of the past century were at last getting served their exorcism papers. Things have moved fast; once-grand hotels and palaces of amusement have come down as swiftly as high-rise condos, SOLD signs, and property valuations have gone up. And, things have moved slowly, in the wake of a lingering economic downturn and the setbacks of Hurricane Sandy. Sometimes things seem to come full circle, as when the skeletal C-8 complex surrendered its footprint to a similarly ill-fated project named originally for Springsteen's "The Rising."

Returning visitors, curious to "see how it's coming back," looked upon an equally curious mix of semiretired landmarks and resurgent treasures; upscale boutiques and fallow lots; destination nightspots and eateries constructed from repurposed shipping containers. Major attractions—big-time music blasts, film festivals, and dance party weekends—came and went, while the traffic (and the metered parking) returned to dormant streets that lurched back to life with food festivals, art happenings, and other events.

An energetic new creative class captured the imagination and the publicity, while Main Street's mix of neighborhood staples (including a new surge of Latino-owned businesses) held down the real-world fort. The first significant new construction in more than a generation came to a Springwood corridor whose residents were more than ready to have their turn.

In the following pages, a remarkable cast of characters demonstrate, each in their own way, how a generation of relative newcomers can work with the true believers to paint positive pictures on a once blank and battered canvas. With the understanding that one person's rising can often represent another's setting sun, Asbury Park, not just the brick and mortar signifiers, but the hearts and minds and souls who represent the city at its best, appears poised to write another new chapter of its relatively short, loud, tumultuous, frankly frustrating, but forever fascinating history.

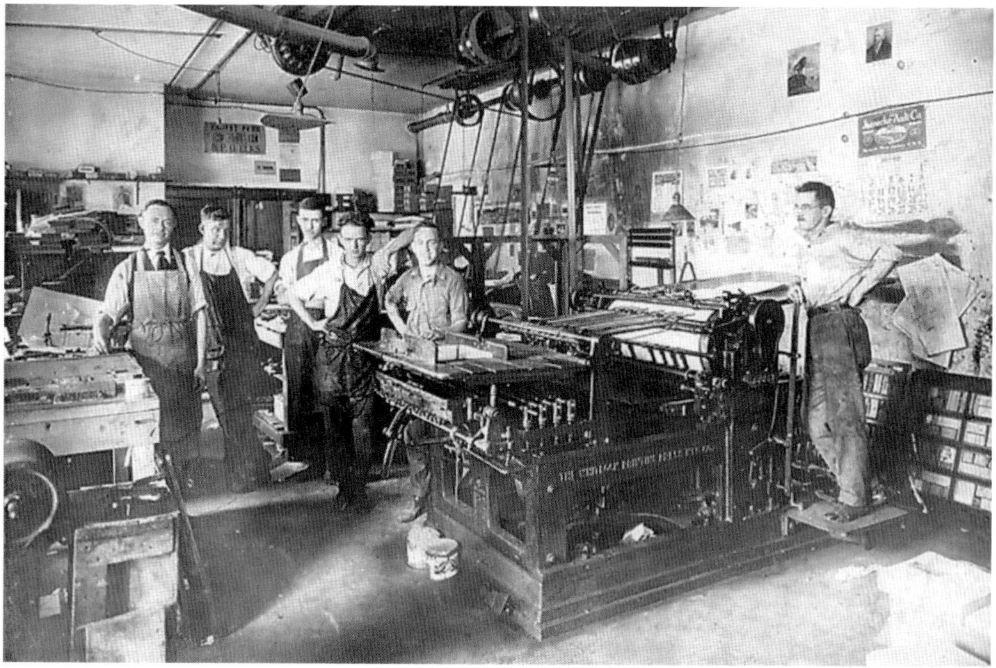

Platin' Place

Its customers included Founder Bradley himself, and for 114 years, Clayton Press quietly and efficiently carried on as downtown Asbury's longest continuously operating business. David Roszel, whose grandfather partnered with original owner Clark Clayton in 1937, stopped the presses in what had become the area's sole remaining letterpress printer in 2014. He closed the Bond Street shop but continues to serve his most faithful clients from an outside location. (Courtesy of Michael Booth and the *Coaster*.)

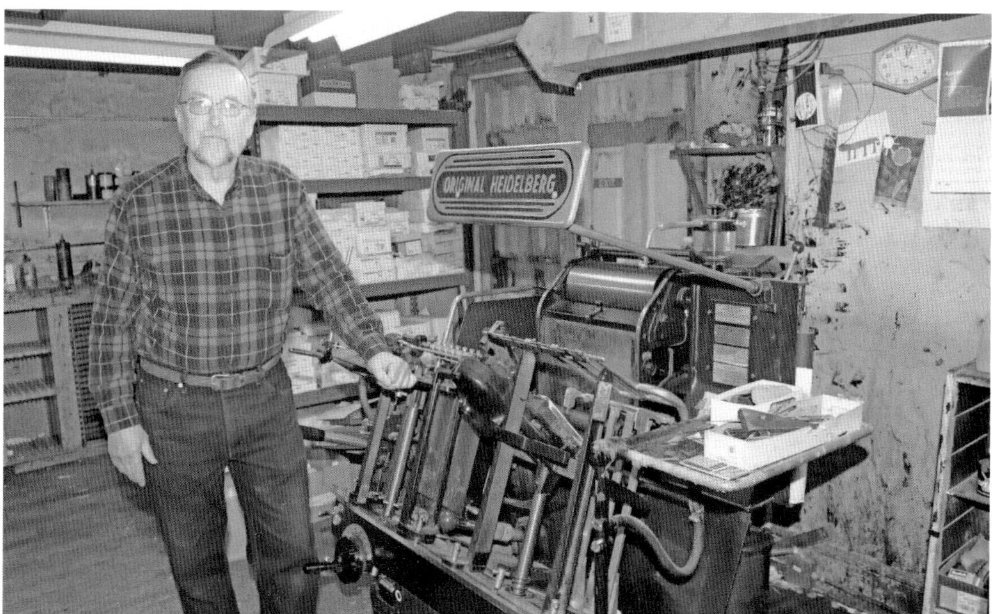

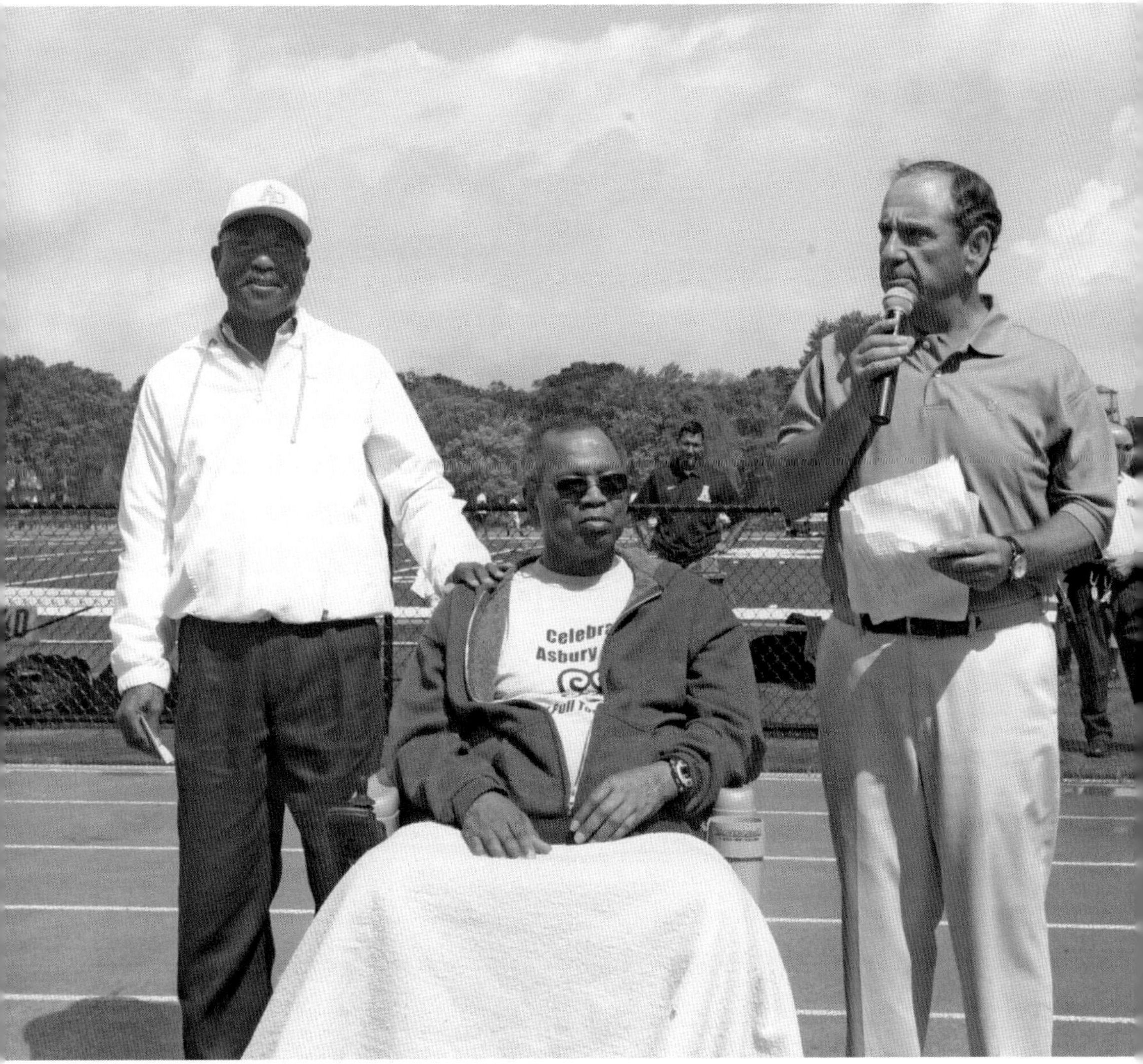

Go Bishops

Tour the Distinguished Alumni Hall of Fame at Asbury Park High School, and one will find numerous people profiled in this book and more. The Sunset Avenue landmark has produced a congressman and several state legislators. Its athletes have set world records and competed in Olympiads and the NFL. Superior court judges and leaders in mathematics, medicine, and academia studied there, as did Grammy-winning composers, opera singers, symphony musicians, multimillionaire investors, entrepreneurs, prominent publishers, and journalists. In the late 1990s, a committee led by Mayor Carl Williams and Judge Ira Kreizman (left and right respectively, with Frank Budd) launched the hall as a vehicle to celebrate some extraordinary graduates and show current students that success is possible, regardless of circumstances. A complete list of inductees, with detailed biographies, can be viewed at aphshalloffame.com. (Courtesy of Michael Booth and the *Coaster*.)

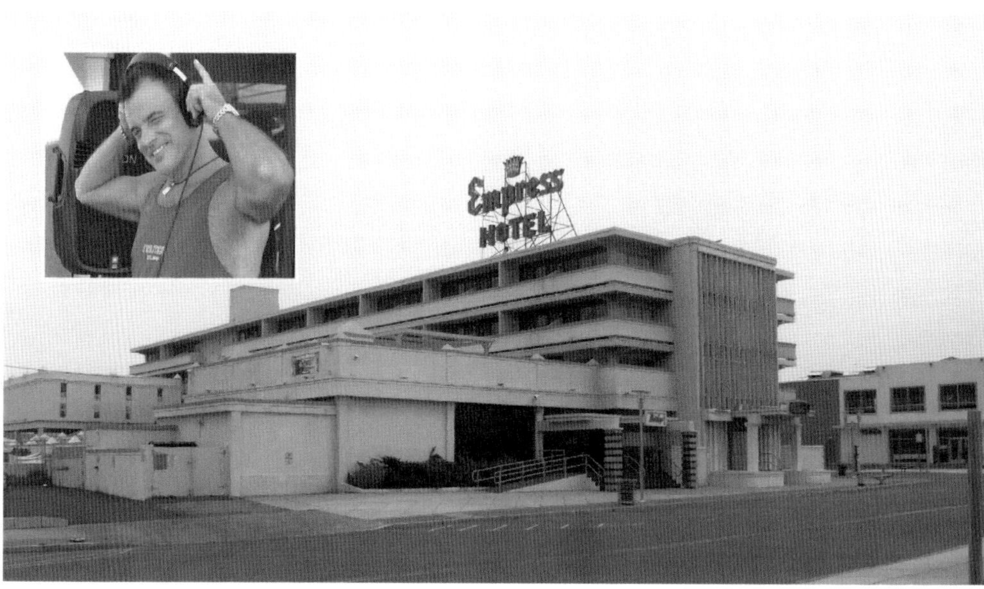

The House That "Vogue" Built
He has produced hits for Madonna, the Pet Shop Boys, and more. As a sought-after remix artist, he lent new dance-floor life to an array of big-name artists. Still, the greatest remix of Shep Pettibone's career might be the Empress, the Ocean Avenue inn (once favored by Judy Garland) transformed by the New York City–based DJ into a luxury lodging and marketed largely to a gay clientele that brought much-needed energy to millennial Asbury. The attached dance club Paradise and Tabú restaurant created a complex that has served as solid anchor to the neighboring boardwalk's often chaotic redevelopment process. (Courtesy of Carol Torre.)

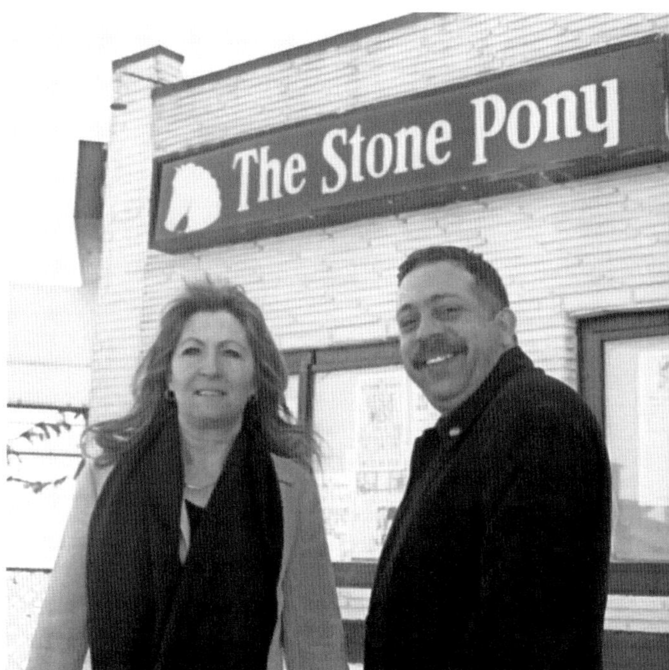

Anno Domenic
When a Jersey City restaurateur named Domenic Santana purchased the Stone Pony in 2000, it was a shuttered hulk, stripped of its old identity and rebranded as Vinyl. Playing the gregarious host to the hilt, the Cuban-born Santana (pictured with Eileen Chapman) had Gov. Christie Whitman rededicate the club, partied after hours with Bruce and crew, and restored the Pony brand to Circuit centerpiece status. He put a human face on the now corporate-owned landmark and performed one of the most crucial rescues in Asbury history. (Courtesy of Michael Booth and the *Coaster*.)

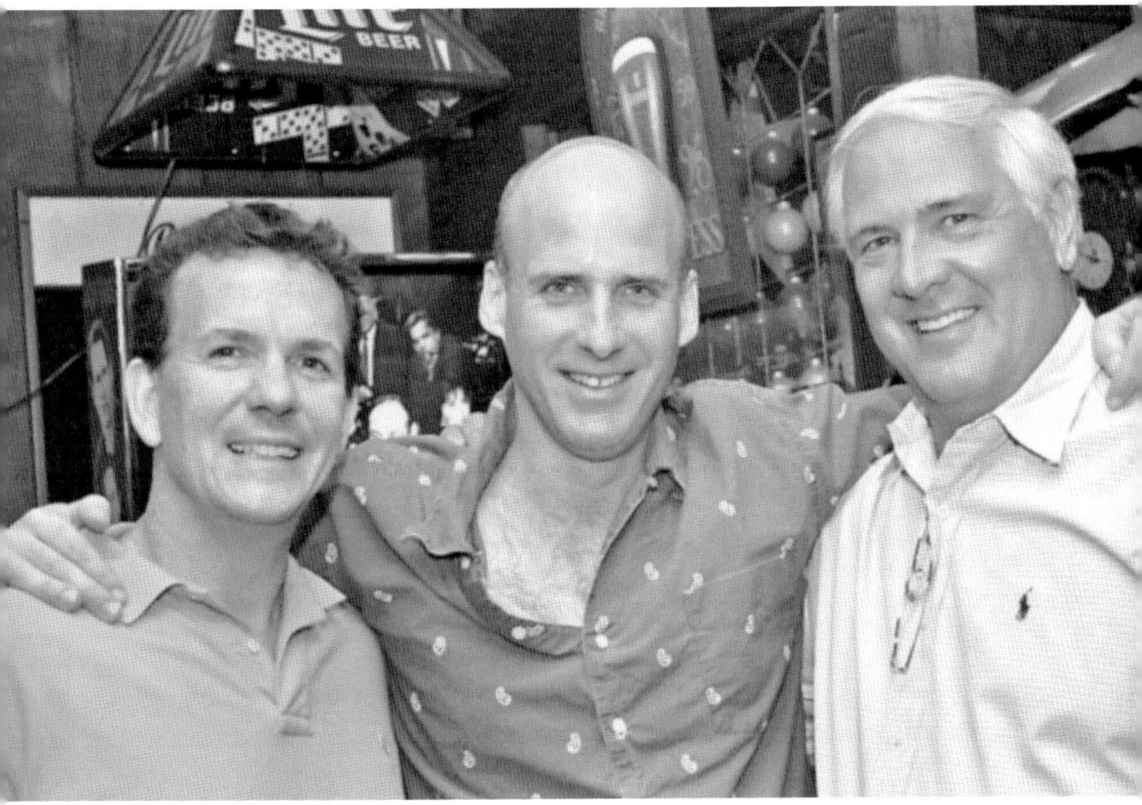

Here to Help

He is pictured here holding down the center between Republican assemblyman Declan O'Scanlon and former Democratic state senator John Villapiano, but while Dan Jacobson ran as an independent in a 2011 New Jersey General Assembly contest (and previously served one term in the legislature as a Democrat), there is nothing middle-of-the-road about his tenure as publisher of the *TriCity News*, the alternative "News and Arts Weekly" that the attorney founded in downtown Asbury Park during the drear winter of 1999.

Arriving on the scene at a crucial turning point in the city's twisted history, and bringing a healthy shot of ballyhoo to Asbury's downtrodden carnival, the onetime Ocean Township councilman caught the cusp of the street wave, cheerleading the downtown's phenomenal rebirth through a print-only product that is provocative, partisan, passionately opinionated, and personalized with the conversationally whip-smart style of its founder. With Red Bank and Long Branch as the sister cities in the troika, Jacobson most certainly could, and most certainly did, lay claim to having influenced much of what is new and exciting in the greater Asbury orbit.

Other web-based projects would follow, including the just-the-facts news source *Asbury Park Sun* and the hipster-culture hagstrom *Asbury Anchor*. But it is his resolutely paper-based flagship freebie *TriCity* that remains the most engaging extension of Jacobson the man and the brand, an endeavor of which the publisher says with a smile, "We're the *TriCity News*. We're here to help." (Courtesy of Michael Booth and the *Coaster*.)

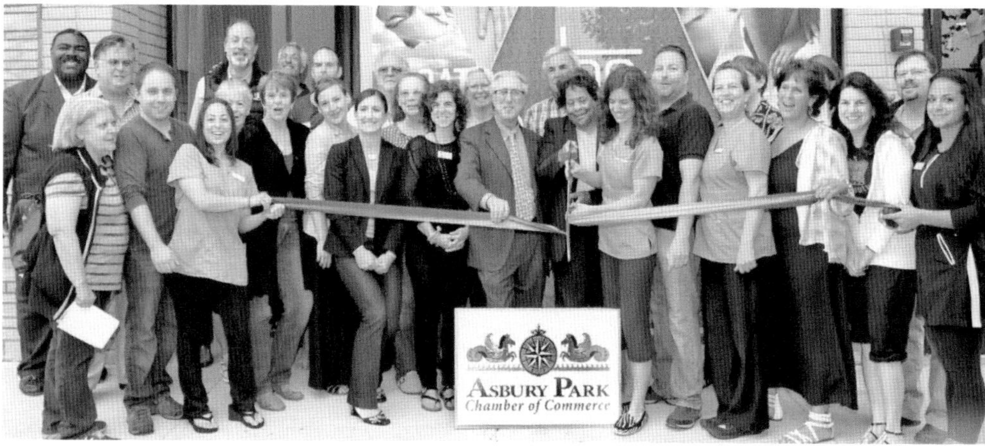

Good Time Gilmour

Yes, Asbury Park has a director of commerce and good times, and while he is more formally the city's head of economic development, Tom Gilmour has embraced the public-welcome spirit of his beach-town bailiwick by playing a highly visible role in the establishment of arts, food festivals, civic events, and the Asbury Park Music Heritage Society. He is pictured here (center) in a familiar setting: assisting Mayor Myra Campbell (with scissors) and fellow Asbury Park Chamber of Commerce members in a new-business ribbon cutting. (Courtesy of Michael Booth and the *Coaster.*)

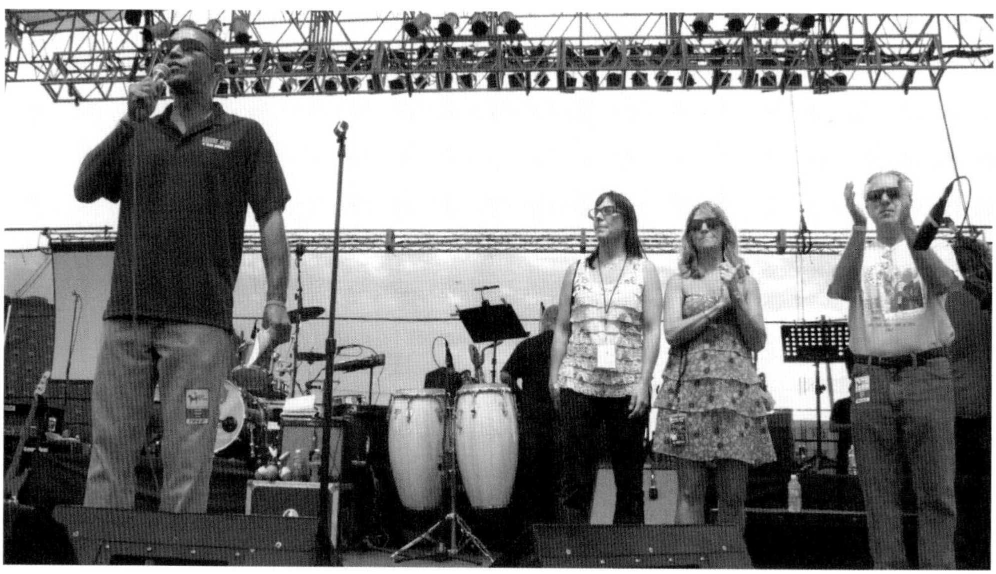

Asbury's Ambassador

He is pictured here (with, from left to right, Susan Pellegrini, Eileen Chapman, and Tom Gilmour, announcing the "Where Music Lives" project from the Stone Pony SummerStage) doing what he does best: welcoming visitors, cheerleading local endeavors, and putting it all together. As an African American and the city's first openly gay mayor, Ed Johnson already appeared a unifying figure, but in the affable, capable UEZ director and college administrator, Asbury Park found a multitasking professional who put its best face forward to the nation. Still sought as a speaker following his retirement from politics, the "mayor emeritus" continues his calling as Asbury's finest ambassador. (Courtesy of John Cavanaugh and the AP Musical Heritage Society.)

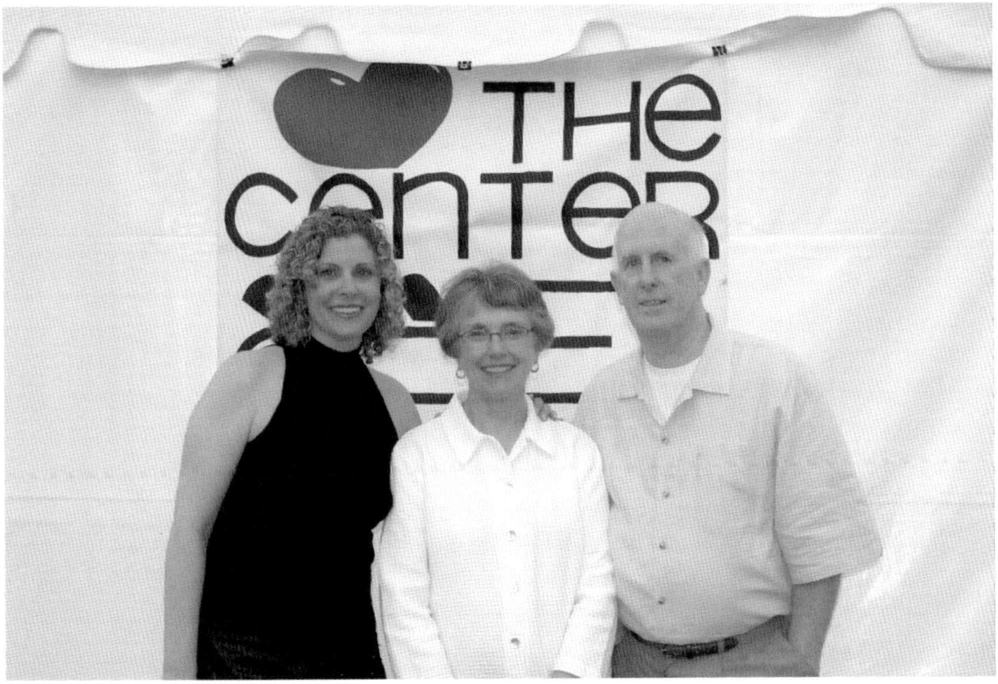

Heart of the City
It began in 1992 as an all-volunteer resource dedicated to the support of local residents living with HIV/AIDS. And, if the Center in Asbury Park seems indicative of a time before the city was rediscovered, it is no less relevant and integral to the well-being of a community that continues to struggle in the new century. Rev. Robert Kaeding (right), his small staff, and more than 70 volunteers have expanded their mission to Center House, a permanent supportive housing facility, and continue to provide meals, transportation, financial assistance, and more to clients throughout Monmouth and Ocean Counties. (Courtesy of Michael Booth and the *Coaster.*)

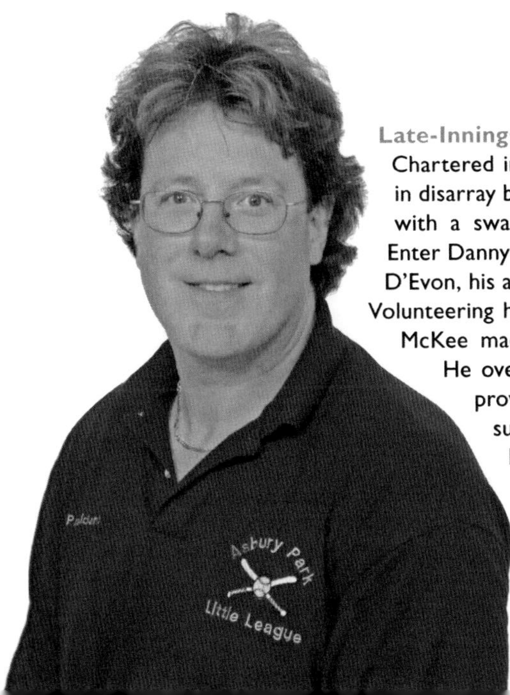

Late-Innings Rally
Chartered in 1955, Asbury Park's Little League program was in disarray by the 2000s, a signifier of the city's fallen fortunes with a swampy sandlot, no equipment, and little support. Enter Danny McKee, an entrepreneur who turned coach when D'Evon, his adopted son with partner Patrick Smith, signed up. Volunteering himself as APLL president and fundraiser in 2005, McKee made the program competitive with its neighbors. He oversaw construction of a state-of-the-art field and provided boys and girls the opportunity to attend summer baseball camp each year. Many APLL players have since achieved great success at the high school level. (Courtesy of Michael Booth and the *Coaster.*)

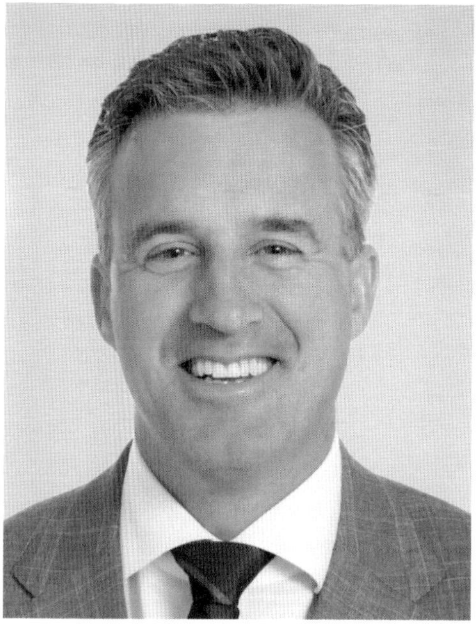

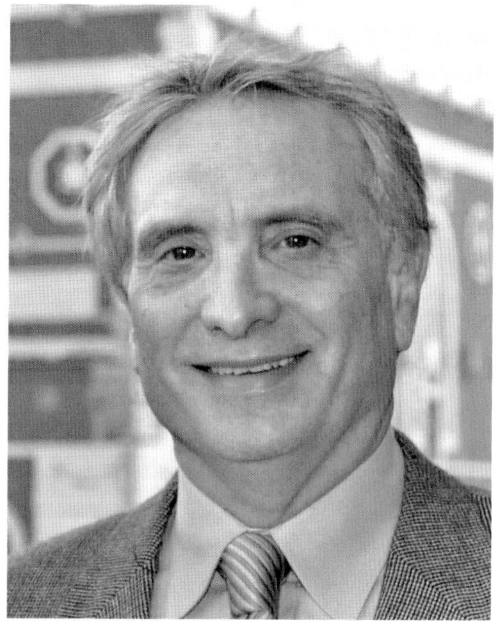

Monuments Men

Although they work different neighborhoods, they are the men most identified with redevelopment in 21st-century Asbury Park. Carter Sackman (left) made headlines with the rescue and reimagining of the Steinbach Building. The Sackman firm's ongoing downtown retail, residential, and entertainment projects include the new House of Independents theatre, part of an entire business district that gained state and national historic registry status thanks to Sackman's efforts. As president of investments for nationwide property managers Madison Marquette, Gary Mottola (right) became the public face of the Asbury Waterfront, a figure of continuity when bankrupted Asbury Partners was folded into NYC-based iStar Financial. MM would assume a stewardship role and minority stake in Convention Hall, the carousel, the boardwalk pavilions, and the Stone Pony. (Courtesy of Michael Booth and the *Coaster.*)

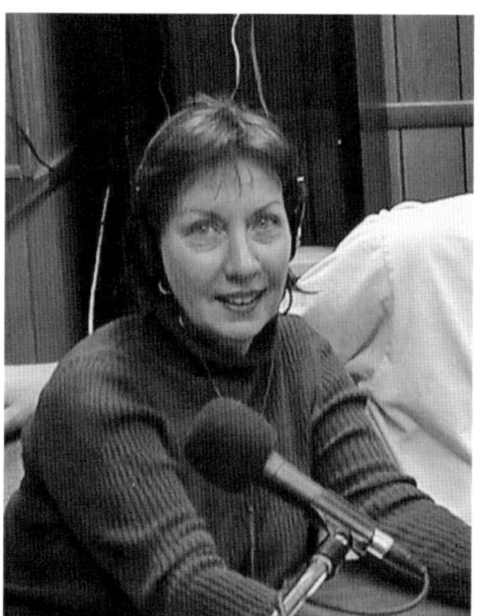

I Cover the Waterfront

She is "a working journalist who can't stop taking notes," one who shows up at council meetings on her own time and dime, grilling the politicians and developers like the National Press Club award-winning financial reporter that she is. For years, Maureen Nevin hosted the hyper-local program *Asbury Radio* (*Restore Radio*) on WYGG, the tiny FM station that served the city's burgeoning Haitian community, amassing material for *Ocean Mile*, her fact-based script drawn from Asbury Park's adventures in redevelopment hell. The former *Press* columnist continues to write nationally on market topics in between e-books like *Avoiding Naples.* (Courtesy of Maureen Nevin.)

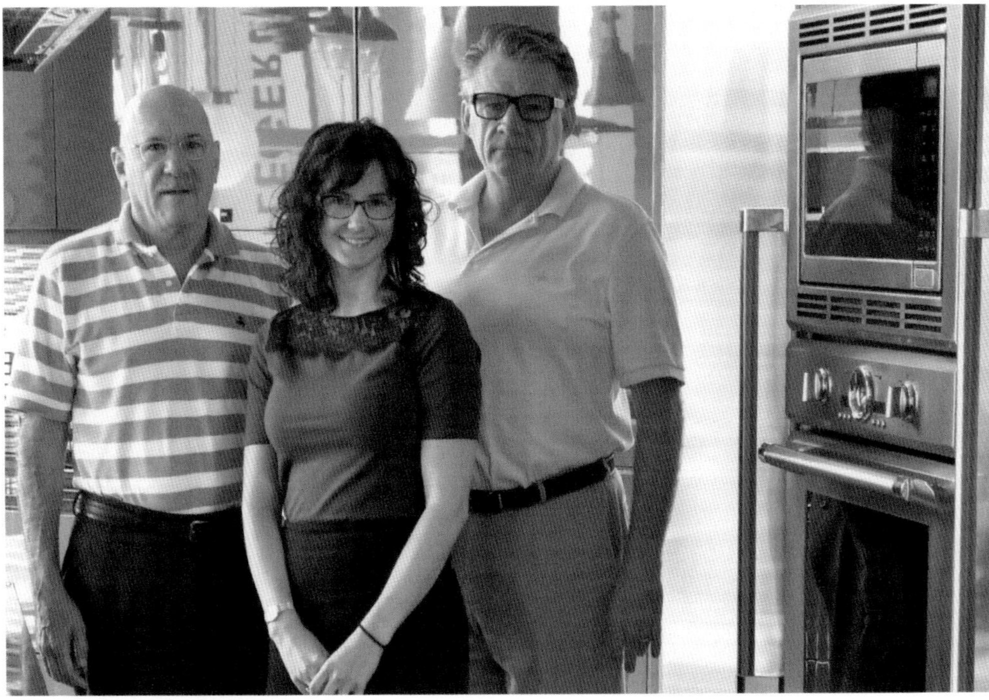

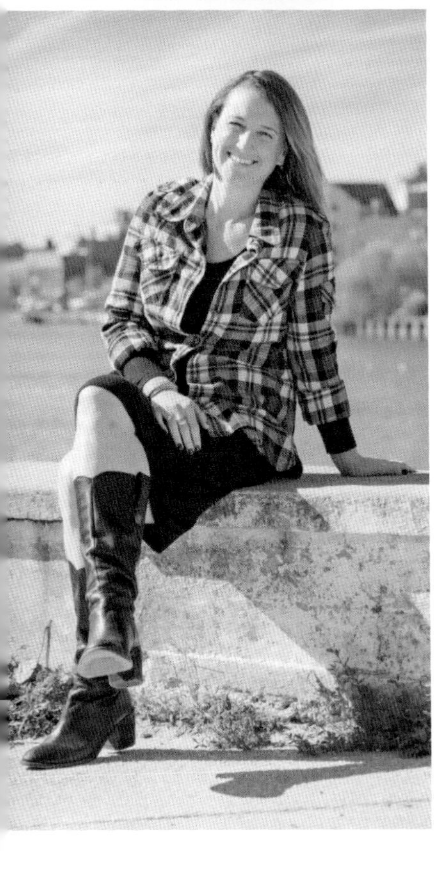

Design Forward

A genuine pioneer in the reimagining of Asbury Park's Cookman Avenue business center—one whose three-story Design Center building brought dramatic sweep and energy to a long-dormant downtown—Robert Legere (right) expanded his bridal/eveningwear concern into Robert Legere Design in 2002. Joined by partner and CEO Steve Troy (left) and design director Krysti Pitterman, the designer created a self-contained showplace for high-end contemporary interiors and contracting services. (Courtesy of Steven Troy.)

Dial M

"Asbury Park is a community that was built on artists," Jenna Zilincar told the *TriCity News*. "And I hope that never goes away." A particularly dynamic example of the new millennial "merchant class" that has transformed the downtown Cookman corridor (both physically and philosophically), the cofounder and president of M Studio oversees a full-service design, marketing, and branding company, one with a reach that extends from neighboring storefronts to national clients from a Bangs Avenue setback that would make Sherlock Holmes pleased. Zilincar joins companies like Knockout/Smith and the Passion Group on this intriguingly creative frontier. (Copyright and courtesy of Sara R. Stadtmiller.)

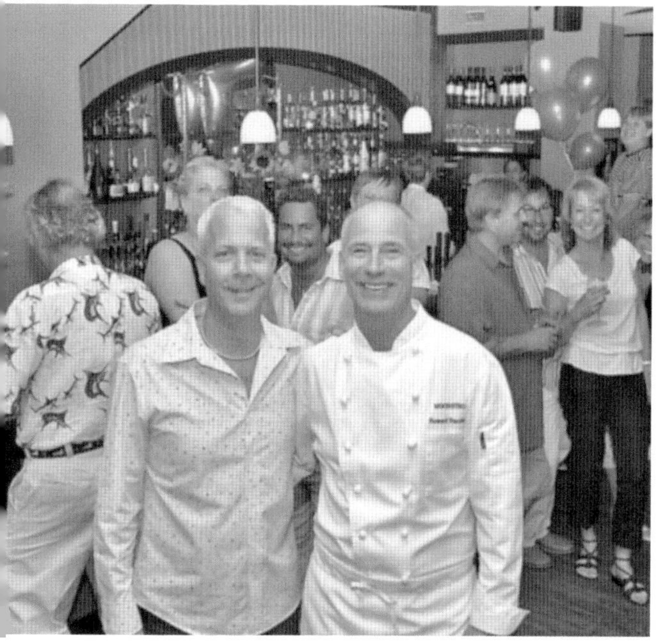

Moon Hits Your Eye

In the *Press*, Andrea Clurfeld noted that the 2002 arrival of Moonstruck "spurred a host of activity—new restaurants, new shops, new spirit—in its new neighborhood. That says something about the kind of respect Moonstruck commands." Indeed, when executive chef Howard Raczkiewicz and co-owner Luke Magliaro moved their hugely popular but not-huge Ocean Grove bistro across Wesley Lake (to a grand old Victorian that once hosted the Deck House), they reimagined Moonstruck as a consistent destination attraction, complete with contemporary American cuisine and a piano bar that regularly hosts impresario Bob Egan's talent showcases. (Courtesy of Michael Booth and the *Coaster*.)

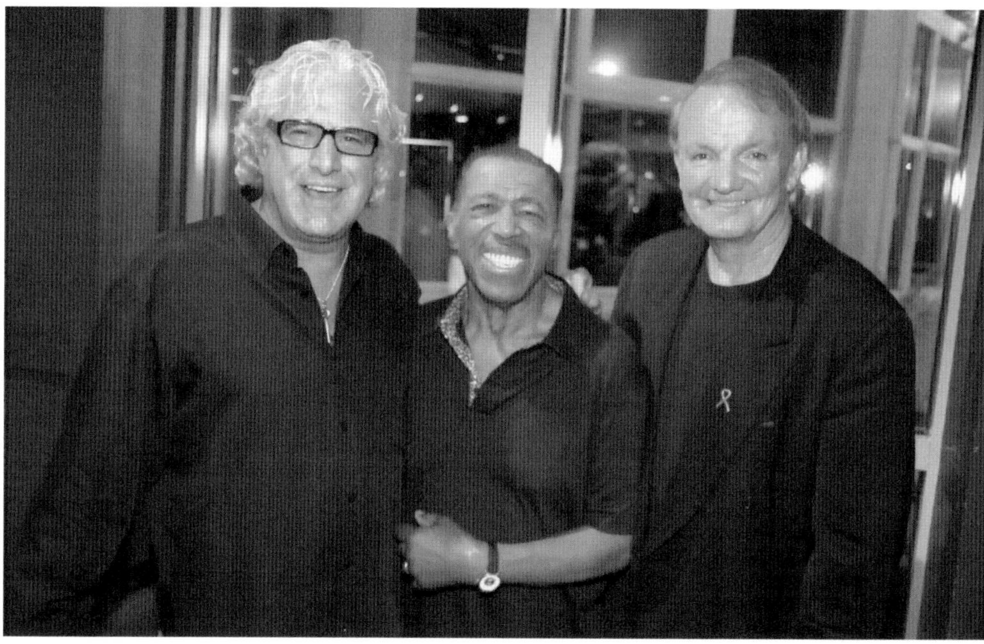

Sing for Your Supper

Few signifiers of the sea change between Asbury old and new are more dramatic than the transformation of the boardwalk's space-age Howard Johnson's into Tim McLoone's Asbury Grille and its swanky second-floor Supper Club. The regional restaurateur, runner, radio host, coach, musician, and humanitarian founder of the nonprofit Holiday Express (right) has hosted jazz greats, Shoreband jams, big-city cabaret, and comedy inside the panoramic penthouse. Realtor and music promoter Sammy Boyd (left) booked hall-of-fame talents like Ben E. King as part of a noteworthy Masters of Music series. (Courtesy of Michael Booth and the *Coaster*.)

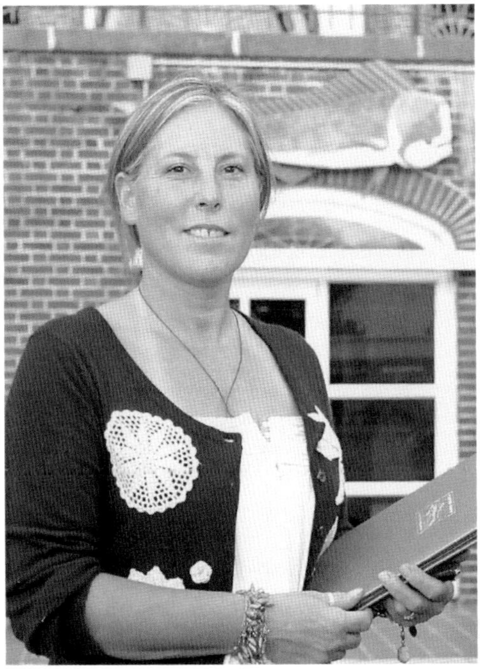

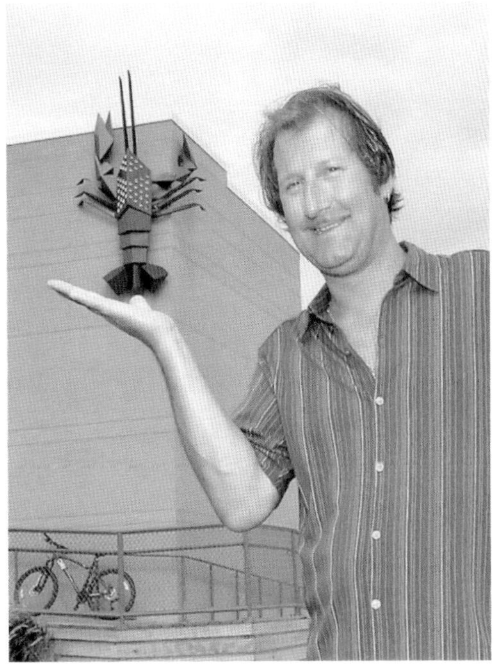

Chairwoman of the Board

Her time at the trailblazing Jersey Shore sushi-fusion site Oshin might have been all that she needed to cement her reputation as a forward-thinking chef and restaurateur, and her status as a recently minted mother to twin daughters might have been all the excuse she required to slow down the professional pace. Despite having been among the area's hardest-hit business owners in the wake of Hurricane Sandy, Marilyn Schlossbach continues to work her concurrent paths of entrepreneur, philanthropist, and activist, adding instruction in the culinary arts, community gardening, and even surfing to a busy mix of activities that range from the high-profile to the pro bono. Together with her husband (fellow surfer, artist, and businessman Scott Szegeski) and music booker/scene legend Peter Mantas (right), Schlossbach has centered her Kitschens Hospitality mini-empire at the 1000 Ocean Avenue pavilion. Under Schlossbach's watch, it is a set of attractions that includes the flagship Langosta Lounge as well as a neighboring bar, two more casual eateries, and the boardwalk's sole surf shop. While the partners also operate dining spots in Shrewsbury and Normandy Beach, it is in Asbury Park that they have become most plugged into local life.

Schlossbach's community projects have included collaborations with nonprofits Clean Ocean Action, Boys and Girls Club of Asbury Park, and Interfaith Neighbors (with whom she established the Kula Café at the new Springwood Center), a Surf Film Festival, and free movie screenings on the beach. Every Thanksgiving and Christmas Day, she teams with Pat Sherman of the nonprofit FEEDing Frenz to transform Langosta Lounge into a free community kitchen, food bank, and clothing distribution center for hundreds of appreciative neighbors. The community has given back, too, helping to fund a grassroots effort to get the Sandy-slammed boardwalk businesses back on line. A series of defunct restaurant ventures and aborted bids for public office have not served to stall Schlossbach's forward momentum, and there is little doubt that this avid wave rider, working mother, and wonder woman will be surfing the crest of the cause any time that the quality of life in her adopted city could use a helping hand. (Courtesy of Michael Booth and the *Coaster*.)

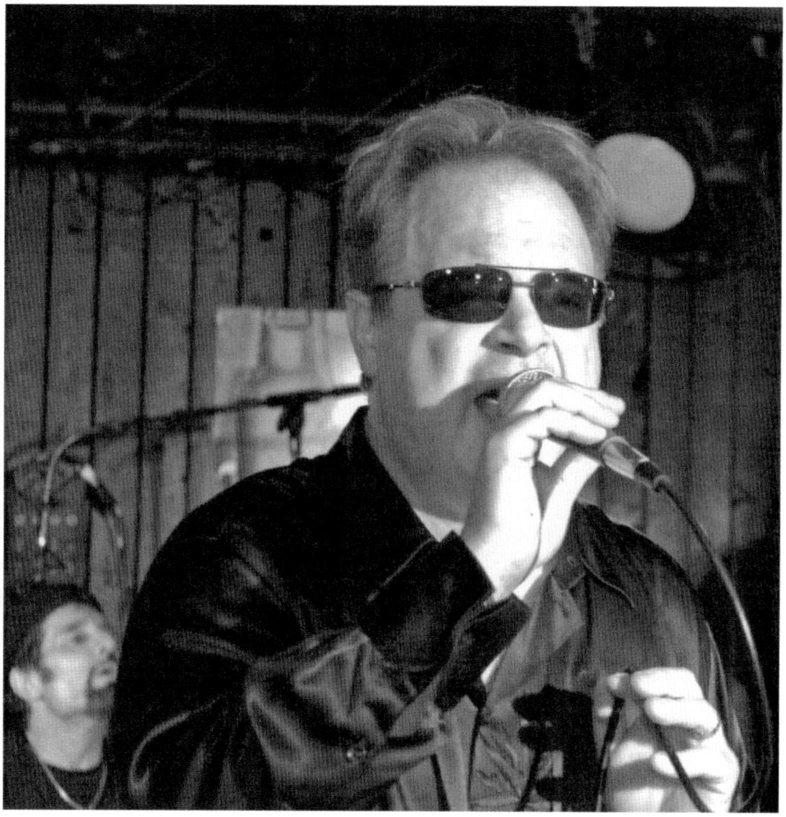

Life in the Fast Lane

The thing that ties the room together—the one factor that unites musical eras past, present, and yet-to-be, straddles the scenes, and gets them all harmonizing—is not a radio station, a magazine, a club, or a band, but one man.

A rare promoter who has lived the business from both sides of the stage, Antonio "Tony" Pallagrosi began his concert-producing career as early as high school, even as he prosecuted a have-trumpet-will-travel musician's career that saw him play in the Shots, Cold Blast and Steel, Charlottesville Allstars, and the Asbury Jukes (plus, with the Miami Horns, the expanded E Street Band). By the early 1980s, he managed clubs like the much-missed Fast Lane, where (with legendary booker Jim Giantonio) he introduced audiences to fledgling acts like U2 and the Police, in addition to John Bongiovi's Atlantic City Expressway. As comanager with future professional wrestler Diamond Dallas Page, he brought original music to the cover band/dance pit Club Xanadu, and by the close of the 20th century he partnered with Jerry Bakal, producing over 4,500 shows as Concerts East (including major events like the Vans Warped Tour) and turning central Jersey's Starland Ballroom into one of the nation's highest-grossing halls.

Continuing to produce regional events under the UMT Presents banner, Pallagrosi has cemented his legacy in the new century via two musically humanitarian endeavors. Through the Light of Day Foundation, Pallagrosi and cofounder Bob Benjamin present an annual slate of high-profile concerts benefiting Parkinson's Disease research (and illuminating the stages of Asbury during the darkest dead-of-winter nights)—events that regularly draw the participation of Bruce Springsteen, Willie Nile, Joe D'Urso, Joe Grushecky, and more.

In 2012, Pallagrosi paid tribute to the veterans of Asbury Park's music scene, from the days of Arthur Pryor to the present, through the creation of the Asbury Angel Project and its virtual hall of fame designed to "honor and memorialize the lives and history of members of the Asbury Park musical community." (Courtesy of Dave Christopher.)

Lord and Lady of the Manor

As front man of locally legendary Lord Gunner (his hat is on the cover of Bruce's *Born in the USA*), Lance Larson evidenced the chops and chutzpah to break out of the 1970s and 1980s Asbury scene. While a series of setbacks (including a near-fatal mugging and a past struggle with heroin addiction) quashed those rock-star dreams, his relationship with Debbie DeLisa allowed him to write a new chapter when the couple acquired the once and future Circuit landmark known as the Wonder Bar. With partner Pat Schiavino aboard, the club (repainted to evoke the iconic Palace Amusements, Tillie and all) came under the Madison Marquette umbrella as a looser, quirkier cousin to the more corporate Pony. Lance and Debbie remain as gracious hosts and spirit guides for a mix that includes Shore-style jams, cult-favorite nationals, and the inimitable Doggie Yappy Hour. (Photo by Mike Kearns, courtesy of the *Coaster*.)

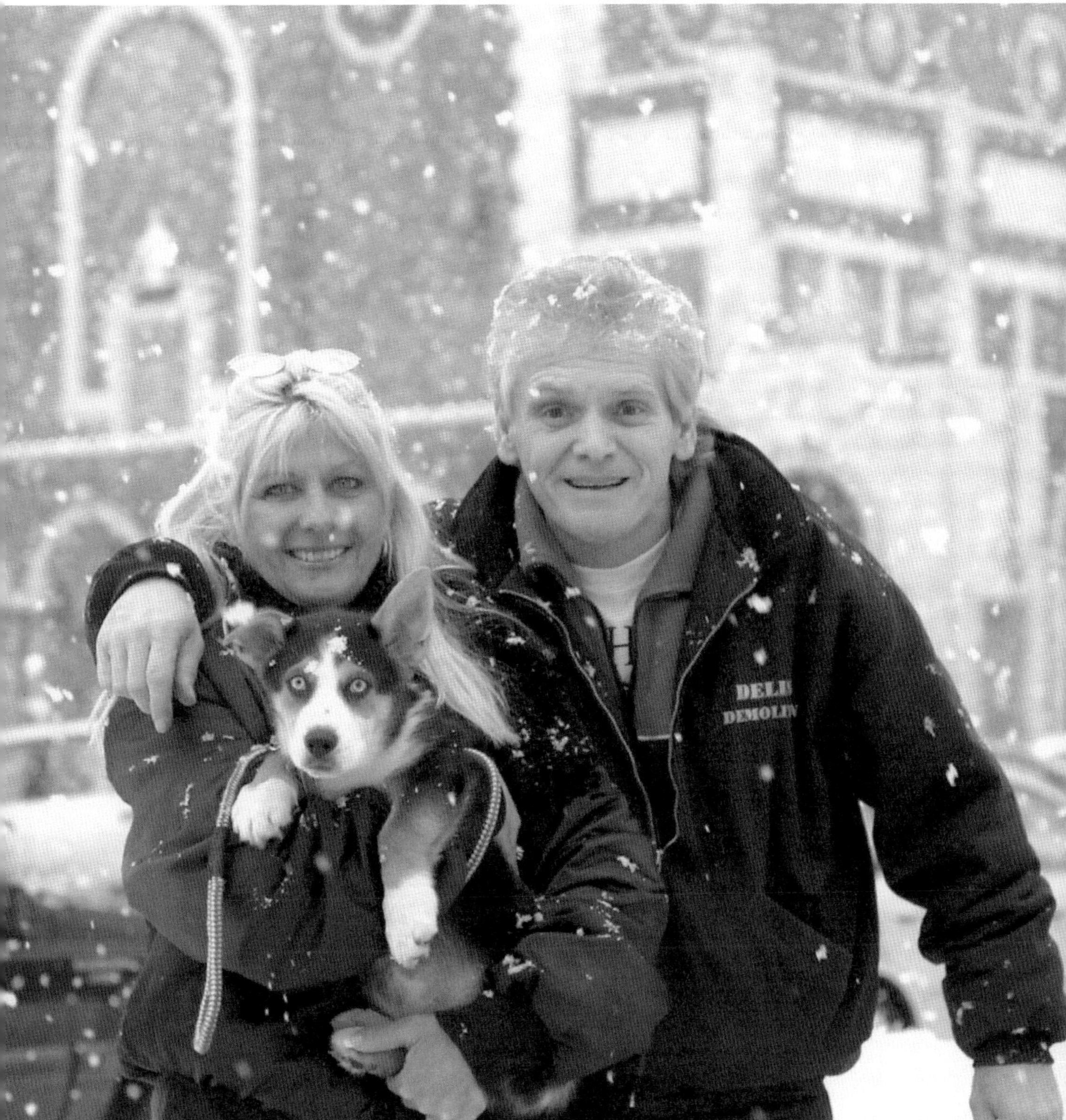

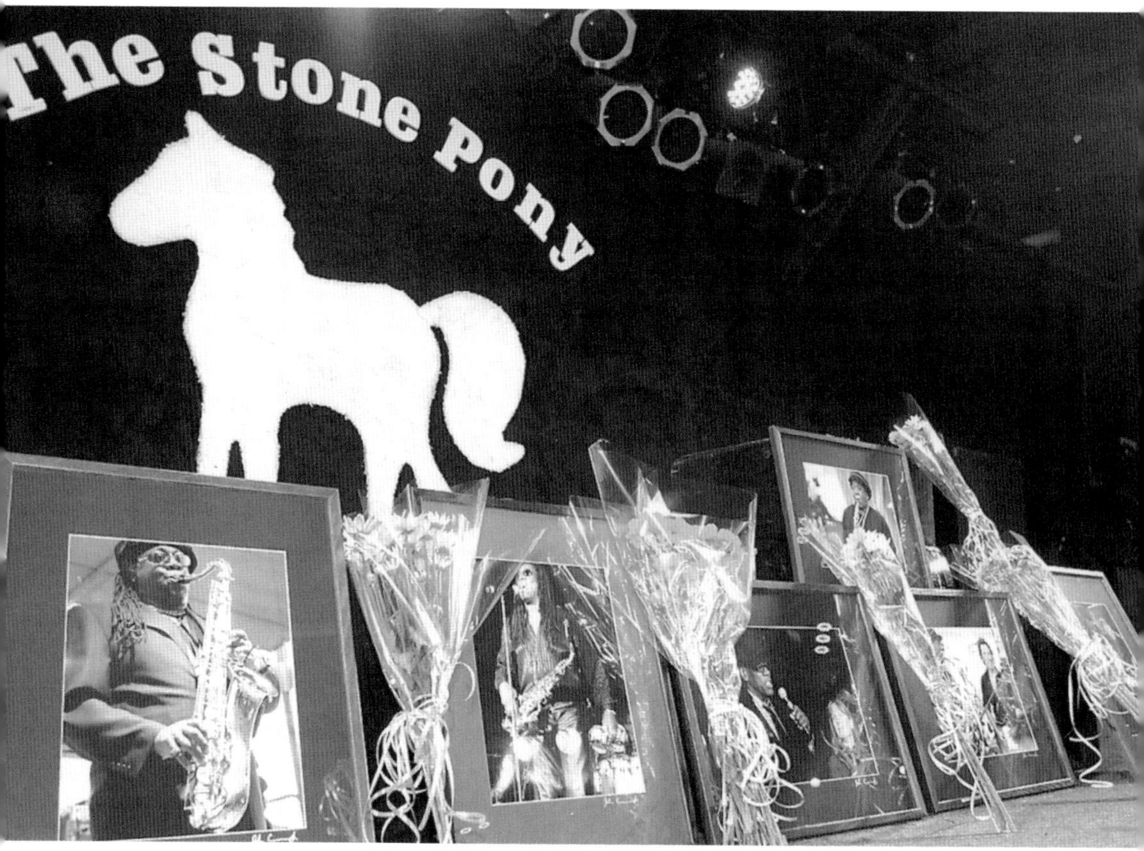

Ask the Angels

The 2011 passing of Big Man Clarence Clemons was more than just a music-scene milestone. The seismic event provided the impetus for the creation of the Asbury Angel Project, founded by Tony Pallagrosi in 2012. Inducting an annual class of departed musical history makers, installing boardwalk plaques, and maintaining an online hall of fame, the project recognizes figures both famous and unjustly forgotten, east-side and west-side, old-timey and timeless, both in front of the audience and behind the scenes. A full roll call of Asbury Angels, with detailed bios, can be viewed at asburyangels.com. (Courtesy of Michael Booth and the *Coaster*.)

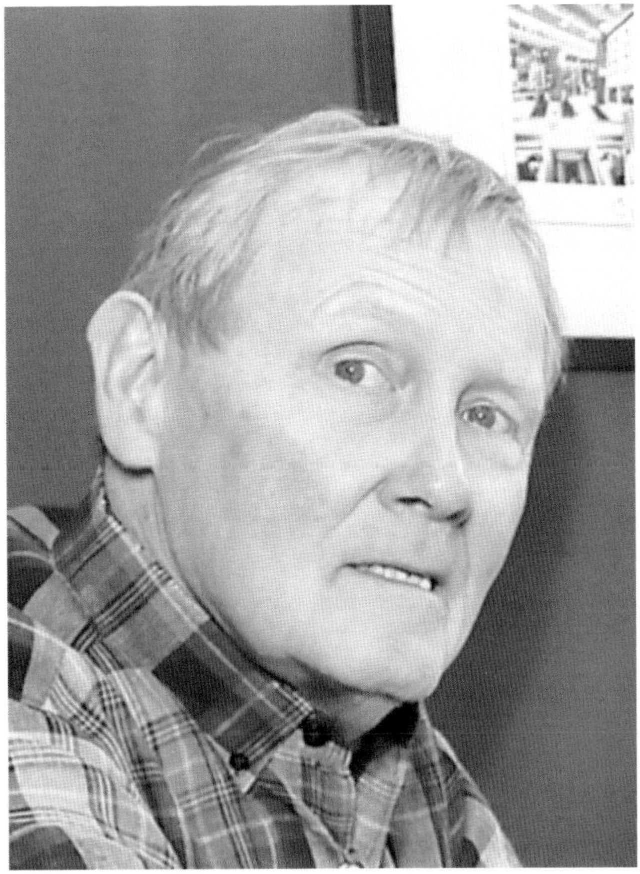

Mac Daddy
"Asbury Park is a neighborhood . . . it's compact," said John McGillion to the *Sun* website. "The people here are very good . . . very liberal, artsy people." Entering the downtown barscape with his quirky, picturesque Johnny Mac's House of Spirits, the tavern keep and his partners quickly expanded their presence to include the former Adriatic (revamped as Kim Marie's), Mary Mac's beer garden, and the planned refresh of the venerable Cameo dive. In 2011, Johnny Mac emerged as a major sponsor of Asbury's premier St. Patrick's Day Parade, spearheaded by city fire official Garrett Giberson. (Courtesy of Michael Booth and the *Coaster*.)

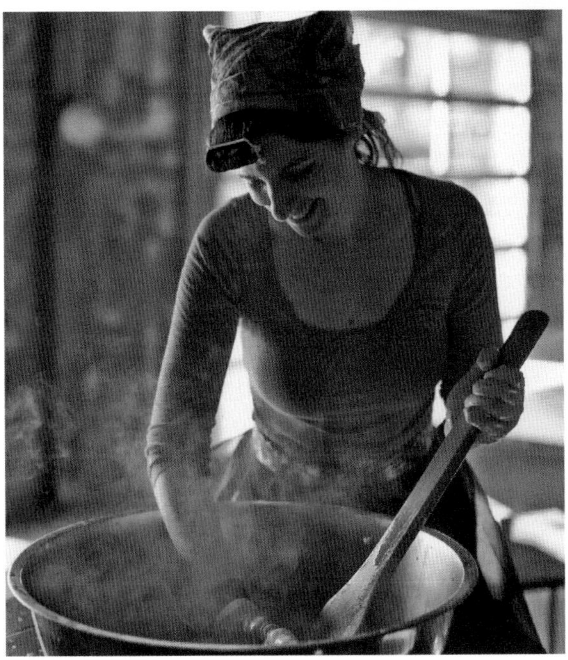

Doors of Perception
Not just a dynamically creative house of ideas, but a brick-and-mortar driver of its host city's physical and demographic transformation, the Smith group (née Knockout) has expanded its reach to a downtown condo building (Eureka) and numerous bar/restaurant projects, including Brickwall, Pascal and Sabine, and the flagship force of nature known as Porta. Creative director Fredrica Vilardi also happens to be the certified head *pizzaiola* of the wildly popular dining room (and even wilder late-night dance club), a place of celebrity sightings, celebrated dishes, and top-rated reviews from the *New York Times*. (Photograph by Andrew Holtz.)

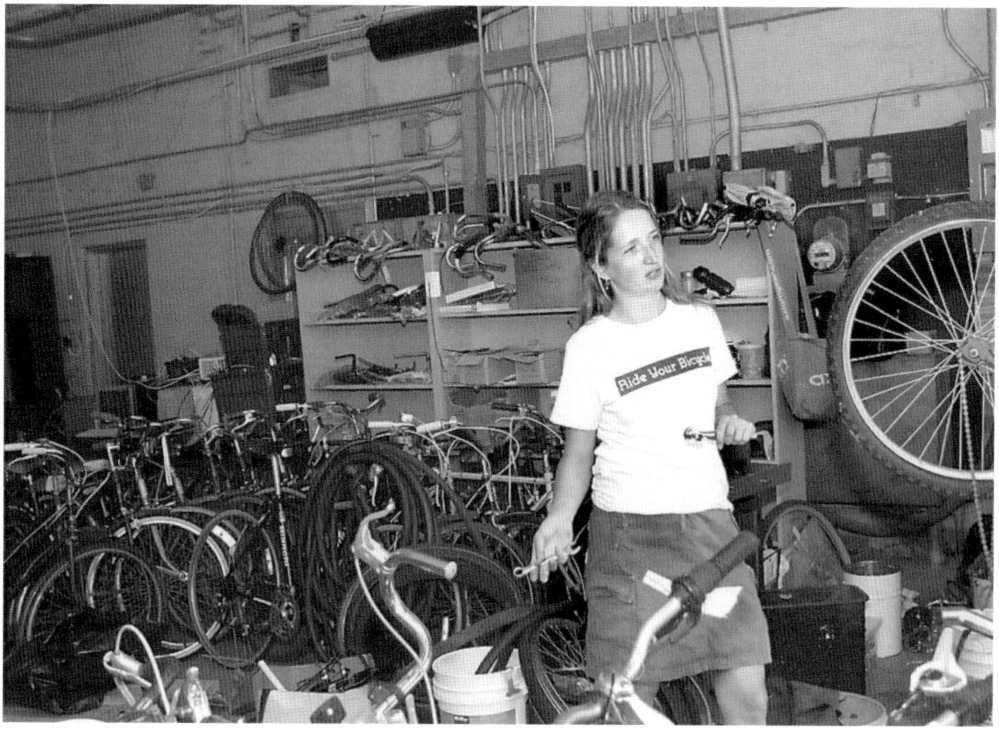

The Spokeswoman

The truth-in-advertising name Second Life Bikes is also a philosophy, and the philosophy often takes the form of humorous daily street-sign sooths by Kerri Martin. Overseeing a volunteer-staffed center for the rescue and refurbishment of all pedal-power makes, styles, and vintages at the corner of Main Street and Springwood Avenue (and maintaining a fighting hold on her warehouse-scale space), Martin aims to match every kid and adult in a struggling town with the wheels (and, in many cases, the skills) they will need to get to where they want to go. (Courtesy of Michael Booth and the *Coaster*.)

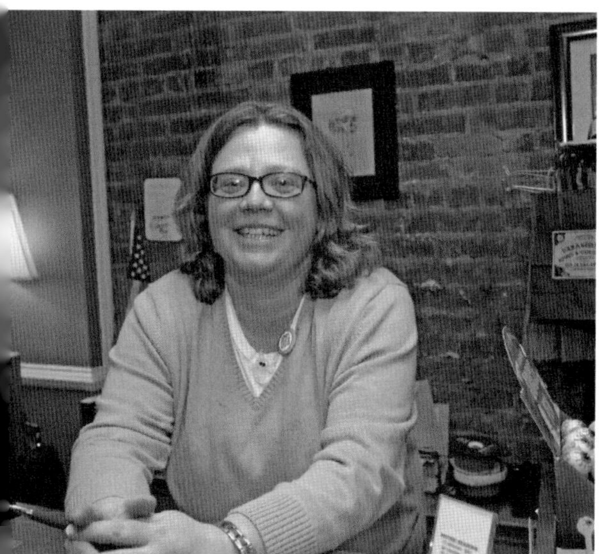

Ghost Town

Kathy Kelly opened Paranormal Books and Curiosities on a Friday the 13th in 2008 and proceeded to turn a fascination with the dead into one of the liveliest businesses in town. The venture expanded into walking ghost tours, year-round ghost investigations, and even a holiday-season festival saluting Santa's associate Krampus. One of the most engaged of the new merchants, Kelly hosts a nexus of past, present, and future in a city of shipwrecked souls and restless spirits, where "anything can happen . . . there's a live-wire buzz about this town." (Courtesy of Michael Booth and the *Coaster*.)

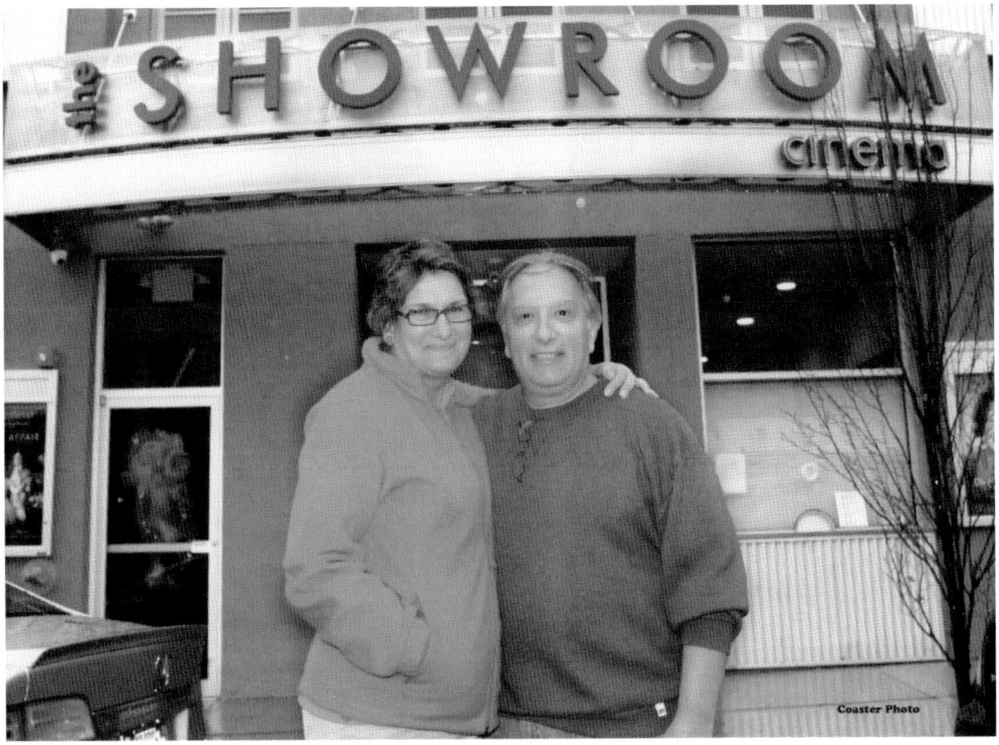

Coming Attractions

Once a city of grand movie houses, Asbury Park greeted its first new nickelodeon in generations when Nancy Sabino and Mike Sodano opened the ShowRoom from a Cookman Avenue storefront in 2008. Focusing on foreign films, indies, and documentaries, the civically engaged veteran filmmakers (*Greetings from the Parking Lot, Rock and a Heart Place*) also used their space as a venue for plays, panels, comedy nights, and concerts. In 2012, the ShowRoom crossed the street to a new three-screen facility, immediately going to the head of the class among area art-house theaters. (Courtesy of Michael Booth and the *Coaster*.)

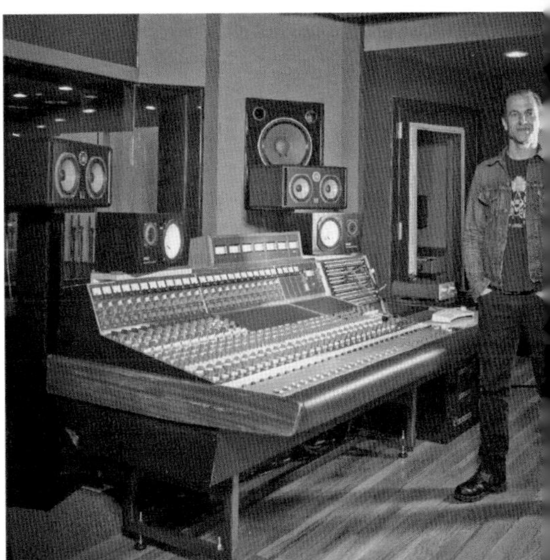

House by the Lake

Some say it's not a scene unless music is "coming out of" a city—and with the advent of Lakehouse Music, Asbury Park took a quantum leap forward. Armed with a collection of vintage instruments (and an ultra-rare 1972 Neve 8024 console), producer/musician Jon Leidersdorff transformed a Lake Avenue warehouse into a complex that features instruction/rehearsal space, Russo music store, Holtz Photography, Mumford's Café, Brian Nelson's music management company, Danny Croak's marketing service Bands on a Budget, and Bret Morgan's Cowerks community. The studio got on the map in 2014, recording Lorde's Golden Globe-nominated "Yellow Flicker Beat." (Courtesy of Jon Leidersdorff.)

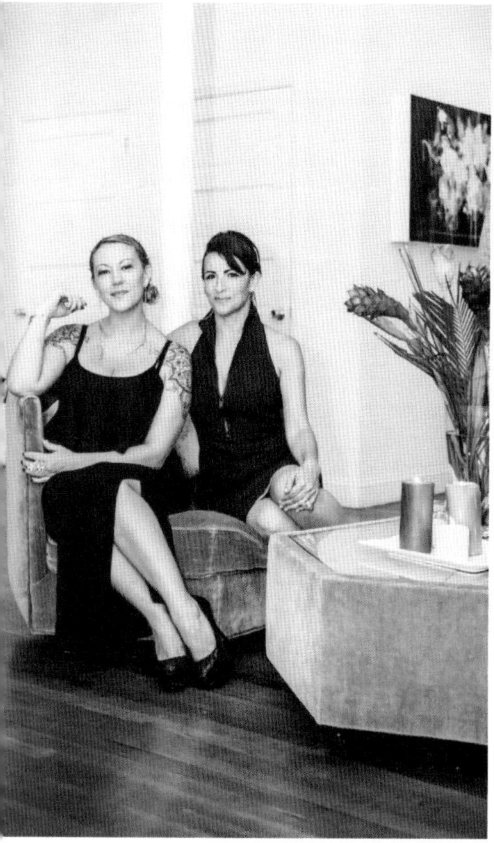

Juicy Jenn

Emerging from the groundhog-burrow of Punxsatawney, Pennsylvania, Jenn Hampton brings a unique mix of Buddhist perspective and old-school business savvy to the city's culture on two crucial fronts. As partner in the Cookman Arts Bloc's Parlor Gallery, Jenn (left, with co-owner Jill Ricci) joined with Michael Walker and Sarah Potter to create a pop-art paradise that has remained in the vanguard of a gallery scene whose outposts have come (Art 629, Palette, Exhibit No. 9) and gone (SICA, Rock Paper Scissors, Knowledge Bennett).

Meanwhile, at Asbury Lanes, the 1960s tenpins taproom turned atom-age arts center, Hampton (with Potter and Mike Lawrence) has carried on from the work of visionary Mel Stultz and provided much-needed continuity throughout regimes that ranged from longtime owners the Ayles family to developers Pat Fasano and Vince Gifford. Hosting resident ghosts as well as local and national bands, burlesque shows, film fests, flea markets, dance-offs, dating games, Sex Toy Bingo, and the odd wedding, all with bowling, Hampton lends her elegant Fellini to a scene that is as much antidote (to the Jersey nightclub norm) as it is alternative. Jenn is pictured below with Potter (left) and Lawrence (center). (Courtesy of Dani Fresh.)

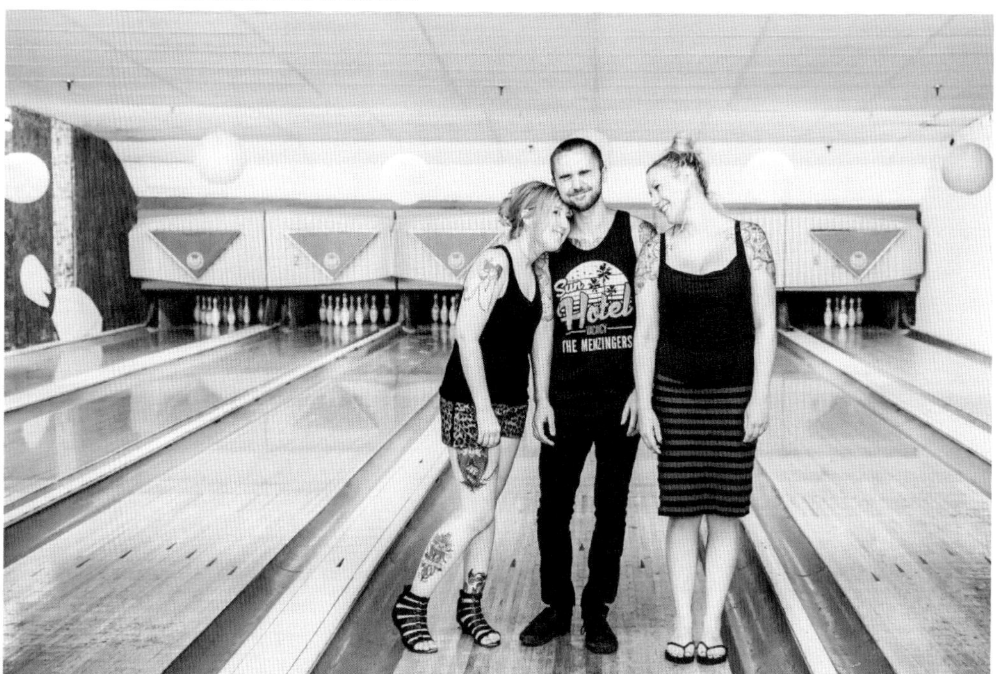

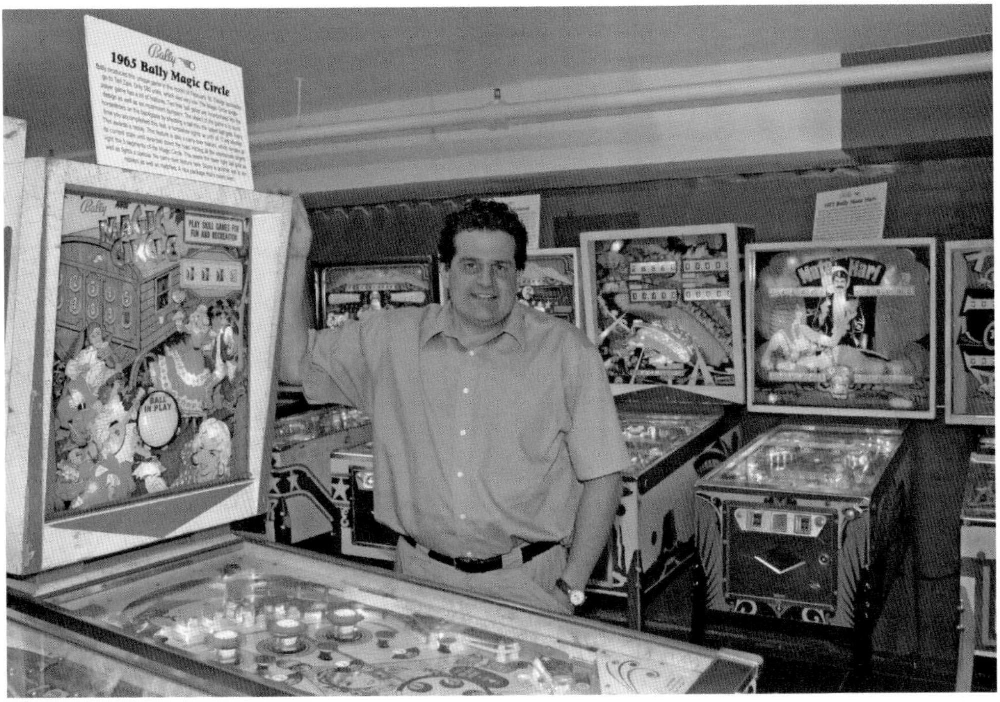

Down on Pinball Way

Whether your nostalgic pheromone of choice is the 1950s–1970s pinball-wizard-era ching of the Bally and Gottlieb, or the 1980s bleep of the Nintendo and Atari, Silverball Pinball Museum has become a fast favorite. Collector and refurbisher Robert Ilvento started the wonderland of breathtakingly restored and fully functional arcade machines (complete with retro party facilities) in the basement of a downtown storefront in 2009; taking his rightful place on the boardwalk in 2010 and surviving even Sandy's salvos to emerge as a crossgenerational destination attraction. (Courtesy of Michael Booth and the *Coaster.*)

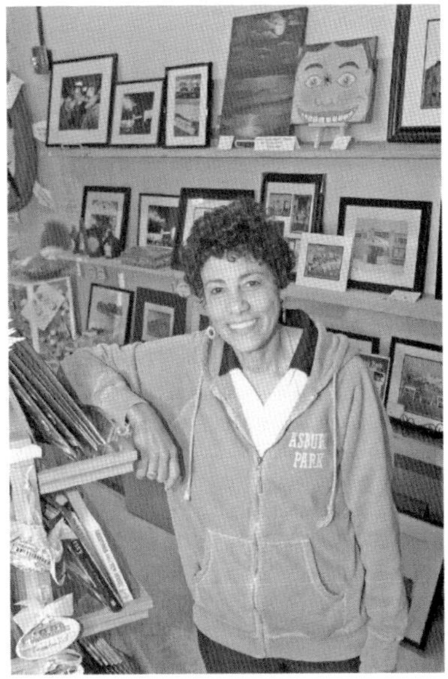

Kay's Mart

"It's the closest thing Asbury Park has to a museum," is how photographer Lobo Jones effusively described Asbury Galleria, the one-of-a-kind gallery and beach store run since 2005 by Kay Harris, now inside Convention Hall's Grand Arcade. A true fan of her hometown's past and a sincere booster of its future, the "Asbury shutterbug" and granddaughter of the legendary sand artist Lorenzo Harris has stamped her own positive personality on a collection of vintage images, books, memorabilia, and souvenirs that has become a must-visit attraction in itself. (Courtesy of Kay Harris.)

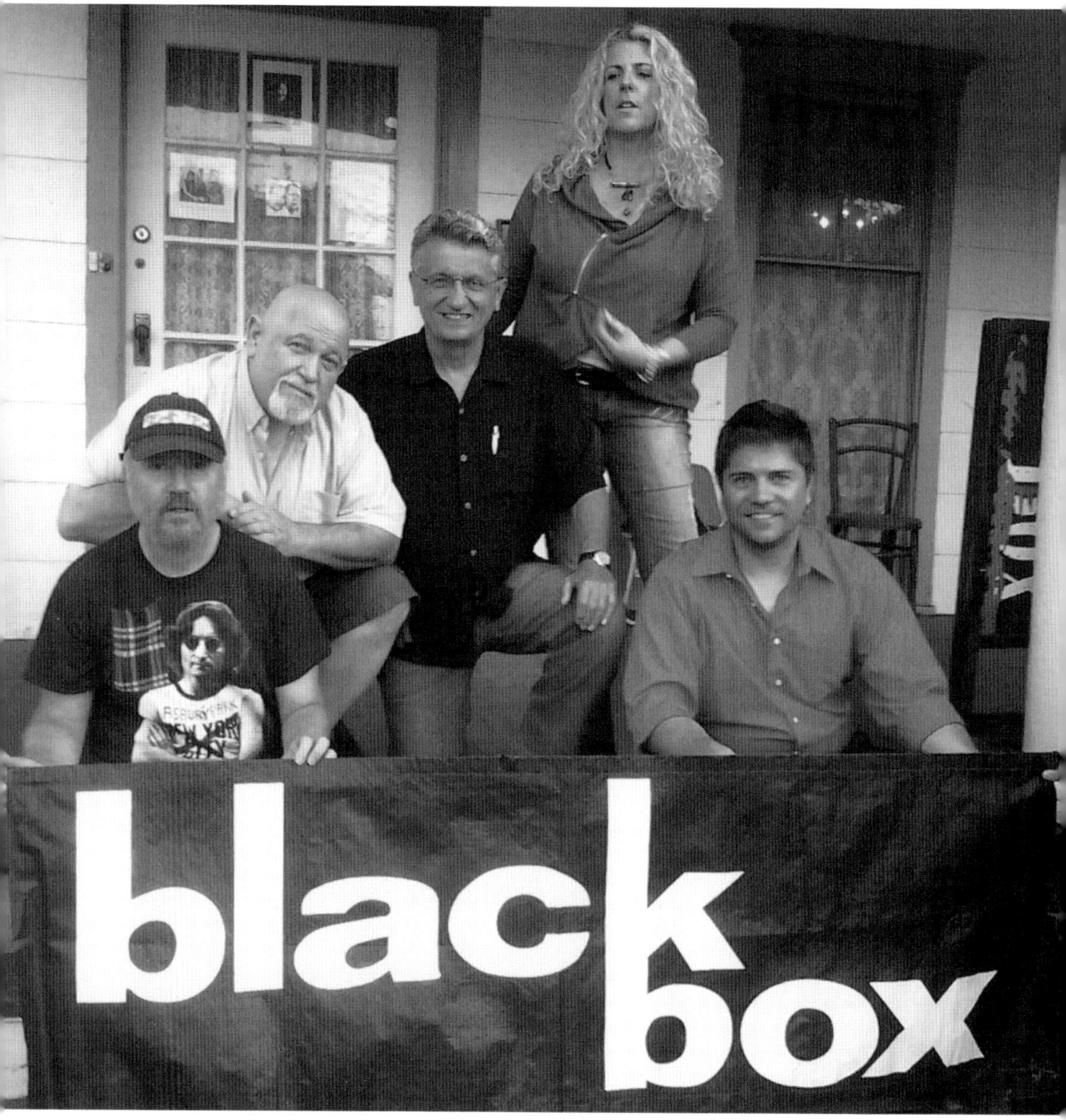

Thinking Inside the Box

The idea of an arts collective, devoid of any asset but its own creative energy, must have seemed so crazy in c. 2000 Asbury Park that it had no choice but to succeed. Coalescing around the core of Terry Thomas, George Hansel, Jan Braverman, and Marie Lawrence (and with the contributions of Maureen Nevin), Black Box of Asbury Park sprang from an outdoor film series. It soon encompassed interactive theater presentations, women's playwright festivals, guest performance artists, writer's workshops, scripted readings, film programs, and more. The faces and venues have changed many times, but the Box has survived and prevailed, an ever-evolving earworm that has excited the city's creative rebirth in ways that resonate far beyond its deceptively modest scale. Pictured from left to right during the summer of 2014 are Black Box principals Jeffrey Seeds, Hansel (since relocated to Europe), Rich Quatrone, Mindy Arcoleo, and Alexis Kozak (Courtesy of Black Box.)

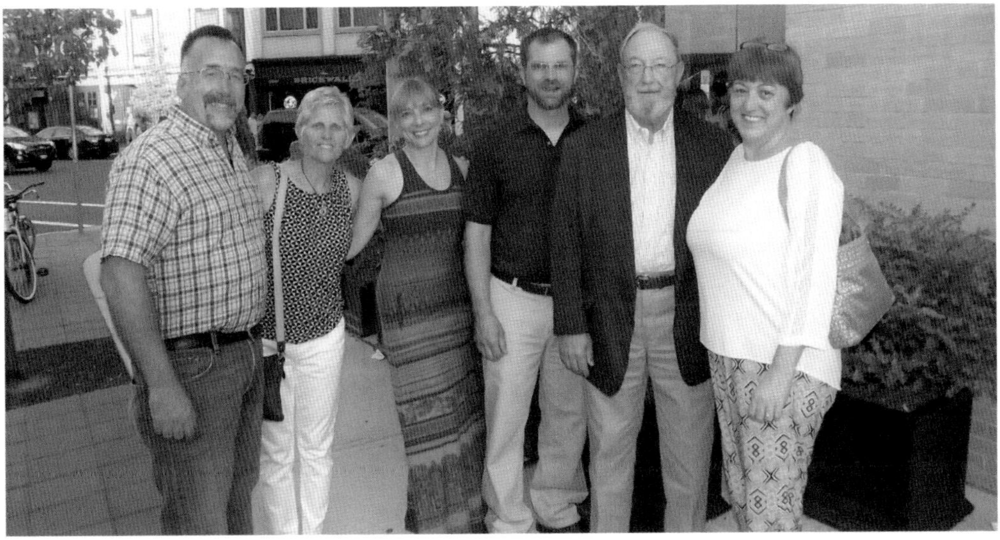

The ReVisionaries

The casting has changed from the founding triumvirate of David Leidholdt, Tom Morrissey, and Stephen Bishop Seeley, and the seasons of frontier theater inside the repurposed Carousel House and VFW transitioned to "hermit crab" engagements at deconsecrated churches and defunct saloons. Under interim artistic director Bob Angelini, the mission of the professional ReVision Theatre Company remains on track as the troupe entered 2014 debt-free, set for summer, and focused on an ambitious new downtown home stage. From left to right, Angelini is pictured with fellow board members Sue Henderson, Jeanne Montano-Giannetta, Kevin Kern, Jules Plangere III, and Judy Whary. Tabitha Falcone DellaPietra is absent. (Courtesy of ReVision Theatre.)

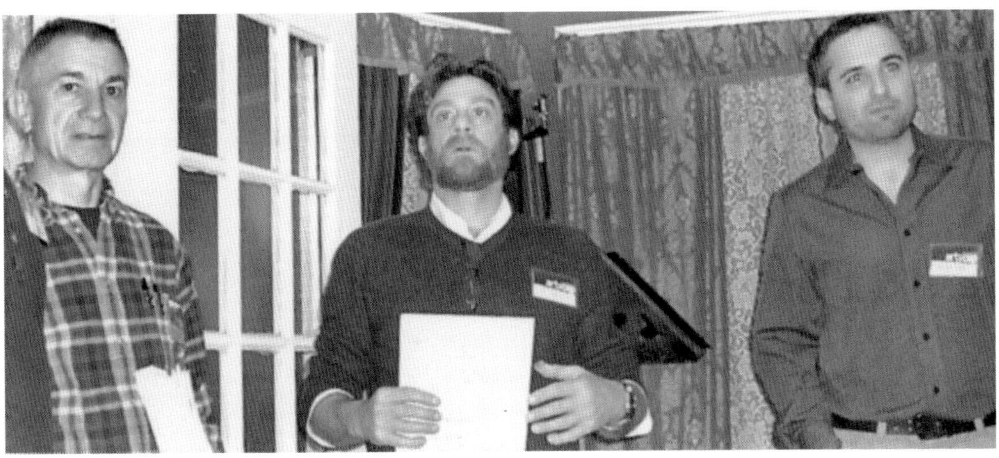

The Arts Capos

Although their good efforts do not always cut the highest profile, the Arts Coalition of Asbury Park (ArtsCAP) has put its energies behind projects both intimately scaled and expansively envisioned—from town-wide festivals, to an "AP in 3 Film Challenge" (with the ShowRoom), and a Little Free Library program (with Anita Weiner and Words! Bookstore) that has placed intriguing reads and compelling constructs in public places around the city. Photographer-educator Dennis Carroll, Tony-nominated actor Lou Liberatore, and comic opera singer-actor Brett Colby are among the neighbors who have invested ArtsCAP with passion and persistence. (Courtesy of Michael Booth and the *Coaster*.)

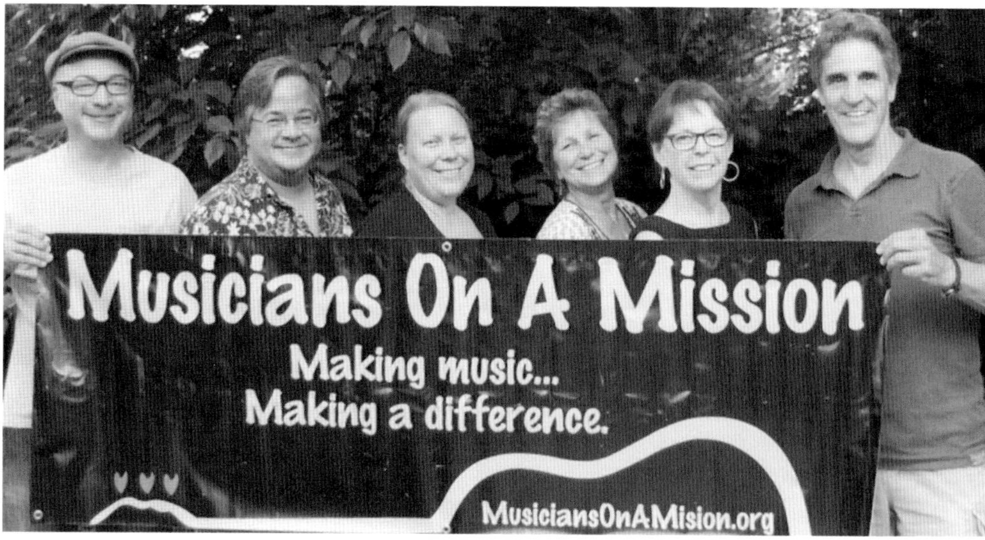

Mission Control

Eric Clapton said musicians are "a soft touch" when it comes to charitable endeavors, and city-based Musicians on a Mission has proven it in just four years, raising thousands for local charities and arts organizations by doing what comes naturally. Founded by mother-daughter duo Cathy Noblick and Jenny Woods in 2010, the nonprofit has grown to encompass some 200 regional volunteers with events highlighted by a Jimmy Webb concert and an all-day MOAM-a-Palooza. Board members include, from left to right, Art Servilla, Jeff Raspe, Woods, Noblick, Brenda Wirth, and Michael Cosentino. Not pictured are Pamela McCoy, Jerzy Jung, Sheli Monacchio, and Matt Scuteri. (Courtesy of Brenda Wirth.)

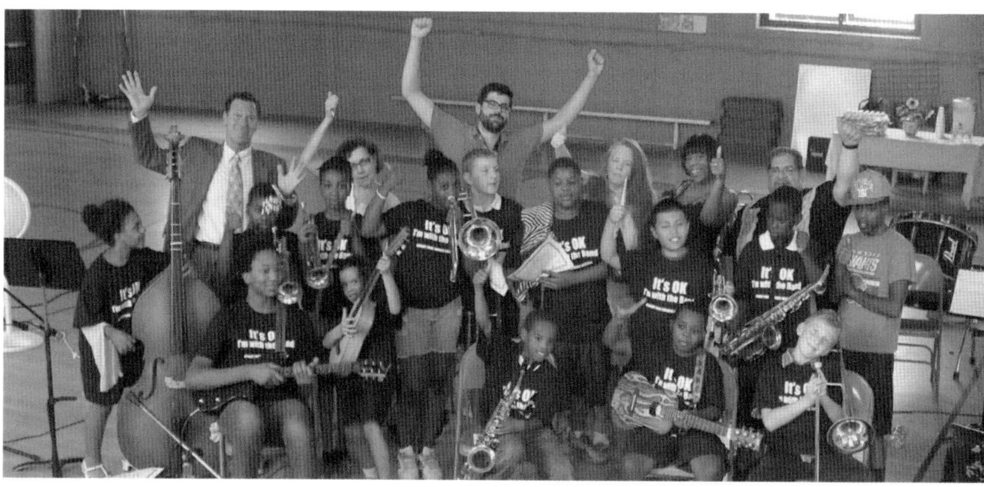

Jazz Hands

It traces its origins as far back as the Kiwanis Boys Club of the 1930s, and its gymnasium on Monroe Avenue has served generations of children since the 1950s. Having entered the new century as the rebranded Boys and Girls Club of Monmouth County, the organization continues to explore new programs for city youth. A partnership with Jazz Arts Project and its artistic director Joe Muccioli seeks to put musical instruments into the hands of every child who wants to make music, and drew *SNL* veteran Joe Piscopo (top left) to a 2014 rehearsal. (Photograph by Roberto Muolo, courtesy of Jazz Arts Project.)

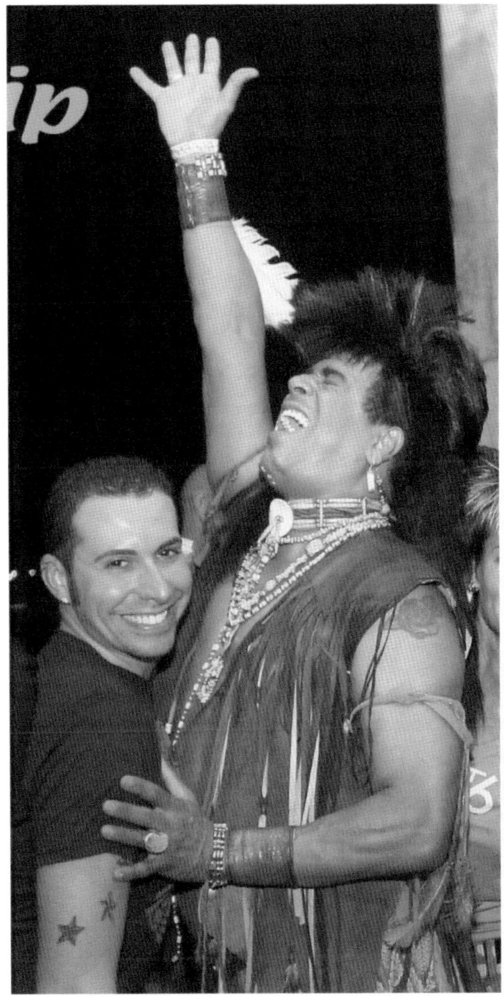

Asbury YMCA

He is a charter member of the disco act that brought gay club culture to the AM radio masses, via monster hits like "Macho Man" and "YMCA." As a Lakota Sioux on his father's side, he had already been dancing in Native American dress when producer Jacques Morali recruited him for what became the iconic lineup of his conceptual pop project. An Asbury resident here in the 21st century, singer, dancer, actor, and producer Felipe Rose (center) continues to perform with and co-manage the Village People while remaining a highly visible figure in the area's arts and philanthropic scene. (Courtesy of Michael Booth and the *Coaster.*)

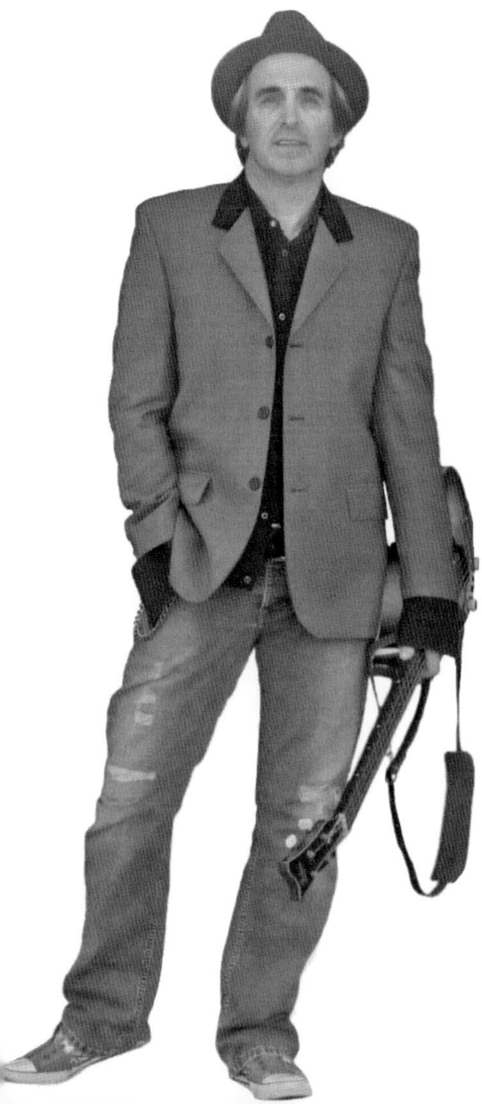

Where Music Moves

He logged hundreds of hours as Paul in Broadway's *Beatlemania*, toured the world as a member of Styx (and a latter-day version of ELO), penned hit songs for industry heavyweights, and raised beaucoup bucks via his all-star tribute and holiday benefits. But while Glen Burtnik is pegged as a "Slave of New Brunswick," it is testament to the allure of Asbury Park that the onetime member of the Pony house band has been embraced as a transplant to the city "Where Music Lives." The musician's musician returned the embrace with a 2011 anthem of that same name. (Courtesy of Glen Burtnik.)

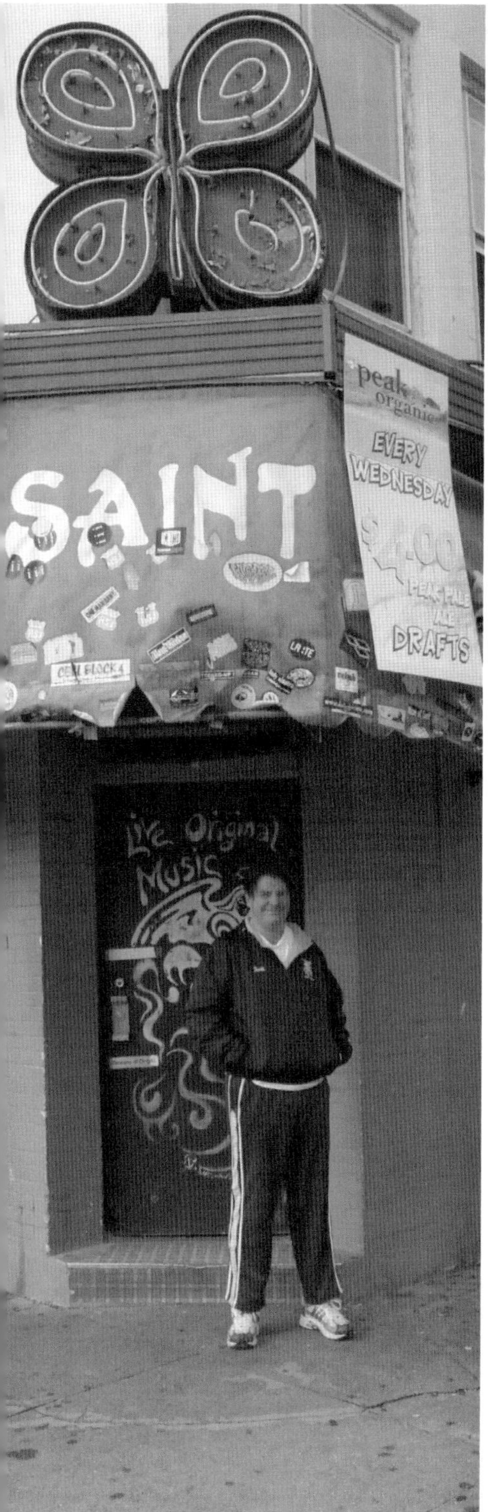

Patron Saint (LEFT)
They started off as the Golden T-Bird Awards, named after the long-gone T-Birds Café on Main Street, and when Scott Stamper moved up the block to the former Clover Club dive, the Saint was canonized. The annual Asbury Music Awards coalesced into a celebration of the myriad sounds that issue from the city's barrooms, boardwalk, boulevards, and bistros. Stamper, who also briefly coproduced the town-wide Wave Festival, books the local and national and the electric and acoustic at his gloriously gritty downtown music box, which the AMAs quickly outgrew in favor of the Stone Pony. (Courtesy of Michael Booth and the *Coaster.*)

Mallets Aforethought (BELOW)
Who knew that Asbury Park was a world capital of marimba music? The universally acknowledged "world's greatest classical marimba player," composer, scholar, publisher, educator, entrepreneur, and inventor Leigh Howard Stevens made Asbury the setting for an annual gathering of international masters of the harmonically hammered instrument. Late spring finds the onetime rock drummer (and founder of the Mostly Marimba/Malletech mini-empire) hosting a series of seminars and best-kept-secret concerts that commandeer some of Asbury's most beautiful churches for bracingly innovative musical events that occur nowhere else on the planet. (Courtesy of Malletech.)

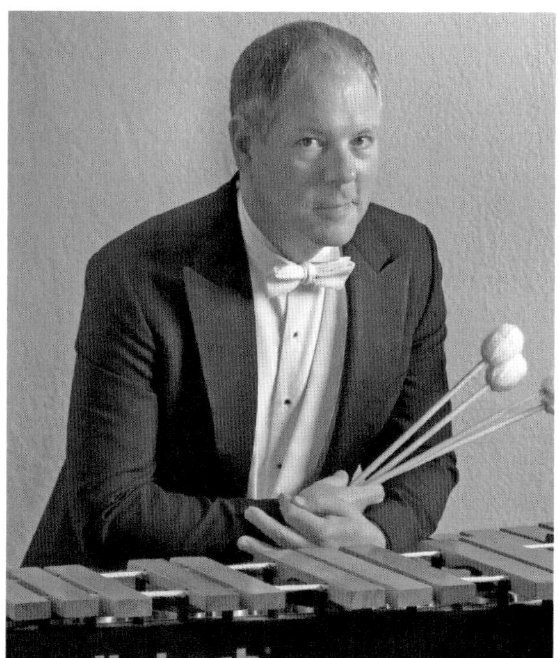

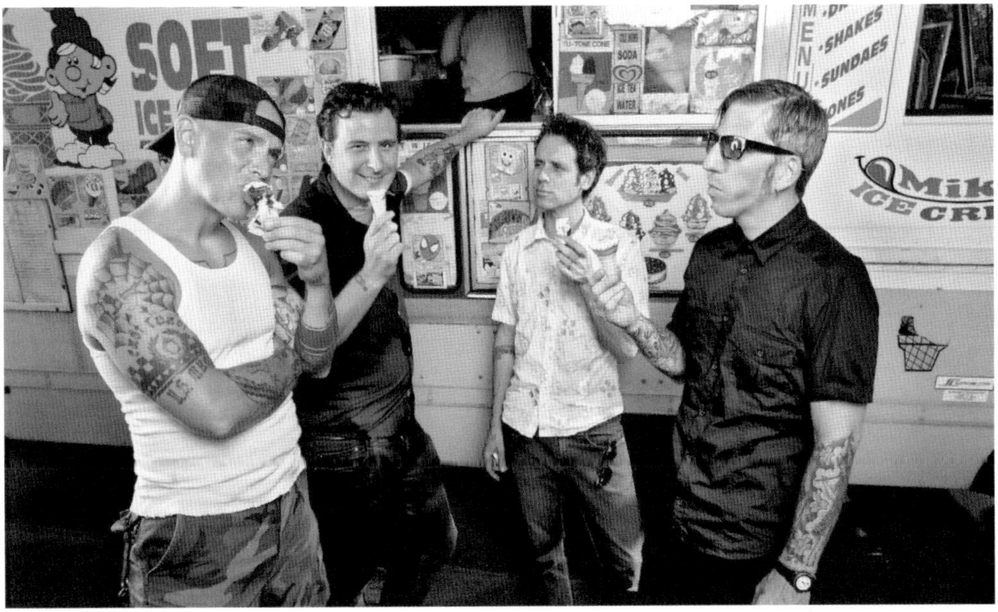

Over Little Eden

They are triangulated as a Brunswick-bred band, but the Bouncing Souls entered the millennium as honorary sons of Asbury, thanks to manager and den-mom Kate Hiltz and her "Little Eden" home base. Housing a basement studio and the offices of the punk band's own Chunksaah Records, the compound serves as world headquarters for global tours as well as for local projects that include Home for the Holidays, an annual post-Yuletide stand of sold-out Stone Pony concerts. Pictured from left to right, the classic lineup of Bryan Kienlen, Pete Steinkopf, Greg Attonito, and Michael McDermott broke for ice cream in 2010. (Photograph by Mike McLaughlin, courtesy of Kate Hiltz.)

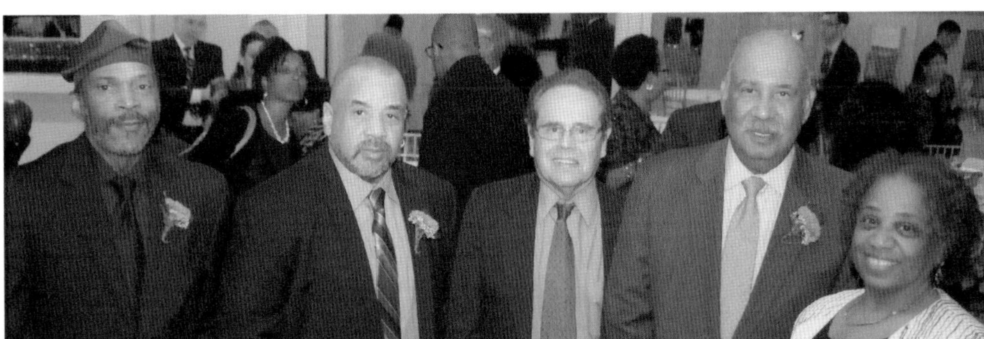

West Side Stories, Continued

At a March 2015 scholarship program dinner, Monmouth County's Brookdale Community College honored five contemporary figures who have helped to write a new chapter in the life of the greater Asbury Park community. Pictured from left to right are Tyrone K. Laws, former director of the West Side Community Center and founder of the educational arts group Kwest for Trust; Daniel A. Harris III, the city zoning board member whose many affiliations include the Asbury/Neptune NAACP and the Men's Ministry at Second Baptist Church; Steven Craig Bogard, cofounder of nondenominational Aslan Youth Ministries; retired BCC administrator Dr. Webster Trammell, coordinator of the city's strategic development plan; and Phyllis Ledbetter of the Asbury Park High School SPOT youth program. (Courtesy of Keith Heumiller and BCC.)

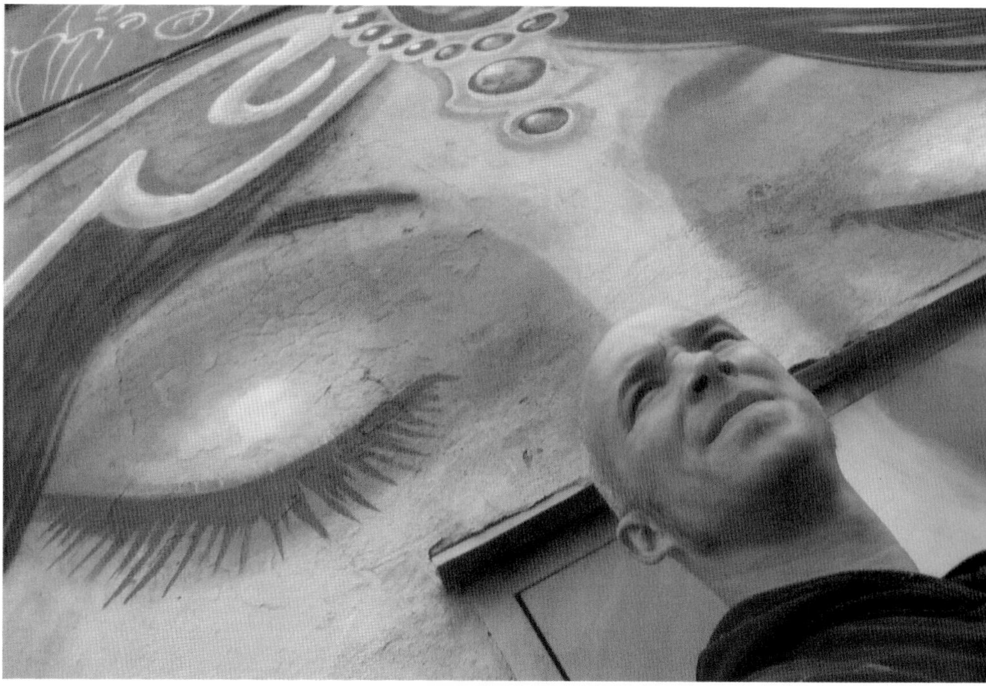

Asbury Pork

His eye-jacking murals on downtown buildings and boardwalk ruins are among the most-photographed and most-shared bits of scenery in millennial Asbury Park, but they are still just one little corner of the world for the artist known as "Porkchop." A frequently exhibited sculptor and painter at Asbury's Parlor Gallery and other settings (and an admitted aficionado of visual erotica), the practitioner of Porktomic art turns heads on a slightly smaller scale, with vivid pop-art statements that range from customized bike helmets and bowling pins, to skeletal sci-fi mannequins and grim figures of nightmare ritual. (Courtesy of Michael Lavallee.)

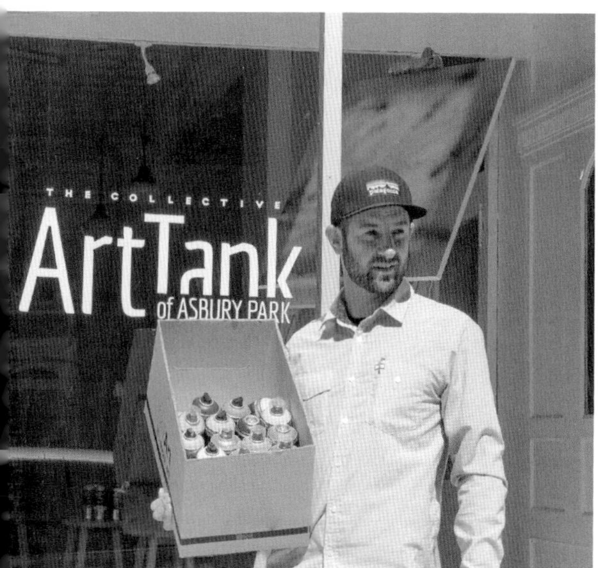

Collective Soul

He has been called a Renaissance man, an *agent provocateur*, even, a "photographer, writer, artist, naturalist, entrepreneur, branding wizard and drone expert" who has long been present on the front lines of anything creative happening in downtown Asbury (when not exploring and documenting South Jersey's Pine Barrens). Through vehicles like Gallery 13 and the hands-on hive of industry and instruction known as the Collective Art Tank, John "Vigg" Viggiano has bridged the lofty gallery scene and the street-level joy of people-powered artworks with community outreach demos, new play readings, and exhibits like Kamelia Ani's Humans of Asbury Park snapshot series. (Courtesy of John Viggiano.)

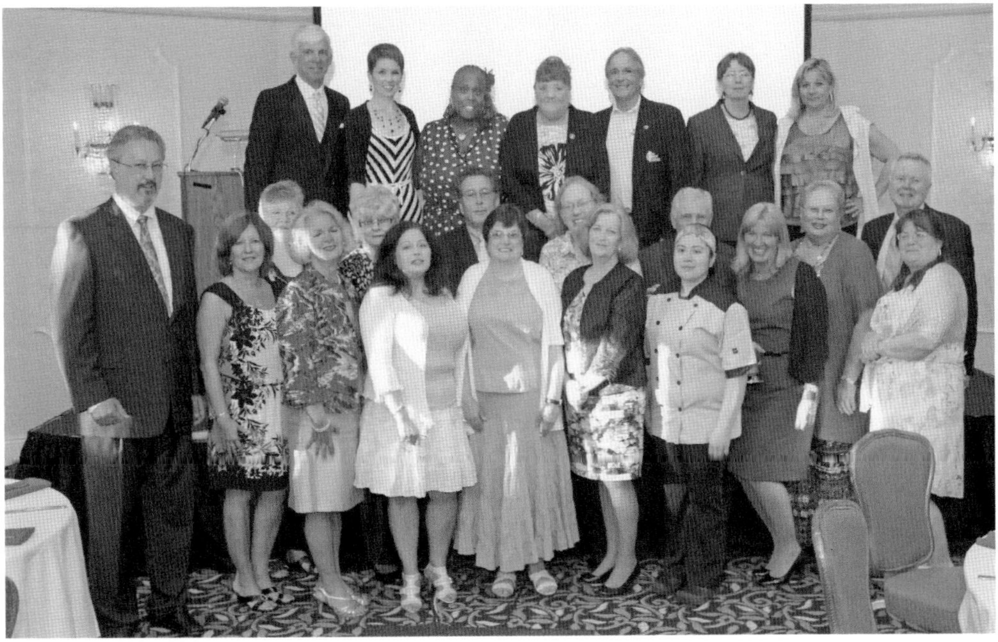

Springwood Spring

The game-changing appearance of the all-new Springwood Center, a public-private-nonprofit partnership on a long-dormant West Side landscape, confirmed what many already knew: that Interfaith Neighbors and executive director Joseph Marmora (hidden in top image) achieved real-world results by forming productive alliances and inspiring the best from their partners. The independent 501(c)(3) grew from a small group of churches into a network of some 45 faith communities, in the process sparing hundreds of families from homelessness, serving countless senior meals, and building numerous affordable housing units. Kicking into overdrive for its third decade, Interfaith fronted a real plan for the West Side, with programs like a Business Development Center incubator for entrepreneurs, and the Kula Café career training facility. Marmora should keep those ribbon-cutting scissors handy, as the times ahead promise an Urban Farm project and a spectacular Asbury JAMS (Jobs, Arts, Music, Science) center at the West Side gateway. (Both photographs courtesy of Interfaith Neighbors.)

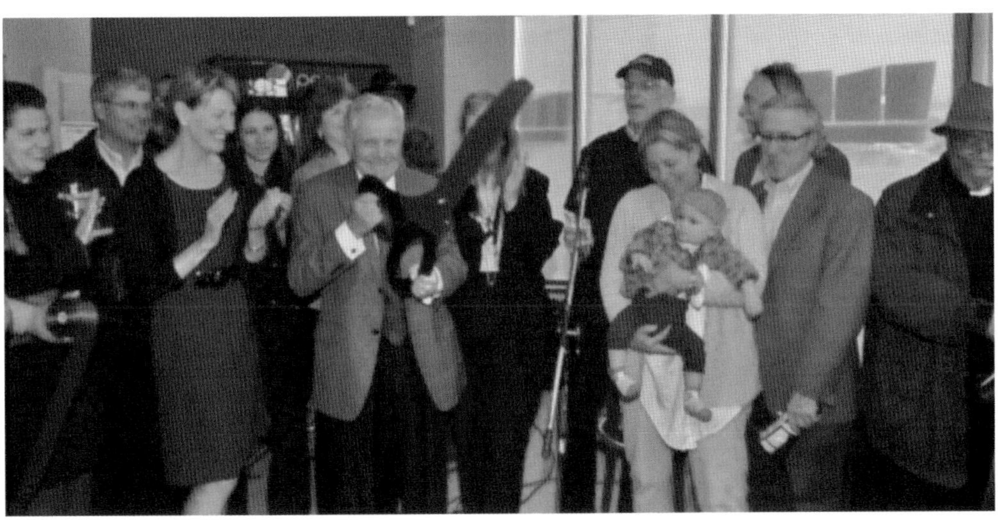

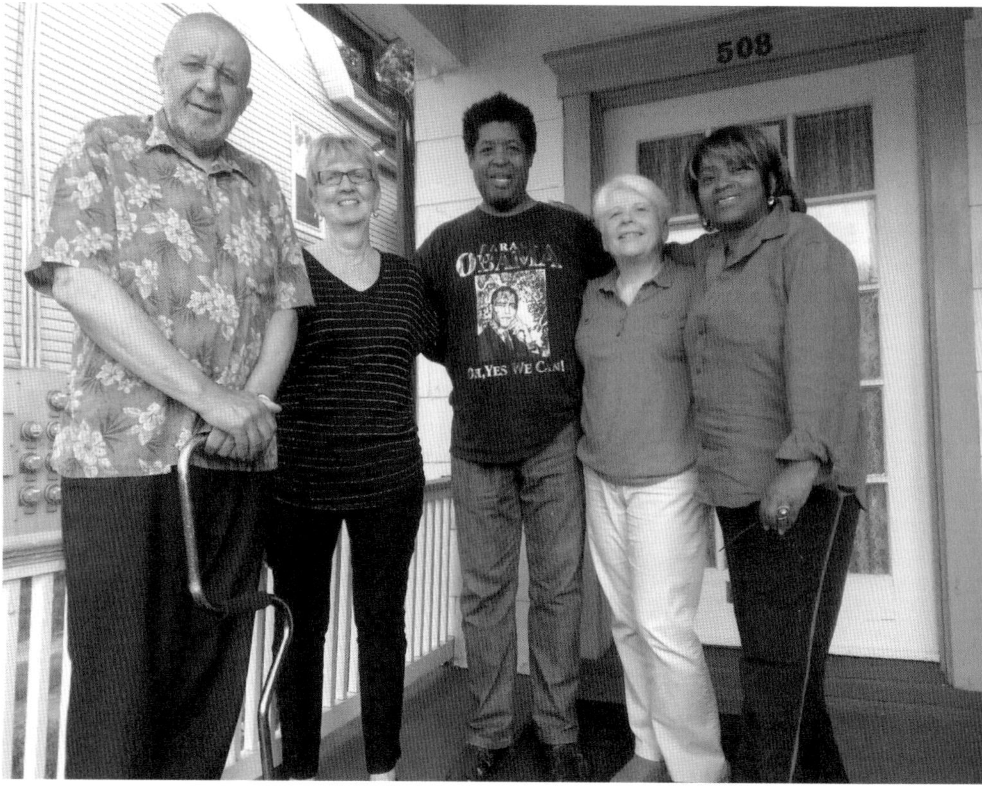

Talk of the Town

"The Dialogue," they call it—not for lack of another name, but because it captures the simple universality of the format. A series of floating community forums, the events evolved from public meetings presented by former zoning board member Pam Lamberton and her teammates on the elected Asbury Park Charter Study Commission, including Duanne Small and legendary local Rita Marano (page 88). It was not long before Pam and retired United Methodist minister Rev. Gil Caldwell were inviting concerned neighbors to some seriously civilized sessions. The conversation continues, and the core of the group (Rev. Caldwell, Pam Lamberton, Conrad Neblett, Linda Phillips, and Halcyon Isaac) could school many world leaders on how to engage, understand, and listen to our fellow human beings. (Courtesy of Diana Moore.)

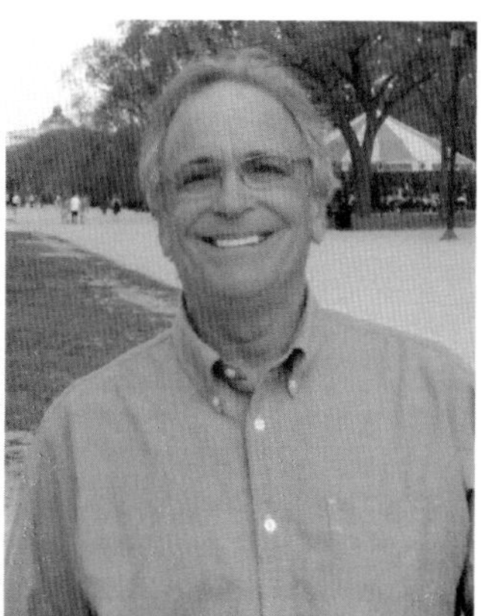

Corps Curriculum

As cofounder of Hope Academy Charter School, Peter Cheney has served as principal of that well-regarded facility since 2001 and as community service coordinator of city-based NJ Youth Corps. The 46-year veteran of Asbury Park's school system works with the State of New Jersey Department of Labor and Workforce Development (and Interfaith Neighbors) to help Asbury's alarming number of dropouts regain their focus. Working toward their GEDs (while assisting a variety of local nonprofits), young adults get academic and skills training from a program that is ready for them, "when they decide they have to make a change." (Courtesy of Hope Academy.)

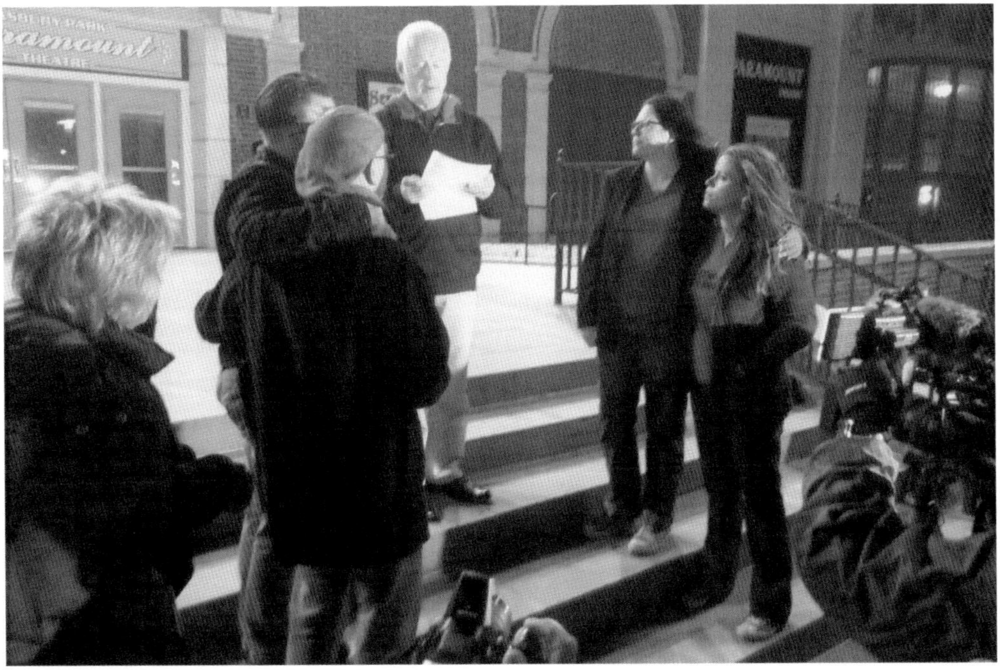

Bells Are Ringing

After years of false starts and delays, same-sex marriage came to New Jersey on October 21, 2013, and at the stroke of midnight on the Asbury Park boardwalk, retired Catholic priest Fr. Tom Pivinski married three couples, including Councilwoman Amy Quinn (right) and Heather Jensen. Also wed were vanguard marriage equality advocates Karen and Marcye McFadden, plus Daniel Baum and Steven Brunner. Following this, Reverend Tom married his own longtime partner in life as well as in Heaven Art and Antiques, Malcolm Navias. (Courtesy of Jeffrey Seeds.)

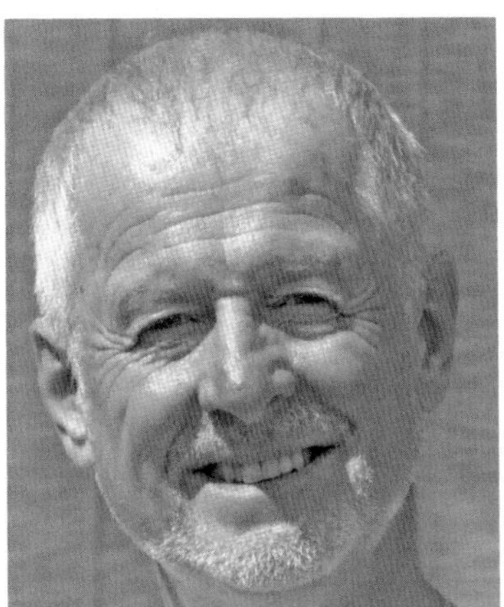

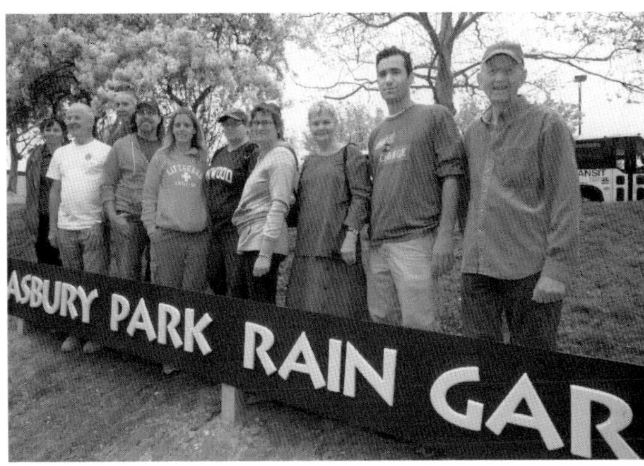

A Tree Grows in Asbury

The Asbury Park Rain Garden, a lush little oasis reclaimed from a drainage ditch adjacent to the James J. Howard Transportation Center, is but one of the projects overseen by Tom Pivinski and a newly reenergized Environment and Shade Tree Commission. The all-volunteer crew of city residents has also established a community vegetable garden as well as neighborhood clean-ups, plantings, and many more endeavors between May and October. (Courtesy of Michael Booth and the *Coaster*.)

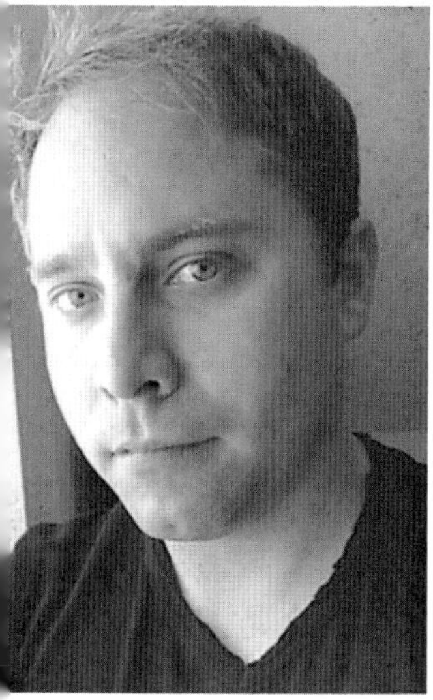

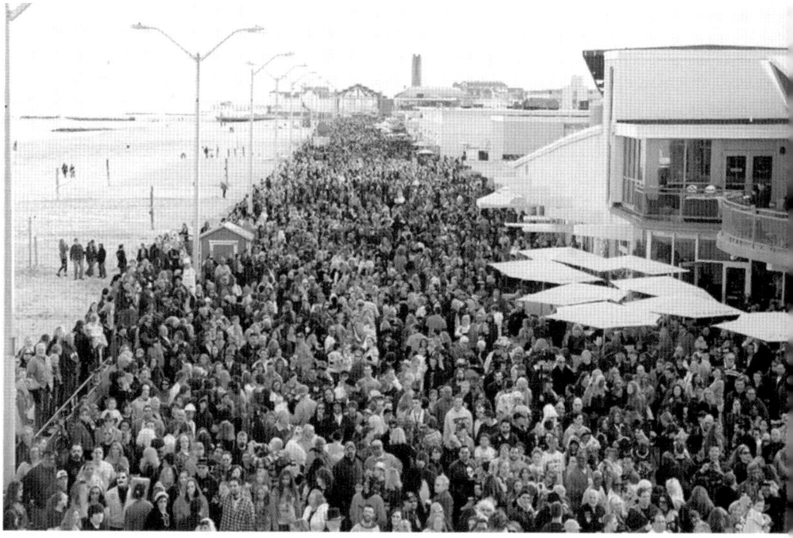

Jason's Revenge

The notion of a zombie walk event elicited a rather cool initial reaction from town fathers, even in walking-dead Asbury Park. But while Jason Meehan was graced with a true zombie's relentless forward momentum, he also had a certain gift of brains, and following a few gear-up editions, the rebranded New Jersey Zombie Walk went for the Guinness with a mass shamble that brought a then-record 4,093 painted participants to the Asbury Park boardwalk in October 2010. Meehan and his cold-blooded crew would reclaim the world record with a jaw-dropping 9,592 marching zombies on October 5, 2013, and the photographer and craft brewer would find vindication the next spring, when the newest member of the Asbury Park Chamber of Commerce accepted its annual Carousel Award for outstanding dedication to the city. (Courtesy of Michael Booth and the *Coaster*.)

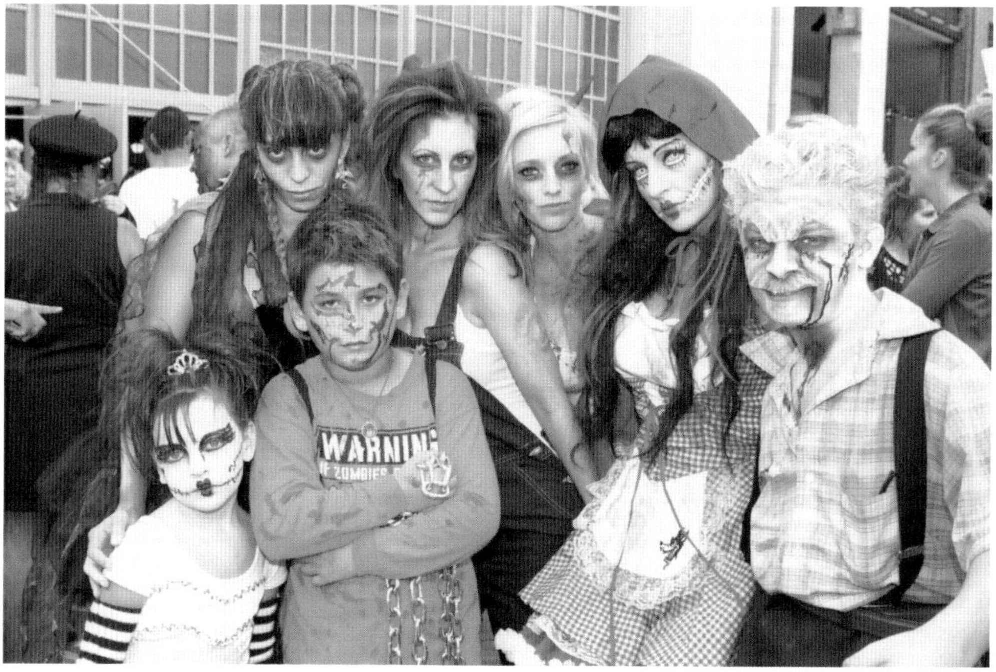

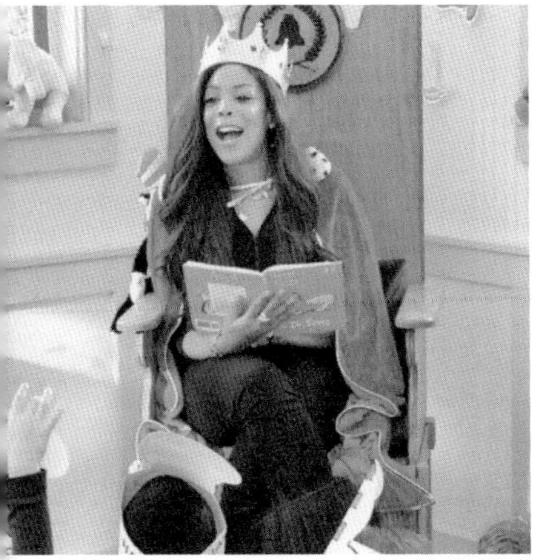

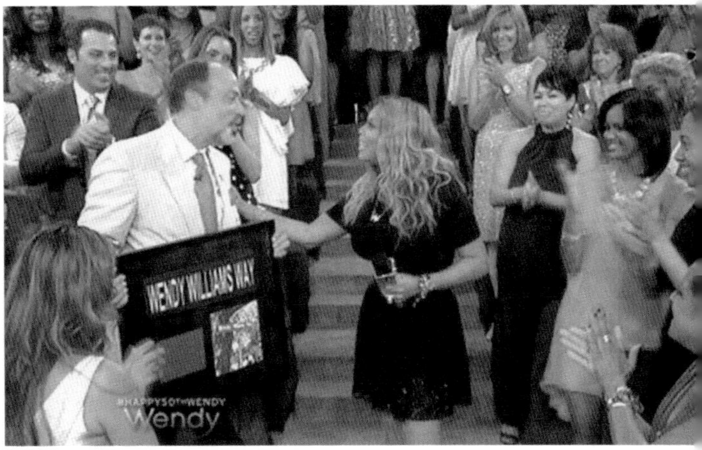

Wendy's Way

She spent the first few years of her life in Asbury Park before moving to Ocean Township with her family (including her father, APHS English teacher and novelist Thomas Williams). But Wendy Williams has embraced her Asbury roots throughout an "overnight" rise from shock radio broadcaster to television talk show sensation and fully branded personality. In July 2014, Asbury Park mayor Myra Campbell rechristened a block of Central Avenue as Wendy Williams Way, while Councilman John Loffredo revealed the accolade to the host on her syndicated program. (Courtesy of Michael Booth and the *Coaster.*)

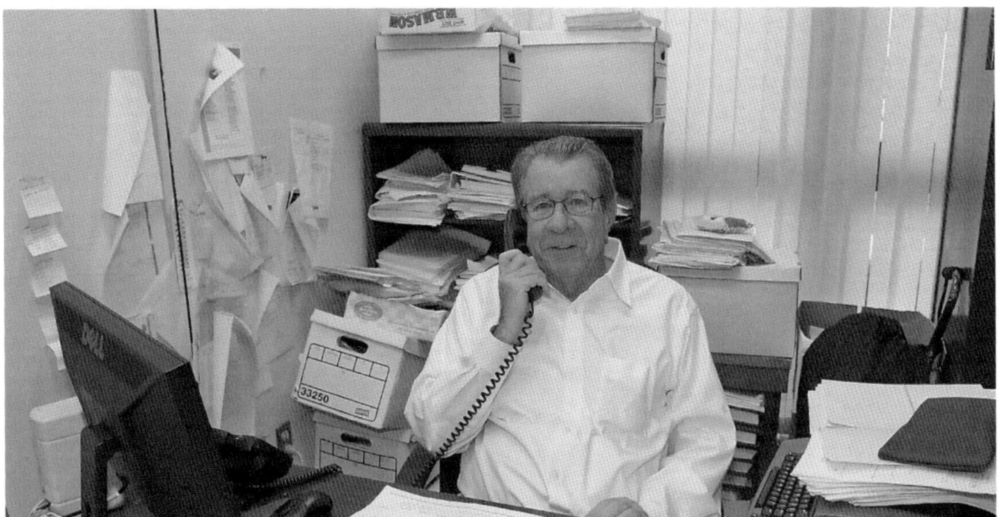

The New Order

Things move fast, here in the city that in 2015 swore in its first-ever directly elected mayor (John Moor), a deputy mayor (Amy Quinn), plus new council members Yvonne Clayton, Jesse Kendle, and Joe Woerner. A new school superintendent, new acting chief of police, and new city manager carried the theme forward—while the retirements of city clerk Stephen Kay (pictured) and deputy city clerk Kiki Tomek wrapped several decades of service and local history. With projects like Festhalle Biergarten, an expanded Lakehouse, The House of Independents, and The Asbury boutique hotel transforming its landscape, Asbury Park continues to confound all attempts to encapsulate its energy between book covers.. (Courtesy of Michael Booth and the *Coaster.*)

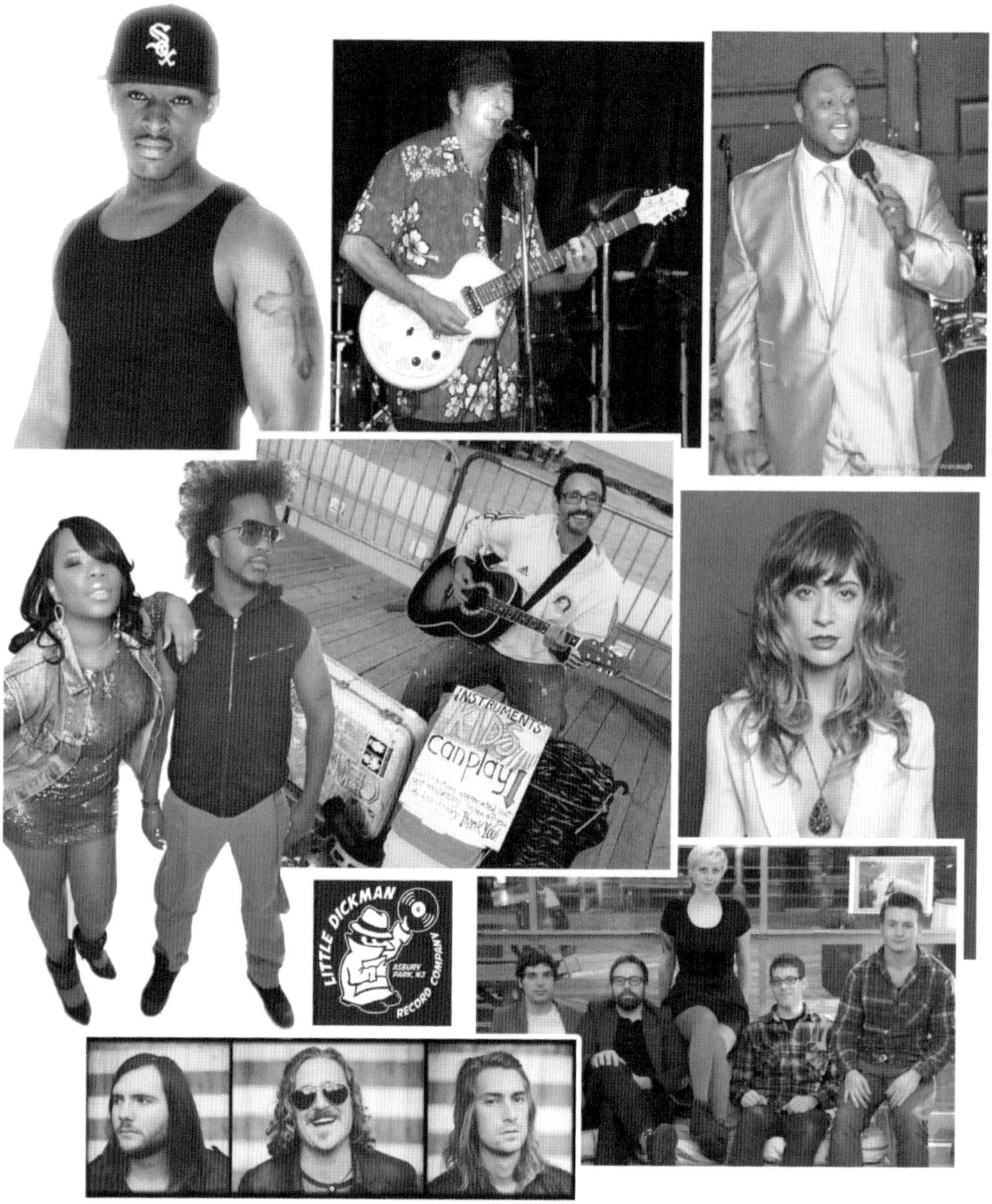

The Beat Goes On

The music continues nonstop in Asbury Park, from (clockwise from top left) Bulletproof Belv's autobiographical hip-hop tales of city life; the old-school jams of Billy Hector, Sandy Mack and Stringbean; the gospel ministry of Tyron McAllister; the breakout bardess Nicole Atkins; the surf-infused pop of Dentist; The Battery Electric and stable of acts from Amy Earixson and Chris Yaniak's Little Dickman Records; the showband groove of Khadijah and The F.L.O.W.—to the karaoke microphone at Georgie's, the show tune fundraisers of Cabaret for Life, a below-radar Latino market, and the Boardwalk, where buskers like Joe "The One Banned Man" Harvard (center) play for change. Author of a fine book on the Velvet Underground, the Boston-bred transplant harbors pointed opinions about the scene—but he will share a song with you, here in a city where quiet time is delightfully *not* part of the social contract. (Courtesy of John Cavanaugh, Dave Christopher, Kristen Driscoll, author's collection.)

BIBLIOGRAPHY

asburyangels.com

Bilby, Joseph and Harry Ziegler. *Asbury Park Reborn.* Charleston, SC: History Press, 2012.

classicurbanharmony.net

Cleary, Fritz. Shore Pioneers, *Asbury Park Press*, 1967–1970.

Froias, Steven. "Walter Reade's Universe Revolved Around Asbury Park" and "Once Around the (Asbury Park) Sun, pts. 1 and 2," posted to AsburyPulp.com, December 2012–January 2013.

Gladwell, Malcolm. "The Pitchman," *The New Yorker*, October 30, 2000.

Jackson, Madonna Carter. *Asbury Park: A West Side Story, Second Edition.* Outskirts Press, 2011.

palaceamusements.com

Pike, Helen Chantal. *Asbury Park's Glory Days: The Story of an American Resort.* Piscataway, NJ: Rutgers University Press, 2005.

Shields, Nancy. "Deep-rooted Asbury family has its history," *Asbury Park Press*, February 15, 2007.

Stine, Don. "Landmark City Building Celebrating 80th Anniversary" and other articles in the *Coaster*, 2009–2014

Troppoli, Donna. "Asbury Park: A Jersey Shore Resort in Deep Purple and Pinstripes," *Garden State Legacy* 21 (2013).

Williams, Carol Gorga. "Match Between Neighboring Towns' Officials Ends 30-Year Run," *Asbury Park Press*, July 12, 2007.

Wien, Gary. *Beyond the Palace*. Trafford Publishing, 2003.

Wolff, Daniel. *Fourth of July Asbury Park*. New York: Bloomsbury USA, 2005.

INDEX

INDEX